AI and Emerging Technologies for a Sustainable Future

(Volume 1)

AI-Driven Technologies for Sustainable Engineering

Shilpa Gupta
Electronics and Communication Department
Chandigarh University, Punjab
India

Ritika Sharma
Computer Science and Engineering Department
Maharaja Agrasen University, Baddi
Himachal Pradesh, India

&

Gokana Mohana Rani
Department of Biological Sciences
and Bioengineering, Inha University
Incheon, South Korea

AI and Emerging Technologies for a Sustainable Future

(Volume 1)

AI-Driven Technologies for Sustainable Engineering

Editors: Shilpa Gupta, Ritika Sharma and Gokana Mohana Rani

ISBN (Online): 979-8-89881-294-2

ISBN (Print): 979-8-89881-295-9

ISBN (Paperback): 979-8-89881-296-6

First published in 2025.

Bentham Science Publishers Pte. Ltd.
No. 9 Raffles Place
Office No. 26-01
Singapore 048619
Singapore
Email: subscriptions@benthamscience.net

BENTHAM
SCIENCE

CONTENTS

PREFACE

In an era where the world is racing with technological developments and simultaneously witnessing growing concerns for the environment, the need for AI in readjusting engineering practices to sustainability is at its most critical point. The interaction of AI-driven technologies and sustainable principles in engineering ensures that there is every opportunity to address complex environmental issues, with optimal resource efficiency and minimum carbon footprint.

This book, AI-Driven Technologies for Sustainable Engineering, investigates how AI may be used holistically to provide creative solutions while also promoting environmental stewardship, economic viability, and social well-being. Predictive analytics provides improved energy efficiency in smart grids, precision agricultural models supported by machine learning, decreased water loss through water-wasting reduction, and many more applications with wide application areas across industries.

We dive into this topic, not just to present current state-of-the-art AI-driven solutions but to encourage readers to question the long-standing paradigms of engineering. This book collects a collection of topics across interdisciplinary lines, such as applications of AI in IoT, education, healthcare, water resources, smart cities, and nanotechnology. Each chapter contains in-depth talks, real-world case studies, and future trends that will be demonstrated in the use of AI for sustainable innovation.

This book concept arose from the observation that while technology is frequently viewed as the source of deterioration when used intelligently, it can reverse these tendencies. With the ability of AI to process huge datasets, generate actionable insights, and automate complex processes, we are now armed with tools that can foster sustainable practices on a scale previously unattainable.

We are deeply thankful to the researchers, practitioners, and thought leaders who have given their expertise to this volume. Their pioneering work and thoughts have made this book extraordinarily rich, bringing enormous value to engineers, researchers, and students who care about a sustainable future.

We hope that this book will be both informative and inspiring.

Shilpa Gupta
Electronics and Communication Department
Chandigarh University, Punjab
India

Ritika Sharma
Computer Science and Engineering Department
Maharaja Agrasen University, Baddi
Himachal Pradesh, India

&

Gokana Mohana Rani
Department of Biological Sciences
and Bioengineering, Inha University
Incheon, South Korea

List of Contributors

Aashima	Department of Computer Science and Engineering, Lovely Professional University, Phagwara, Punjab, India
Adepu Sree Lakshmi	Department of CSE (AI&DS), Faculty of Science and Technology (IcfaiTech), ICFAI Foundation for Higher Education, Hyderabad, India
Anjum Rouf	Department of Computer Science and Engineering, Lovely Professional University, Phagwara, Punjab, India
Bimal Raj Dutta	Department of Electronics and Communication Engineering, Chandigarh University, Chandigarh, Punjab, India
Cherukuri Gunalakshmi	Department of Computer Science and Engineering, Centurion University of Technology and Management, Vizianagaram, Andhra Pradesh, India
G. Madhavi	Mahatma Gandhi Institute of Technology (Autonomous) affiliated with Jawaharlal Nehru Technological University, Hyderabad (JNTUH), Hyderabad, Telangana, India
Gulab Singh	Department of Bio-nanotechnology, Chaudhary Charan Singh Haryana Agriculture University, Hisar, Haryana, India
Harbinder Singh	Department of Electronics and Communication Engineering, UCRD, Chandigarh University, Chandigarh, Punjab, India
Kandipati Rajani	Department of Electrical & Electronic Engineering, Vignan's Lara Institute of Technology & Sciences, Vadlamudi, Andhra Pradesh, India
Ketanpreet Kaur	Bahra College of Law, Patiala, Punjab, India
Love Singla	Department of Microbiology, Maharaja Agrasen University, Baddi, Himachal Pradesh, India
Madhu Bala	Department of Computer Science and Engineering, Lovely Professional University, Phagwara, Punjab, India
Nripinder Kaur	Amar Shaheed Baba Ajeet Singh Jujhar Singh Memorial College, Bela, Punjab, India
P.S.G. Aruna Sri	Department of IoT, Koneru Lakshmaiah Education Foundation, Green Fields, Vaddeswaram, Andhra Pradesh, India
Poka Venkata Sai Jayanth	Department of Electrical & Electronic Engineering, RVR&JC College of Engineering, Guntur, Andhra Pradesh, India
Rajni Sharma	Department of Biotechnology, Maharaja Agrasen University, Baddi, Himachal Pradesh, India
Rama Devi Gude	Computer Science and Systems Engineering, Lendi Institute of Engineering and Technology, Jonnada, Andhra Pradesh, India
RamaKoteswaraRao Alla	CSE-AIML Department, RVR&JC College of Engineering, Guntur, Andhra Pradesh, India
Ranjit Kumar Bindal	Department of Electrical Engineering, Chandigarh University, Chandigarh, Punjab, India
Routhu Daswanta Kumar	Department of Computer Science and Engineering, Centurion University of Technology and Management, Vizianagaram, Andhra Pradesh, India

Routhu Shanmukh Department of Computer Science and Engineering, Centurion University of Technology and Management, Vizianagaram, Andhra Pradesh, India

Sheetal Department of Zoology, Maharaja Agrasen University, Baddi, Himachal Pradesh, India

Shifa Shah Department of Computer Science and Engineering, National Institute of Technology, Srinagar, Jammu & Kashmir, India

Sunil Kumar Department of Electrical, Electronics and Communication Engineering, Galgotias University, Greater Noida, UP, India

Tabassum Rahim Department of Computer Science and Engineering, National Institute of Technology, Srinagar, Jammu & Kashmir, India

Vaibhav Department of Electrical Engineering, Chandigarh University, Chandigarh, Punjab, India

Vaibhav JaDon Department of Electrical Engineering, Chandigarh University, Chandigarh, Punjab, India

CHAPTER 1

Nanomaterials in the AI Era: Revolutionizing Research, Design, and Applications

Rajni Sharma[1,*], **Love Singla**[2] and **Gulab Singh**[3]

[1] *Department of Biotechnology, Maharaja Agrasen University, Baddi, Himachal Pradesh, India*

[2] *Department of Microbiology, Maharaja Agrasen University, Baddi, Himachal Pradesh, India*

[3] *Department of Bio-nanotechnology, Chaudhary Charan Singh Haryana Agriculture University, Hisar, Haryana, India*

Abstract: Nanomaterials, distinguished for their unique properties and diverse applications, are at the forefront of scientific and technological innovation. A transformative development in this field is integrating Artificial Intelligence (AI) into nanotechnology to discover, design, and apply materials at the nanoscale. By harnessing AI's ability to process complex data sets, researchers can predict material behaviors and develop methods to manufacture nanomaterials with tailored functionalities. AI is also revolutionizing nanomaterial characterization, delivering unparalleled imaging, spectroscopy, and structural analysis precision. Simultaneously, nanomaterials are advancing AI hardware, especially in neuromorphic computing and energy-efficient processes. While this chapter explores various applications such as healthcare innovations, environmental monitoring, sustainable energy solutions, and next-generation electronics, it highlights that these represent only a fraction of the potential where AI and nanomaterials converge. However, this integration raises challenges, including ethical considerations, environmental impacts, and safety regulations. The synergy between AI and nanotechnology holds immense promise for driving the discovery of next-generation nanomaterials across multiple industries, shaping a more sustainable and innovative future.

Keywords: Artificial intelligence (AI), Machine Learning (ML), Material characterization, Nanomaterials, Nanotechnology, Neuromorphic computing, Sustainable energy.

INTRODUCTION

Nanomaterials, characterized by their dimensions in the nanoscale (1–100 nm), exhibit enhanced properties due to quantum effects, high surface area-to-volume ratio, and unique atomic arrangements. These attributes have made nanomaterials

* **Corresponding author Rajni Sharma:** Department of Biotechnology, Maharaja Agrasen University, Baddi, Himachal Pradesh, India; E-mail: sharmarajni578@gmail.com

essential across various industries, enhancing electrical, optical, and mechanical performance. Their applications span drug delivery systems, diagnostics, tissue engineering [1], energy storage solutions like batteries and supercapacitors, and sustainable energy technologies, including solar cells and fuel cells [2]. In environmental sustainability, nanotechnology addresses critical challenges, such as water purification, where materials like titanium dioxide play a vital role in photocatalysis, and graphene revolutionizes membrane technology for desalination. Similarly, nanoelectronics, a specialized branch of nanotechnology, has been pivotal in miniaturizing electronic components, enabling advancements in compact and efficient devices [3].

The rapid integration of Artificial Intelligence (AI) into nanotechnology has further transformed the field. AI excels in processing massive and complex datasets, enabling breakthroughs in predictive modeling, optimization, and materials discovery. While AI has revolutionized domains like biology, chemistry, and materials science, its specific integration into nanotechnology is particularly impactful. AI-driven Machine Learning (ML) models have significantly improved property predictions, optimized synthesis conditions, and accelerated the discovery of new materials [4]. Such advancements address the limitations of traditional material design approaches, which are often manual, slow, and costly. In nanomaterials research, AI enhances High-Throughput Experimentation (HTE) by efficiently analyzing intricate datasets from simulations or experiments, reducing the time required to identify materials with desired functionalities [5]. AI-based computational models also predict material behavior under specific conditions, minimizing costs associated with trial-an--error processes. These innovations enable the discovery of functional nanomaterials tailored for particular applications in healthcare, electronics, and energy [6]. By focusing on unique benefits, such as the functionalization of nanomaterials for optimized biological, electronic, and energy applications, AI-driven research promises to redefine the future of nanotechnology. This convergence of AI and nanotechnology accelerates discovery and addresses pressing challenges in sustainability and innovation [7].

NANOMATERIALS AND THEIR APPLICATIONS

Nanomaterials are materials that have been engineered to be extremely small at the scale of nanometers and, therefore, possess new functional properties vastly superior to bulk materials due to quantum effects and very high surface-area--o-volume ratios. This demonstration of properties such as increased strength, conductivity, and reactivity has made them very useful in many contexts [8].

There are several types of nanomaterials, which include:

- **Nanoparticles:** Spherical particles, commonly metal (gold, silver), oxides (zinc oxide, titanium dioxide), or polymers, have applications in catalysis, biomedicine, and energy storage [9].
- **Nanocomposites**: Hybrid materials with nanoparticles within a matrix improve their mechanical, thermal, or electrical properties. Nanocomposite materials are used in a broad range of applications, such as in the automobile, aerospace, and building industries [10].
- **2D Materials**: Thin sheets of materials such as graphene, molybdenum disulfide (MoS_2), and hexagonal boron nitride display unique electronic, optical, and sensing properties [11].

Nanoparticles also have potential applications in nanoscale technology, including components of quantum dots and other nanostructures. They exhibit different properties from the bulk material, which are generally expected to alter depending upon a specific size, such as Nanowires and nanotubes (such as carbon nanotubes). Nanorods (Dimensional structures) have beneficial properties like mechanical strength and high electrical conductivity, increased surface area for catalyzing reactions, and sensors, which make them attractive for use in certain application types like flexible electronics, energy storage, and drug delivery.

Applications of Nanomaterials in Various Sectors

Nanomaterials are used in various spheres of daily life, as shown in Fig. (**1**). Some of them are described below:

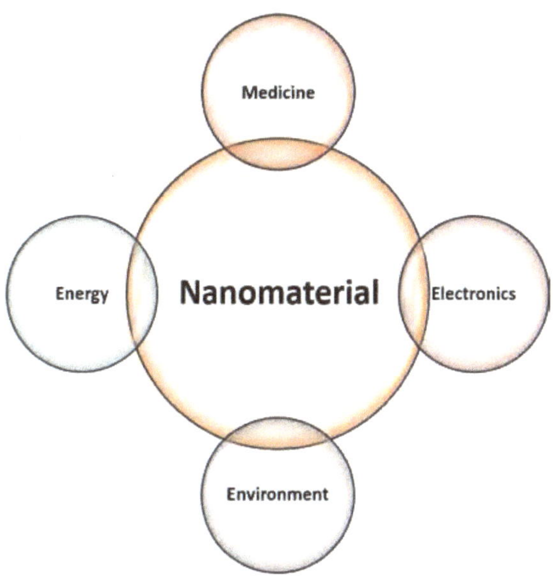

Fig. (1). Applications of nanomaterials in different fields.

1. **Medicines:** Nanomaterials have revolutionized medical applications, mainly drug delivery through various types of nanoparticles like liposomes, micelles, and polymer-drug conjugates that offer targeted and controlled drug release, thereby reducing side-effects and improving therapeutic results, such as gold nanoparticles, which are currently being used for treatment in cancer, both imaging and treatment. In medical diagnostics, quantum dots are essential nanomaterials for bioimaging with improved contrast and sensitivity [1].
2. **Electronics**: One industry that is gaining significant dividends in yield enhancers through the use of nanomaterials is the electronics industry, with carbon nanotubes and graphene being only a pair among many others. Their improved electrical conductivity, strength, and flexibility make them essential in developing future transistors, sensors, and conductive films [12]. For instance, transistors based on carbon nanotubes are predicted to outperform silicon-based transistors in speed and energy efficiency, whereas the application of graphene into flexible electronics leads to abundant possibilities [13].
3. **Energy**: The application areas of nanomaterials in energy management and conversion technologies are nanostructured electrodes like silicon nanoparticles and graphene, which improve the energy density and charging rates in batteries. Materials at the nanoscale are also applied in solar cells to enhance light absorption by exploiting nanomaterials, known as developments in renewable applications (*e.g.*, quantum dot solar cells and perovskite-based photovoltaics) [14].
4. **Environment**: Nanomaterials are widely used for applications such as water purification, pollution control, and waste management. Together with the ability to filter out heavy metals and organic pollutants from water, carbon-based nanomaterials such as graphene oxide offer great potential [15]. In addition, titanium dioxide nanoparticles have been applied to the photocatalytic degradation of pollutants present in air and water, which represents a green pathway for environmental remediation [16].

Challenges in the Traditional Research and Development of Nanomaterials

1. **Expensive:** The production of nanomaterials of high quality, for the most part, remains metastable and costly to synthesize, especially the creation of these at an industrial scale. A lot of difficulties are known to be encountered when manufacturing materials that have the same set of properties, as we know, in the alterations involved with producing graphene. Permalink — Nanomaterial commercialization is limited only by expensive and unscalable production pillars [11].
2. **Time-Consuming Processes**: Conventional approaches to the discovery and refinement of nanomaterials, frequently by using substantial experimental

efforts, are time-consuming. There is a higher chance that the desired outcome will come about from this method, but it also increases the scope of variables that must be tested (the synthesis conditions and material properties can vary widely) [17].

3. **Reproducibility and Scaling**: Scaled-up production of nanomaterials that possess unique properties certainly poses a challenge due to variations in desired properties across production volume, particularly in applications like nanoelectronics, where precision control over material dimensionality is all the more critical. Store multiple synthesis paths for inconsistent end usage behavior [18].
4. **Health and Safety issues**: Some applications, particularly biomedical and environmental applications. There are serious health concerns regarding the toxicity of some nanomaterials for safe handling, usage, and disposal. The use of nanomaterials in recirculating systems may lead to their complicated interactions with biological systems; hence, they should be carefully studied for long-term health effects [19]

AI has surfaced as a game-changer in addressing these challenges. Machine learning algorithms allow researchers to analyze large datasets, predict material properties, and improve the synthesis of materials more efficiently than traditional experimental methods, such as Nanoparticle Research Using Pattern Recognition Faster and Quieter with AI [20]. AI-driven methods also help in enhancing the reproducibility of the results by finding out the conditions under which something can consistently be produced [4].

Application of AI in Nanomaterial Research

Role of AI in Accelerating Nanomaterial Discovery and Synthesis

AI has been transforming several dimensions of nanomaterial research, mainly in the exploration, manipulation, and creation of new materials. In the past, new nanomaterials have been discovered through expensive and time-consuming trial-and-error experimentation. However, research has significantly sped up with the help of AI, which uses techniques like Machine Learning (ML), which is data-driven and can provide accurate predictions [20]. AI can help with process optimization to synthesize nanomaterials so that, for instance, only two experiments would need to be performed until the required experimental conditions like temperature, pressure, and concentration were identified [21]. For example, when optimized using AI models, the synthesis of carbon nanotubes (CNTs) is of much higher quality and takes less time than if conventionally synthesized. AI-based models can also relate synthesis conditions with material properties by considering extensive amounts of experimental and theoretical data, providing the means to predict outcomes that were previously unattainable. As a result, AI has made it possible to bypass lengthy experimental steps in computational methods for researchers. In such a context, AI is an accelerator for exploring new materials, automating the identification of promising new materials with specified properties from large datasets [4].

High-Throughput Screening and Data Mining in Nanomaterial Research Using Artificial Intelligence

When we think of finding nanomaterials, High-Throughput Screening (HTS) for Nanomaterials is one of the most evident cases where the impact of AI can be observed. High-Throughput Screening (HTS) is a testing method in which researchers can conduct millions of random combinations of tens or hundreds of materials. A researcher states, "Of course, the number of potential material compositions grows as a power-law combinatorial explosion, making it infeasible. This is the void that AI fills, making it possible for predictive models to be built, which can quickly sift out thousands of potential cases if only those with a high enough likelihood of success are tested [17]."

Machine learning-based algorithms could scan existing databases, such as Materials Project and Open Quantum Materials Database (OQMD), to predict suitable NPA candidates for different applications [6]. AIs thus can help scientists quickly sift through vast quantities of data and suggest which materials are worth investigating further in synthesis or experiment. The use of Artificial Intelligence (AI) has led to a new chapter in material High-Throughput Screening (HTS), which may be employed as novel energy storage and conversion materials (*e.g.*, battery electrodes, solar cell materials) [4].

In addition, using data mining techniques on experimental data offers possibilities to uncover latent structures and trends. For example, AI algorithms can be influential in identifying correlations between a nanomaterial's composition and its performance attributes, which are non-intuitive or extremely difficult to find by traditional means [7]. With this new experimental data, these models can then be refined over and over again, and AI-based predictions will keep getting better with time, speeding up the material discovery.

Prediction of Material Properties and Behaviors Using Machine Learning Models

To understand the properties and behaviors of nanomaterials and to predict what happens to them over time under a variety of conditions, scientists have been taking cues from models built with Machine Learning (ML). Such models enable users to accurately predict electrical, mechanical, and thermal properties [22], which is helpful in the sense that materials can be screened virtually rather than through tedious and costly experimental measurements. One such example is the band gap of semiconductors, which has been used as a model system for its predictive value in electronic and photovoltaic devices. They can even do the same for small nanomaterials, *e.g.*, 2D materials and quantum dots, in order to facilitate the rational design of materials that are predictable and optimal in terms of their electronic behavior [23].

ML has also been used to predict mechanical properties (hardness, elastic modulus, and fracture toughness) of nanomaterials like graphene and nanocomposites. It can be employed, for example, by researchers to develop models to predict the mechanical performance of novel materials, such as high-strength and high-ductility nanocomposites used in an array of industries by training on large amounts of pre-existing experimental data [17].

In addition, for thermal properties, AI models can predict the thermal conductivities of materials as well, which is essential when designing materials that we are tuning and using in heat dissipation and energy storage applications. Some references found where ML algorithms have been used to produce nanomaterials with better thermal conductivities for Thermoelectric and Heat exchangers in industrial usages [9]. Table **1** shows the application of artificial intelligence in different properties of nanomaterials.

Table 1. Applications of AI-driven ML models for predicting the properties of nanomaterials.

Property	Nanomaterial	AI/ML Application
Band Gap	2D materials, quantum dots	Predicting electronic properties
Mechanical Properties	Graphene, nanocomposites	Predicting hardness, elasticity, and fracture toughness
Thermal Conductivity	Nanostructured thermo-electrics	Predicting thermal properties for heat dissipation

Applications of AI for Discovering New Nanomaterials with Desired Features

AI applications have already yielded several vital findings in nanomaterials research. As an example, batteries need improved materials. In one case, researchers applied AI models to discover more effective materials for components of lithium-ion batteries that would increase energy density, enhance charging speeds, and prolong lifespan. A clear case in point is the discovery of a new lithium iron phosphate ($LiFePO_4$) cathode material with higher performance than its predecessors, where an AI algorithm carried out most of the work [20].

Added to that, in the catalysis area, new nanoparticle catalysts have been developed by AI for hydrogen generation. Researchers identified the previously unreported high-efficacy nano-catalysts in hydrogen evolution reactions by predicting activity and stability for all-metal alloys using ML models [4].

Flexible electronics and nanomaterials for dark matter detection are designed with artificial intelligence. Additionally, by using Ml models to find nanomaterials that could be suitable for both more flexible and wearable electronics, like carbon nanotube or 2D materials (MoS_2). The performance of flexible devices has begun to surpass that of his invention because these models are specifically designed to improve the required electrical and mechanical properties for high-end applications [13].

Usage of AI for Nanomaterial Design and Optimization

AI's Role in Optimizing Material Synthesis Processes

In the case of nanoparticles, parameters like temperature, pressure, concentration, and reaction time need to be fine-tuned for them to synthesize nanomaterials. Conventional methods and systems have long depended upon try-and-error experimentation, which is time-consuming as well as resource-exhaustive. Instead, AI models analyze empirical data and determine correlations between variables (hence estimations of those values) with fewer experiments [20].

In the synthesis of carbon nanotubes (CNTs), for instance, parameters like catalyst composition, temperature, and precursor gas concentration are to be controlled tightly. Taking advantage of previous experimental results can optimize these conditions by utilizing a machine-learning algorithm that calculates the best combination or highest likelihood of producing CNTs with specified properties (*e.g.*, length and diameter) [17]. Related to nanoparticle formation, AI has been applied to optimize nanoparticle synthesis by optimizing the conditions for controlled size and morphology of nanoparticles that affect performance in, *e.g.*, drug delivery or catalysis [4].

It can also simulate the computationally expensive and complex multi-variable interactions during nanomaterial synthesis, thereby providing insights into small changes in synthesis conditions that lead to significant changes in material properties. For example, deep learning has been used to predict temperature and concentration changes that affect the size and shape distribution of gold nanoparticles with superior synthesis protocols.

Preclinical Development Using Predictive Modelling of Nanomaterial Design

Machine learning has been effective in controlling the design of nanomaterials with any specific properties (morphology, size, and functionality) because of AI's predictive modeling capabilities. Through machine learning, vast nanomaterial properties can be documented along with the structures, and they can determine whether an architecture is good at working or not, with this method of at least 100 percent accuracy [22]. One example is designing nanomaterials of different shapes, such as rods, spheres, or sheets, and their associated mechanical, electrical, and optical properties from predictive models by Smita Dev and Mark Asta. These models are applied not only to guide the experiments but also to design functional nanostructures and their application in drug delivery applications, energy-storing devices, etc. Artificial Intelligence (AI) models have been employed to predict the synthesis parameters responsible for tuning the size distribution of nanoparticles, a crucial aspect while leveraging them as catalysts and bioimaging agents. Smaller nanoparticles are generally more catalytically active, whereas larger particles can be more stable under a reaction condition. Predictive models streamline reaching the correct size distribution more efficiently than standard generalizing treatment methods [23]. In addition, AI has been used for predicting the functionalization of nanomaterials with revolutionary surface modifications that increase their biocompatibility or catalysis efficacy. A prediction model has also been employed to design nanomaterials functionalized with groups that have some function in biomedicine applications, such as targeted drug delivery [9]. These models allow us to simulate methods of functionalizing the surface before we do anything expensive and time-consuming.

Optimisation via AI Platforms of Nanomaterials for Specific Applications

Moreover, AI significantly boosts the optimization of nanomaterials for intended functions such as energy storage, drug delivery, catalysis, etc. Working together with experimental data, AI merges it with the computational models to perform high-throughput screening of candidate materials, which show the best performance for any dedicated application by predicting their properties.

- **Energy Storage**: AI was used widely to improve the performance of nanomaterials for energy storage devices like batteries and supercapacitors. AI has also predicted that nanostructured materials such as graphene and silicon nanoparticles would enhance lithium-ion battery capacities, but it provides little insight into the impact on the energy density of those batteries or the speed at which they can be charged [21]. AI is used to optimize electrode materials for supercapacitors as well, targeting nanomaterials that can achieve high surface area and conductance [4].

- **Biomedical:** Pharmaceuticals have used AI to engineer nanoparticles for targeted drug delivery. These data can be used to train predictive models for designing nanoparticles with specific size ranges and surface charges, as well as functionalizations that will assist in making these particles reach the correct tissue or cell type more efficiently. In fact, AI has been used to tune drug release kinetics from nanoparticles to slow the burst and provide the tuneability necessary to achieve limited and sustained release, which is key in enhancing therapeutic efficacy while diminishing side effects [22].
- **Catalysis**: AI has shown a potent means for the optimization of catalysis-relevant nanomaterials, such as nano-catalysts with high activity for chemical reactions (hydrogen production, CO_2 reduction), designed using machine learning algorithms [7]. For example, the best composition and structure of a nano-catalyst (*e.g.*, metal alloy nanoparticles) under a particular catalytic activity or stability associated with specific reaction conditions can be predicted by AI models.

Case Studies on AI's Impact on the Design of High-Performance Nanomaterials

The application of AI in nanomaterial design has been particularly successful in lithium-ion batteries. Additionally, novel electrode materials such as lithium iron phosphate ($LiFePO_4$) have been discovered by AI-driven models that show the ability to improve energy density and cycle life as compared to traditional materials. A slight increase in energy barrier to the AI could be obtained by optimizing particle sizes and distribution of these materials using an AI approach, replicating commercial battery applications better [20]. One of the very recent works in the catalysis area is about the utilization of AI for designing new nano-catalysts to split water molecules for generating hydrogen. One catalyst with efficient and durable catalysis ability for hydrogen evolution reactions. The AI models find that a specific combination of alloy nanoparticles made up of nickel and molybdenum would form a highly expressed metal/metal-oxide interface to generate hydroxides on surfaces. AI-driven optimization has led to a number of clean energy technologies [4]. AI algorithms have also been used to design metallic nanomaterials for flexible electronics, which may find applications in things like wearable and malleable displays. AI models have been developed to tailor mechanical properties by bending or stretching graphene and carbon nanotube electrical conductors. Next-generation electronic devices have also greatly benefited from such AI-driven materials [23]. The integration of AI with nanomaterials in various sectors, such as energy storage, hydrogen production, electronics, and drug delivery, is given in Table **2**.

Table 2. Applications of optimized nanomaterials with their role in AI.

Application	Optimized Nanomaterial	Role of Artificial Intelligence
Lithium-Ion Batteries	$LiFePO_4$ nanoparticles	Predicting particle size and distribution.
Hydrogen Production Catalysts	Ni-Mo alloy nanoparticles	Optimizing composition for efficiency and stability.
Flexible Electronics	Graphene, carbon nanotubes	Predicting mechanical properties for flexibility.
Drug Delivery	Functionalized nanoparticles	Designing for targeted delivery and release profiles.

Application of AI for Nanomaterials Characterization and Imaging

Image Analysis and Interpretation at the Nanoscale Encouraged by AI-based Approaches

Materials characterization at the nanoscale level is used to specify the structure, morphological attributes, and properties of nanostructured materials using essential techniques like Atomic Force Microscopy (AFM), Transmission Electron Microscopy (TEM), etc. Unfortunately, the imaging data tends to be high resolution at the nanoscale, so many tedious steps are often required to interpret these *via* software solutions. AI-based techniques, including machine learning (ML) and deep learning (DL) approaches, have been shown to be effective in automating and improving the analysis of those images, thus enhancing throughput while maintaining accuracy.

For example, in AFM, which creates surface topography maps for materials, AI models can automatically identify and label different surface features, such as nanoparticles or imperfections on the surface, without human intervention [24]. With AI algorithms, the task can be significantly accelerated and made more objective. An image can be segmented into individual regions, or edges can be detected; nanoscale structures are better quantified by these means than when done manually. In TEM, the most complete images of internal structures on an atomic scale, AI can analyze large datasets of images to identify features such as crystal lattices, grain boundaries, and defects [25]. With the large data generation in TEM experiments, machine learning models help in providing much faster and more robust interpretations. AI-based computer image analysis also benefits in improving contrast and resolution in nanoscale imaging. Deep learning methods and filters allow researchers to process images, increase resolution, and even reconstruct 3-D data from acquired 2-D images. Provide results in a more detailed and accurate visualization of the selected nanomaterials, hence enabling researchers to investigate deeper into the structural and behavioral characterizations [21].

Enhanced Accuracy and Speed in Characterizing Nanomaterials Using AI

Nanomaterial characterization speed and accuracy can be significantly enhanced using AIs. Indeed, traditional characterization methods are typically less than ideal, with manual analysis, which can be subjective and error-prone, particularly for large datasets or subtle features. On the other hand, AI algorithms use predefined models to perform analysis and give a regular and biased answer each time.

AI has the ability to work with loads of data in a short time. For instance, machine learning algorithms can process hundreds or even thousands of AFM or TEM images in a fraction of the time that it would take a human researcher and possibly even improve results. It is beneficial primarily for high-throughput experiments that require quick characterization [24]. In addition, AI models can capture tiny details within the data during manual analysis that might be missed otherwise. There, for example, in electron spectroscopy or microscopy, ML already helps with the detection of atom coordinates, crystal defects, and structures, which are hard to distinguish with conventional means. It's convenient for materials such as graphene, which can be drastically altered in its properties and change the small particulars of its structure [26].

This increases the accuracy of measurements. For instance, AI-based algorithms help us in AFM with better analysis of force-distance curves, which leads to more accurate quantification of surface properties, including roughness, stiffness, and adhesiveness [4]. High-fidelity mapping like this is necessary if we have accurate models of nanomaterial physics, which could be put to use in designing new nanostructures for biomedical or energy applications.

Automating and Optimizing Nanomaterial Imaging with the Help of AI

AI plays a key role in automating and optimizing nanomaterial imaging procedures, resulting in more efficient workflows that require less human oversight, causing fewer mistakes. Existing Scanning probe tip imaging, Such as atomic force microscopy, is usually done in an ad hoc way, so the setup, operation, and interpretation have a high variability. At multiple points, this strategy can be automated, from image acquisition to AI algorithms for data analysis, and yield faster and more reproducible results.

- **Control other instruments**: The AI model can adjust the scanning parameters for AFM or TEM to focus, exposure, and scan speed, and improve the quality of image acquisition online. Instead, it reduces the time for manual corrections and promises accurate data [21]. Automated image acquisition is ideal for high-throughput environments like those in which a massive number of samples must be imaged rapidly.
- **Image Conditions Optimization**: AI can be used to optimize imaging conditions; for instance, in TEM, working with auto electron beam settings correction will result in your sample getting less damage and still getting high-quality images. This will, for instance, allow machine learning models that predict the best operational conditions given the material being imaged and avoid being over-exposed to potentially harmful conditions whilst maintaining high-level images [20]. This is particularly relevant when using sensitive (organic nanostructures or biological) samples.
- **In-Image Pathology**: This includes real-time image analyzers to provide instant feedback to the operator. For example, it allows for changes during imaging (*e.g.*, refocusing), modification of scan parameters to image better-defined regions, dynamic control, etc. In this manner, AI helps in online imaging optimization, resulting in fewer post-acquisition corrections and better efficiency in the overall investigation [25].
- **Automation of Image Segmentation and Feature Detection:** The tedious manual work of segmenting images at the nanoscale and finding relevant features (which can be highly variable) can be extensively automated through AI, which does not have the same limitations. For example, segment single nanoparticles or defects on the surface and automatically analyze their size, shape, and distribution from AFM images. This system could accelerate the characterization, and it was also more accurate compared to subjective manual analysis [24]. Moreover, the integration of AI in imaging workflows led to the development of closed-loop systems. An iterative process of learning is performed by these AI algorithms as they keep taking in more and more data and updating the imaging parameters needed to get the best images for acquisition. These systems are particularly relevant for advanced imaging tools (*e.g.*, scanning probe microscopy or high-level electron microscopes), where the imaging conditions need to be kept constant to obtain accurate data [26].

AI in Nanomaterial Applications

Nanomedicine: AI-Enabled Nanomaterials for Drug Delivery, Diagnostics, and Therapy

Nanomedicine areas like targeted drug delivery, diagnostics, and therapies expect the properties of nanoparticles to enhance selective distribution and action at diseased sites, either alone or as add-on values on existing drugs like rifampicin, through controlled release, requiring lower dosage by stabilizing Geneticin, etc. Artificial Intelligence (AI) has vastly contributed to improving the design, synthesis, and usage of nanomaterials for medical purposes.

Drug Delivery

AI with nanomaterials could effectively encapsulate drugs and release them directly into the desired cell or tissue, thereby reducing side effects and improving treatment efficacy. A Machine Learning (ML) framework to predict nanoparticles for biological interactions, such as predicting biodistribution, cellular uptake, and drug release profiles of nanoparticles. It has been employed to optimize the size, conformation, and surface characteristics of nanoparticles to promote active targeting of cancer cells while minimizing uptake by normal tissues [27]. AI also allowed for the creation of targeted drug delivery setups (innovative drug delivery systems), where nanomaterials are programmed to release drugs according to predefined physical stimuli (pH, temperature, or enzymatic activity) in vivo. These AI-driven models are instrumental in predicting material composition and which functionalization is necessary for these stimuli-responsive systems, which is essential in a personalized medicine approach [27].

Medical Diagnostics

The nanoparticles are designed for use in biosensors and imaging agents and have great importance when it comes to medical diagnostics. Gold nanoparticles or quantum dots can be targeted towards specific cancer pathways; AI models are able to predict surface modifications that make these nanoparticles most effective for use in diagnostic assays (to detect biomarkers at very low levels) of a panel of diseases, such as cancer or cardiovascular conditions [28].

Medicine/Therapy

In medical treatments, AI is helping to design nanomaterials that can be used for Photothermal Therapy (PTT) and Photodynamic Therapy (PDT). AI models help to design the nanomaterials for the conversion of light to heat (in PTT) or production of the reactive oxygen species (ROS) after cellular uptake, leading to the specific treatment of cancer cells [29]. Predictive models are based on Artificial Intelligence (AI) to determine the properties of nanomaterials, such as size, surface charge, and light absorption, for optimal therapeutic effects.

Nanoelectronics: AI-Enabled Design of Nanomaterials for Transistors, Sensors, and Semiconductors

- **Nanoelectronics:** AI-based design of nanomaterials for transistors, sensors, and semiconductors. For instance, advancements in the design and optimization of nanomaterials for use within nanoelectronics, such as transistors, sensors, and semiconductors, require exact electrical, thermal, and mechanical properties.
- **Transistors**: In the area of transistor technology, the conditioned superiority in electrical conductivity and flexibility provided by graphene and carbon nanotubes (CNTs) compared to bulk materials helps in smaller transistors, allowing future electronics to be made. However, the electrical properties of these nanomaterials are being predicted and optimized using AI models that analyze massive datasets of material properties and synthesis conditions [4] by simulating doping, defect engineering, and structural modifications on the electronic properties of nanomaterials using artificial intelligence [23].
- **Sensors**: Nanomaterials have drawn significant attention for the development of sensors with a large surface area and tunable properties towards their environmental responses using materials like metal oxides and 2D nanosheets (*e.g.*, MoS2, black phosphorus). These nanomaterials, in combination with AI-driven models, could further assist in the optimization of material composition, morphology, and functionalization to enhance gas/chemical/biosensors with higher sensitivity and selectivity. AI technology has been utilized in the development of sensors based on nanomaterials that can detect minute amounts of environmentally relevant gases (CO_2 or NO_2) essential for environmental monitoring and industrial safety [30]. On the way to developing nanosensors, AI plays a crucial role in designing better response time, durability, and energy efficiency. Such predictive models can allow the simulation of a variety of nanomaterial configurations that can behave in different environmental conditions, enabling the construction and manufacture of robust and reliable sensors.
- **Semiconductors:** AI is used in designing nanomaterials for semiconductors to improve the efficiency and performance of electronic devices, including quantum dot nanomaterials for optoelectronics. AI can problematize the electronic band structure and optical properties of these materials to architect nanomaterials with fine-tunable optoelectronic characteristics for use on displays, LEDs, and solar cells. This speeds up the time-to-market of improved-performing new semiconductors in practical applications [20].

Energy and Environment: AI in Designing Nanomaterials for Energy Storage and Environmental Solutions

AI is helping design nanomaterials for energy storage and various environmental solutions. The most significant global problems are related to clean energy and pollution control.

Energy storage: AI is handy in optimizing nanomaterials for batteries, supercapacitors, and fuel cells. AI models are used to design electrodes with silicon nanoparticles and graphene composites for enhanced energy density, cycle life, and charge/discharge rates in lithium-ion batteries [21]. It uses AI to identify twists in material structure and composition that alter the performance of the battery, guiding scientists to develop improved electrode materials [31]. AI has been employed to design micro/mesoporous architecture and surface area of nanomaterials (*e.g.*, carbon-based materials) in supercapacitors that impact their energy storage capability. By showing the ideal conditions for the synthesis of these nanomaterials, the predictive model gives more effective energy storage devices [22].

Environmental Solutions: AI-driven designs of nanomaterials for water purification, pollution control, and carbon capture. The most common nanomaterials used for water treatment are zeolites, carbon nanotubes, and metal-organic frameworks. AI innovative design programs are vital to predict the efficacy of these materials as adsorbents and regenerable sorbents. It is an essential factor in designing modular sorption materials for pollutant selective removal based on adsorption [26]. The use of AI-developed nanomaterials for water purification is a key research area. These materials are capable of adsorbing contaminants like heavy metals and pesticides [7]. Potential uses include environmentally friendly advanced nanomaterials that capture CO_2 directly out of the air and, therefore, can either be used or buried, with carbon-removing technology being one such example in both cases [24].

AI-Driven Approaches for Sustainable Nanomaterial Design and Development

The Contribution of AI in Creating Green, Degradable, or Recyclable Nanomaterials

AI is straddling efforts to produce nanomaterials that are green in nature, biodegradable, and recyclable. Although such traditional nanomaterials are known to be effective in numerous applications, they can also possess environmental and health risks due to their environmental persistence and possible toxicity. This is where AI-driven approaches are being used to find and develop high-performance, sustainable nanomaterials.

Green nanomaterials, nature-originated eco-friendly nanomaterials (*e.g.*, cellulose nanofibers, chitosan), are used in various fields, from packaging to water detoxification. In each step, material science is using AI to accelerate the overall synthesis of these materials, taking into account performance and sustainability constraints. It allows artificial neural networks to predict the mechanical and chemical properties of biodegradable nanomaterials from their composition itself to make them strong as well as degradable under natural conditions [32].

AI also facilitates the development of recyclable nanomaterials by predicting material lifecycles and their behavior under different environmental conditions. Predictive models can determine whether nanomaterials break down and can be recovered, helping to design materials that can be easily recycled or reused in new applications [22]. This is an essential factor in the context of circular economy principles, where materials are intended to leave waste and are disposed of at their disposal rate into the production cycle.

Optimizing Material Efficiency and Reducing Waste Using AI

This will improve the use of nanomaterials in industry and minimize waste at all stages from synthesis to post-processing and through to applications. Legacy methods for material development are typically tedious trial-and-error processes that result in extra waste. For this, AI models (*e.g.*, genetic algorithms and deep learning) can help by predicting the best synthesis parameters (temperature, pressure, concentrations, etc.) for fast production [33]. AI-driven simulations are integrated to discover ideal nanomaterial compositions with the trade-off of fewer raw materials for a given performance. They can even predict the best-performing nanomaterials combination, mitigating strength, conductivity, or catalytic efficiency, which would eventually lead to lower consumption of rare or more expensive materials [30]. Material conservation at both the fabrication and application stages. In addition, AI-based optimization methods are gaining popularity in green chemistry for designing greener and less toxic synthesis routes of nanomaterials. AI aids the transition to greener nanomanufacturing approaches by modeling chemical reactions that reduce waste and energy spent [4].

Frontiers in Green Nanotechnology and Environmental Remediation Based on Artificial Intelligence

AI innovations are being implemented in areas like green nanotechnology. This area not only creates nanomaterials from renewable resources by eco-friendly methods but is also one spot where the impact of AI is significant. AI models also allow the discovery of more sustainable synthesis routes, i.e., involving plant extracts or bio-sourced solvents that can be used in place of toxic chemicals and eventually perfecting these processes for scale-up capacity [31].

Improved nanomaterials in Environmental Remediation that are AI-based on Models for Air, Water, and Soil Pollution Purification. Design AI-based technologies for the removal and degradation of contaminants like heavy metals, organic dyes, and greenhouse gas adsorption using nanomaterials, *e.g.*, Metal-Organic Frameworks (MOFs) such as graphene-based composites, etc. Predictive learning with adsorption capacity of GO and rGO as remediation materials [20]. This includes advancing the AI-facilitated design of photocatalytic nanomaterials, which are used to degrade pollutants with the help of light. This is because AI acts as a primary tool for property screening and potential utilization of nanomaterials in photocatalysis *via* size, shape, and composition tweaking, thereby improving their efficacy in the Photocatalytic degradation treatment of contaminants.

For example, in the case of Carbon Capture and Storage (CCS), by using artificial intelligence, it is possible to design nanomaterials that can be used for efficient absorption of CO_2 and other greenhouse gases from the atmosphere or industrial activities. Corroborate the sort of AI-driven breakthroughs that these are, which are powerful when it comes to climate change and addressing cleaner energy and industrial systems [7].

AI for Sustainable Nanomaterials

Developing Green, Biodegradable, and Recyclable Nanomaterials with AI

The role of sustainable nanomaterials in reducing the environmental impact of this technology is fundamental. Use of AI in the identification and production of non-toxic, biodegradable nanomaterials. The designs are utilized in making AI models biodegradable as they are produced from polyesters and polylactic acid (PLA) basic commodity polymers that serve a pinnacle of applications to bottling and packaging, including agriculture consumer goods sectors along with in biomedical products used for medical device usages or surgical implants where their degradability affect stress-free disposal process focusing on material waste issues by these complex calculations, machine learning algorithms can estimate the biodegradability of materials using informative molecular properties making it possible for scientists to build newer recyclable and degradable material [4].

The design of nanocomposites that could be dismantled and reused once end-o--life requires AI. The identified materials are studied using AI models to predict how they would behave in the recycling of these different recycling processes while retaining their material performance properties after reprocessing [20]. This work will contribute to developing the computationally anticipated extensive recycling performance of nanomaterials by providing valuable insights into sustainable material design for circular economies [21].

Optimizing Material Efficiency and Reducing Waste Using AI

This will improve the use of nanomaterials in industry and minimize waste at all stages from synthesis to post-processing and through to applications. Legacy methods for material development are typically tedious trial-and-error processes that result in extra waste. For this, AI models (*e.g.*, genetic algorithms and deep learning) can help by predicting the best synthesis parameters (temperature, pressure, concentrations, etc.) for fast production [33]. AI-driven simulations are integrated to discover ideal nanomaterial compositions with the trade-off of fewer raw materials for a given performance. They can even predict the best-performing nanomaterials combination, mitigating strength, conductivity, or catalytic efficiency, which would eventually lead to lower consumption of rare or more expensive materials [30]. Material conservation at both the fabrication and application stages. In addition, AI-based optimization methods are gaining popularity in green chemistry for designing greener and less toxic synthesis routes of nanomaterials. AI aids the transition to greener nanomanufacturing approaches by modeling chemical reactions that reduce waste and energy spent [4].

AI-Driven Innovations in Green Nanotechnology and Environmental Remediation

AI comes with the help of machine learning; significant progress has been made related to green nanotechnology by designing greener nanomaterials. For example, AI-driven models have been developed for the rational design of nanomaterials targeting applications in environmental remediation, such as carbon capture, water purification, and soil detoxification.

Artificial Intelligence in Developing Efficient Adsorbent Nanomaterial for Water or Air Pollutants Capture. AI also helps predict the adsorption capacity and regeneration efficiency of materials such as Metal-Organic Frameworks (MOFs), graphene, or carbon nanotubes for pollutant removal and recycling [28]. Furthermore, AI models capture toxic organic contaminants, especially pesticides and microplastics, which are a crucial factor in the challenge to an environment that prevails in water resources scenarios for sustainable development to use in producing photocatalytic nanomaterials, which convert sunlight into chemical reactions for degrading pollutants or converting CO_2 to energy resources. By fine-tuning the size, architecture, and constitution of these photocatalysts, AI is capable of achieving optimum performances in terms of degradation of pollutants or transformation to less harmful products [20].

AI-Driven Nanomaterial Integration and Fabrication

AI in Improving Precision and Scalability of Nanofabrication Techniques

AI in nanofabrication has a high promise for resourceful and large-scale production techniques like lithography, self-assembly, and Chemical Vapor Deposition (CVD), which have revolutionized new ultraprecision industrial norms. Although all the previously mentioned methods are essential in controlling nanostructures' dimensions and properties, it is not easy to maintain the consistency of most of them on a large scale.

To improve the precision of nanoscale lithography, new models using AI for image recognition and reinforcement learning are in development. Next, AI can monitor and manipulate in real time the production process to steer it back into deviation-free mode when it appears. This ensures that nanostructures are synthesized with minimal defects [26]. AI is also involved in the processing terms known as self-assembly, a procedure where nanomaterials automatically form into advantageous 3-D shapes. Using predictive AI models, these processes can be emulated and ideal conditions for constructing more robust nanostructures [7].

Scalability presents an enormous hurdle in nanomanufacturing. Furthermore, AI models are used to bring lab-scale nanofabrication protocols to an industrial level of production, from AI-driven process optimization in CVD, which guarantees that large-scale production has the same quality and properties as small-scale experiments. It is essential for industries working in high volumes and using nanomaterials like electronics [22].

Enhancing Nanoscale Process Control Using AI Models

The ability to have high-reliability control over nanoscale phenomena is central to the realization of nanomaterials and devices. Using AI models to observe massive amounts of data from in-situ monitoring systems, which collect real-time data on temperature, pressure, and material behavior during fabrication processes, offers an added level of control. Allowing for uniformity and quality in areas on the scale of square meters, i.e., AI engineers can predictably affect by varying many different inputs to a nanostructure when using techniques such as ALD or spin coating. AI-mediated fine control of process parameters minimizes variance in nanofabrication, which is the key to near-zero-defect manufacturing [20].

AI models are also interwoven with feedback control systems for updating nanoscale fabrication processes. So this helps the nanomaterials to have the desired thickness and morphology. These improvements are being used in areas such as nanoelectronics and photonics, where precision on the few-nanometer scale is crucial [30].

AI for Integrating Nanomaterials into Complex Devices and Systems

Applications of AI include the incorporation of nanomaterials into complex devices and systems, such as flexible electronics, biosensors, and quantum applications. Nanomaterials can introduce unique high electrical conductivity, flexibility, and sensitivity properties, but due to their shape, these ideals for specific applications require the process of design and optimization. For example, in flexible electronics, AI is employed to predict how nanomaterials such as graphene or carbon nanotubes behave under various mechanical loads and environmental conditions. It results in more resilient circuits that can be used in wearables or foldable devices [20]. Also, the AI-based models have led to a new class of biosensors designed by integrating nanomaterials for medical diagnostic biomarker quantification. These models predict the optimal material pairs to give the highest sensitivity and specificity in disease detection applications.

For quantum computing and photonic devices, AI helps in perfecting the combination of nanomaterials having specific quantum or optical entities. With AI models that can realistically replicate any material interacting with light or certain quantum states. To design novel quantum dots, nanowires, nanophotonic structures, *etc.*, for future high-performance computing and communication systems [7].

CHALLENGES AND ETHICAL CONSIDERATIONS

Data Privacy and Intellectual Property Concerns in AI-Powered Nanomaterial Research

AI could be employed more extensively in nanomaterial research that is centered around issues of data privacy and Intellectual Property (IP). The source of data may be very far away from the research group or companies that use AI models on nanomaterials. These data sources require a lot of storage and bandwidth to transfer relevant files. Sharing of such data can be risky due to misuse or exploitation (proprietary patents, confidential company information). It is crucial to keep data breaches that allow sensitive advancements in technology to be stolen or commercially exploited without consent in a secure manner.

Ethical and Safety Challenges in the Deployment of AI in Nanomaterial Design and Applications

Another key area for responsible AI distribution is to address the ethical gap of using them in nanomaterial design. AI-designed nanomaterials are especially suited for applications like nanomedicine that come into contact with biological systems. AI-assisted means will expedite the development of new nanomaterials that should be accompanied by testing in regard to toxicity, biocompatibility, and environmental impact. These wrong-sized materials could present unexpectedly high health and environmental hazards if the safety of AI-designed nanomaterials is not adequately evaluated.

There is also the ethical mandate to have transparency on systems arriving in nanomaterial research. For example, material designed or optimized makes sense for several reasons, including machine learning algorithms. Designers and developers need to strive so that systems can be understood and decisions can be connected to intelligible models.

Regulatory Considerations for the Use of AI in Nanotechnology Industries

In the nanotechnology sector, AI integration works at the intersection of existing safety and environmental standards to bring technology into the industry. Most of the regulations on nanomaterials tend to regard the potential hazards associated with the same properties. This confluence of AI playing a rapid design and scale-up role in the materials themselves adds greater complexity to traditional material testing and approval mechanisms, with the rapid innovation AI is enabling to these new materials.

It is necessary to change the guidelines and frameworks established by governments and regulatory authorities for using AI in nanotechnology. These guidelines should include evaluations of the safety and environmental impact assessments of AI-driven nanomaterial designs, capturing data, managing intellectual property considerations, *etc*. Regulatory cooperation at the global level is also crucial because AI and nanomaterial technologies transcend several industries and even international boundaries.

FUTURE DIRECTIONS AND EMERGING TRENDS

The AI landscape in nanomaterials research is quickly changing due to developments in AI, ML, quantum computing, and automation technologies. AI should make an even bigger difference in the discovery, design, and testing of nanomaterials. A significant trend is the growing use of AI simulations, as it helps researchers model materials' behaviour under different circumstances without expensive physical tests [4]. This will make it possible for new, high-tech nanomaterials with superior performance to be discovered at a rate and level of accuracy that would have been unfathomable in the past. Now, two new interdisciplinary frontiers include AI and nanotechnology. Instead, AI coupled with biotechnology has helped in the creation of intelligent nanomaterials programmed precisely for either drug delivery or biosensing on demand, as well as novel 3D tissue engineering. AI may develop in the era of precision-designed nanomaterials interfacing with biological systems, characterized by increasingly predictive matching through synthetic biology for personalized medicine and therapeutics [28].

In such a scenario, AI systems can conceptualize experiments ranging from hypothesis generation to material synthesis and testing with minimal human interference in an autonomous laboratory. These kinds of systems promise to cut the discovery time and costs for nanomaterials, meaning entire design spaces will be accessible [7]. AI also empowers the matter and can train the stimulus-responsive nanomaterials that are capable of altering their properties or behaviors in response to external stimuli. AI can be used to predict the evolution of materials in time and space, as well as for future design of reconfigurable materials for applications such as innovative coatings, self-healing materials, or reconfigurable electronics [4].

The potential of AI-nanotechnology for innovation is crucial for a wide variety of improvements in other industry sectors. This could include the discovery of nanomaterials with direct and less invasive methods for treating diseases like cancer or neurological disorders through nanomedicine. For energy storage, AI-designed nanomaterials could transform battery technologies, creating more efficient and longer-lasting energy storage systems [28]. For example, in environmental sustainability, artificial intelligence will help advance green nanotechnology, including new nanomaterials that eliminate waste, sequester carbon, or optimize clean water treatment. At the same time, AI systems get more intelligent and more independent, and they find completely new materials that lead to nanotechnology regeneration in terms of living [21].

CONCLUSION

Artificial Intelligence (AI) seems to be a game-changer in nanomaterials, as it has catalyzed research and applications in various areas. A critical outcome of nanotechnology is that AI has accelerated the discovery, design, characterization, and application to produce advanced materials that have designed properties. These have led to the employment of machine learning in predictive modeling, AI-driven automation in synthesis, more sophisticated characterization techniques, and several others that have generated new ways for advancements. Collaborations between AI and nanotechnology are enabling numerous new possibilities, from autonomous research systems to the inclusion of nanomaterials in smart devices, as well as more sustainable materials. It is clear that AI and nanotechnology will enable a new wave of discoveries in the years to come by tackling some of the grand challenges faced by society today, from health and environment to energy access. Taking such collaboration to its fullest will not only enhance innovations but also help us to manage the scientific, moral, and regulatory complexity that these advancements bring with them, channeling a future where AI and nanotechnology collaborate for the public good.

REFERENCES

[1] R. Xu, D. Wang, and Y. Zhang, "Nanomaterials for Biomedical Applications: A Review of Current Advances and Future Trends", *J. Nanobiotechnology,* vol. 21, no. 1, pp. 56-75, 2023. [PMID: 36805678]

[2] L. Chen, Z. Li, and S. Zhang, "Nanomaterials in Energy Storage and Conversion: The Role of AI in Advancing the Field", *Energy Mater. Today,* vol. 15, no. 4, pp. 451-467, 2022.

[3] S. Iijima, "Nanotechnology and Electronics: The Influence of Carbon Nanomaterials on the Development of Next-Generation Devices", *Nano Today,* vol. 10, no. 1, pp. 30-43, 2021.

[4] K.T. Butler, D.W. Davies, H. Cartwright, O. Isayev, and A. Walsh, "Machine learning for molecular and materials science", *Nature,* vol. 559, no. 7715, pp. 547-555, 2018. [http://dx.doi.org/10.1038/s41586-018-0337-2] [PMID: 30046072]

[5] H. Guo, W. Sun, W. Lu, Q. Sun, M. Wang, and L. Xu, "Machine learning approach for predicting the fracture toughness of bulk metallic glasses", *Philos. Mag.,* vol. 105, no. 17, pp. 991-1005, 2025. [http://dx.doi.org/10.1080/14786435.2025.2484719]

[6] D. Jha, L. Ward, A. Paul, W. Liao, A. Choudhary, C. Wolverton, and A. Agrawal, "ElemNet: Deep learning the chemistry of materials from only elemental composition", *Sci. Rep.,* vol. 8, no. 1, p. 17593, 2018. [http://dx.doi.org/10.1038/s41598-018-35934-y] [PMID: 30514926]

[7] Y. Zhuo, A. Mansouri Tehrani, and J. Brgoch, "Predicting the band gaps of inorganic solids by machine learning", *J. Phys. Chem. Lett.,* vol. 9, no. 7, pp. 1668-1673, 2018. [http://dx.doi.org/10.1021/acs.jpclett.8b00124] [PMID: 29532658]

[8] B. Bhushan, *Springer Handbook of Nanotechnology.* Springer, 2017. [http://dx.doi.org/10.1007/978-3-662-54357-3]

[9] X. Zhang, Q. Zhao, and T. Feng, "Machine learning modeling for predicting thermal conductivity of nanostructured materials", *J. Appl. Phys.,* vol. 126, no. 5, p. 054303, 2019.

[10] V. Mittal, *Nanocomposites: Synthesis, Structure, Properties, and New Application Opportunities.* Wiley, 2020.

[11] Y. Gao, F. Deng, R. He, and Z. Zhong, "Spontaneous curvature in two-dimensional van der Waals heterostructures", *Nat. Commun.,* vol. 16, no. 1, pp. 1-10, 2025. [http://dx.doi.org/10.1038/s41467-025-56055-x]

[12] A. Akbarzadeh, M. Samiei, and S. Davaran, "Magnetic nanoparticles: preparation, physical properties, and applications in biomedicine", *Nanoscale Res. Lett.,* vol. 7, no. 1, p. 144, 2012. [http://dx.doi.org/10.1186/1556-276X-7-144] [PMID: 22348683]

[13] C. Lee, X. Wei, and D. Kim, "Flexible electronics: Advances and challenges of nanomaterials", *Adv.*

Funct. Mater., vol. 31, no. 5, p. 2005925, 2021.

[14] P.V. Kamat, "Quantum dot solar cells: The next big thing in photovoltaics", *ACS Energy Lett.,* vol. 5, no. 3, pp. 709-711, 2020.

[15] I. Ali, C. Peng, and I. Naz, "Water purification using graphene composites: A review", *Environ. Sci. Pollut. Res. Int.,* vol. 26, no. 3, pp. 1825-1839, 2019.

[16] O. Carp, C.L. Huisman, and A. Reller, "Photocatalytic titanium dioxide: From the fundamentals to applications", *Appl. Catal. B,* vol. 73, no. 1–2, pp. 179-188, 2021.

[17] C. Xiang, D. He, and X. Wang, "Machine learning in nanomaterials: Properties, design, and applications", *J. Nanomater.,* vol. 21, p. 156, 2021.

[18] K.P. Loh, Q. Bao, and P.K. Ang, "Graphene and carbon nanotubes in nanoelectronics", *Adv. Mater.,* vol. 22, no. 9, pp. 1399-1411, 2019.

[19] G. Oberdörster, V. Stone, and K. Donaldson, "Toxicology of nanoparticles: A historical perspective", *Nanotoxicology,* vol. 1, no. 1, pp. 2-25, 2007. [http://dx.doi.org/10.1080/17435390701314761]

[20] J. Schmidt, M. R. Marques, S. Botti, and M. A. Marques, "Recent advances and applications of machine learning in solid-state materials science", *npj Comput. Mater.,* vol. 5, no. 1, p. 83, 2019. [http://dx.doi.org/10.1038/s41524-019-0221-0]

[21] L. Zhu, H. Peng, and Z. Fan, "AI-driven green nanotechnology for environmental sustainability", *Environ. Sci. Nano,* vol. 8, no. 3, pp. 1021-1038, 2021.

[22] D. Dhokane, A. Shaikh, A. Yadav, N. Giri, A. Bandyopadhyay, S. Dasgupta, and B. Bhadra, "CRISPR-based bioengineering in microalgae for production of industrially important biomolecules", *Front. Bioeng. Biotechnol.,* vol. 11, p. 1267826, 2023. [http://dx.doi.org/10.3389/fbioe.2023.1267826] [PMID: 37965048]

[23] A.P. Burgard, P. Pharkya, and C.D. Maranas, "Optknock: A bilevel programming framework for identifying gene knockout strategies for microbial strain optimization", *Biotechnol. Bioeng.,* vol. 84, no. 6, pp. 647-657, 2003. [http://dx.doi.org/10.1002/bit.10803] [PMID: 14595777]

[24] Y. Zhang, Y. Zhao, and T. Cui, "Deep learning for nanoscale imaging and spectroscopy", *Adv. Intell. Syst.,* vol. 2, no. 5, p. 1900143, 2020.

[25] M.B. Oviedo, "Fast and interpretable classification of small x-ray diffraction datasets using data augmentation and deep neural networks", *npj Comput. Mater.,* vol. 5, no. 1, p. 60, 2019. [http://dx.doi.org/10.1038/s41524-019-0196-x]

[26] S.V. Kalinin, B.G. Sumpter, and R.K. Archibald, "Big–deep–smart data in imaging for guiding materials design", *Nat. Mater.,* vol. 14, no. 10, pp. 973-980, 2015. [http://dx.doi.org/10.1038/nmat4395] [PMID: 26395941]

[27] J.K. Patra, G. Das, L.F. Fraceto, E.V.R. Campos, M.P. Rodriguez-Torres, L.S. Acosta-Torres, L.A. Diaz-Torres, R. Grillo, M.K. Swamy, S. Sharma, S. Habtemariam, and H.S. Shin, "Nano based drug delivery systems: recent developments and future prospects", *J. Nanobiotechnology,* vol. 16, no. 1, p. 71, 2018. [http://dx.doi.org/10.1186/s12951-018-0392-8] [PMID: 30231877]

[28] H. Chen, Z. Li, and J. Zhang, "AI for designing biodegradable nanomaterials for environmental applications", *J. Mater. Res.,* vol. 36, no. 4, pp. 250-265, 2019.

[29] C. Li, L. Bai, and J. Liu, "AI-enhanced biosensors based on nanomaterials for early disease detection", *Biosens. Bioelectron.,* vol. 149, p. 111823, 2020.

[30] Y. Feng, L. Zhu, and X. Jiang, "AI-enabled gas sensing using nanomaterials: Challenges and prospects", *Nano Energy,* vol. 56, pp. 595-609, 2018.

[31] C. Cath, S. Wachter, B. Mittelstadt, M. Taddeo, and L. Floridi, "Artificial intelligence and the 'good society': The US, EU, and UK approach", *Sci. Eng. Ethics,* vol. 24, no. 2, pp. 505-528, 2018. [PMID: 28353045]

[32] H. Chen, Z. Li, and J. Zhang, "Smart drug delivery systems for cancer therapy", *J. Control. Release,* vol. 294, pp. 263-279, 2019.

[33] G.R. Rudramurthy, M.K. Swamy, and U.R. Sinniah, "Nanomaterials in cancer therapy", *Front. Pharmacol.,* vol. 9, p. 1364, 2018.

CHAPTER 2

Artificial Intelligence Technique Application in Maximum Power Point Tracking for Solar Photovoltaic Systems

RamaKoteswaraRao Alla[1,*], **Kandipati Rajani**[2] and **Poka Venkata Sai Jayanth**[3]

[1] *CSE-AIML Department, RVR&JC College of Engineering, Guntur, Andhra Pradesh, India*

[2] *Department of Electrical & Electronic Engineering, Vignan's Lara Institute of Technology & Sciences, Vadlamudi, Andhra Pradesh, India*

[3] *Department of Electrical & Electronic Engineering, RVR&JC College of Engineering, Guntur, Andhra Pradesh, India*

Abstract: This work presents a comparative analysis of two Maximum Power Point Tracking (MPPT) methods used in solar energy systems. Artificial Neural Networks (ANN) and Perturb and Observe (P&O) are the methods considered in this work. P&O algorithm offers ease of implementation and performs well under uniform irradiance, but it exhibits oscillations around the steady-state operating point during rapid environmental changing conditions. Additionally, its efficacy in monitoring the MPP (Maximum Power Point) under shading conditions is not appreciable. To overcome these shortcomings and to enhance the system efficiency, an advanced MPPT technique, such as ANN based, has been used in this work. ANN-based MPPT technique can alleviate this burden by automatically learning these relationships through training data. However, the accuracy of MPP tracking is highly dependent upon the quality of the chosen data. By providing a comprehensive evaluation of these MPPT controllers, this chapter empowers the readers to select the most effective solution for maximizing solar power extraction.

Keywords: Artificial Neural Network, Maximum Power Point Tracking, Perturb and Observe, PV System.

INTRODUCTION

The rising demand for electrical energy, coupled with diminishing fossil fuel reserves, has propelled renewable energy sources to lead as a potential solution. Among these, solar energy has emerged as the leading one [1]. Photovoltaic (PV)

[*] **Corresponding author RamaKoteswaraRao Alla:** CSE-AIML Department, RVR&JC College of Engineering, Guntur, Andhra Pradesh, India, India; E-mail: ramnitkkr@gmail.com

Shilpa Gupta, Ritika Sharma & Gokana Mohana Rani (Eds.)

systems offer a clean and environmental friendly method for converting solar energy into electricity. Compared to other renewable energy sources, PV systems require minimal maintenance and generate minimal noise [2].

However, they are also subject to limitations such as expensive installation charges and poor efficiency. PV system's output depends on both irradiance (solar radiation) and temperature. To optimize power generation, the system must operate at its maximum power point. Using maximum power point tracking strategies, this is accomplished. For solar power systems to maximize their production, especially those that use PV panels, MPPT is essential [3].

Sunlight intensity fluctuates throughout the day due to factors like weather and shading. MPPT algorithms address these variations by continuously monitoring the system parameters [4]. The relationship between voltage and current produced by a solar panel is non-linear, with a specific voltage point corresponding to the highest power output. MPPT ensures that the panels operate at this MPP for optimal power generation. MPPT guarantees that the greatest amount of electricity from the solar panels is captured under various conditions by continually monitoring the MPP.

Several MPPT techniques exist in the literature, each suited to a specific application. Among these, the perturb and observe approach is broadly used because it is straightforward and simple. However, it exhibits limitations in tracking the MPP during rapidly changing environmental conditions. To address these shortcomings and ensure faster MPP tracking under dynamic environmental conditions, different MPPT techniques are introduced in a recent study [5]. These techniques include fuzzy logic control and artificial neural networks. This paper compares the P&O and ANN-based MPPT methods. Section II will explore PV module modelling, while Sections III and IV will explore DC-DC converter and MPPT principles. Section V presents the simulation results, followed by a concluding discussion in Section VI.

PV MODULE

Fig. (**1**) depicts the circuit model of a photovoltaic cell [6]. The primary current source, denoted by I_{ph} (photocurrent), represents the current generated within the cell due to the absorption of solar irradiance by photons. This current exhibits a near-linear relationship with irradiance, implying that higher irradiance levels result in a proportionally higher photocurrent. A junction diode is connected in parallel with the current source. This diode simulates the non-ideal behaviour of a p-n junction in the PV cell. A small leakage current, denoted by I_D (diode current), flows through this diode even under open-circuit conditions (when no load is connected). A shunt resistance (R_{sh}) represents a leakage path for current within the cell. A small current, denoted by I_{Rsh} (shunt current), flows through this resistor due to imperfections in the cell. The final output current (I), also known as the load current delivered by the PV system, is the summation of these three currents [7].

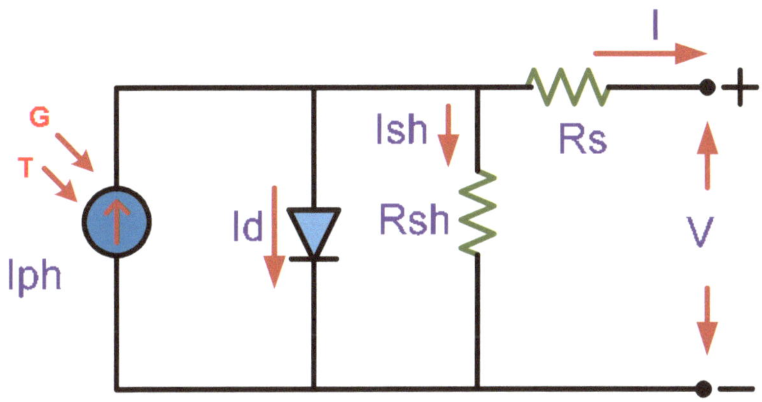

Fig. (1). Practical solar cell circuit.

Mathematically, the output current (I) can be expressed as in Equations 1 and 2

$$I = I_{L,cell} - I_d - I_{sh} \quad \textbf{(1)}$$

$$I = I_{L,cell} - I_D\left[\exp\left(\frac{V_{cell} + R_S I}{V_T a} - 1\right)\right] - \frac{V_{cell} + R_S I}{R_{sh}} \quad \textbf{(2)}$$

From the equation given above, Io is the reverse saturation current. This means that when there is no solar radiation or under dark conditions, the diode is reverse-biased, then the current flowing in the diode is the reverse saturation current.

BOOST CONVERTER

Fig. (**2**) illustrates a typical DC-DC boost converter circuit employed in photovoltaic (PV) systems. The goal of this converter is to raise the input DC voltage level to a higher output DC voltage level [8]. It is necessary to compute the inductor's ripple current in order to build a boost converter with optimal efficiency and dependability [9].

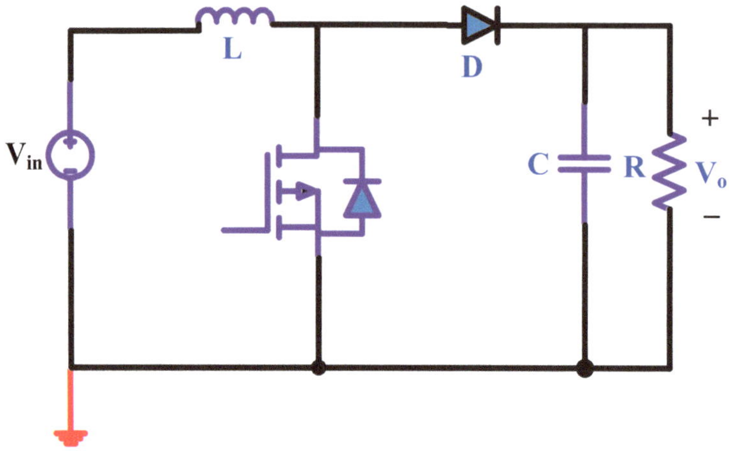

Fig. (2). DC-DC boost converter.

The equation is written as

$$\Delta I_L = (0.2 \text{ to } 0.4) \times I_{OUT(max)} \times \frac{V_{OUT}}{V_{IN}} \quad \textbf{(3)}$$

20 to 30 percent of the output current is a reasonable estimate for ripple current. The value of the inductor from the boost converter can be calculated through the ripple current equation as given in Equations 3 and 4.

$$L = \frac{V_{IN} \times (V_{OUT} - V_{IN})}{\Delta I_L \times f_s \times V_{OUT}} \quad \textbf{(4)}$$

The above equation is the design value of the inductor inside the boost converter.

MPPT TECHNIQUES

- **A. Perturbation and Observation (P&O):** The Perturb and Observe algorithm is a popular MPPT approach in photovoltaic (PV) systems because of its inherent simplicity [10]. This method operates by iteratively adjusting the operating voltage of the photovoltaic array in small increments. Following each adjustment, the P&O algorithm calculates the resulting change in output power. As the power output grows, the P&O algorithm will continue to perturb the voltage in that direction, assuming it's approaching the maximum power point. Conversely, if the output power decreases, the P&O algorithm changes the way of its voltage perturbations. While this approach effectively tracks the MPP, it has limitations, like tracking at the local maximum peak sometimes [11]. The continuous search for the optimal operating point leads to oscillations around the true MPP. These oscillations can result in some energy loss. Additionally, the P&O algorithm's effectiveness diminishes under partial shading conditions, where the MPP itself becomes more dynamic and less predictable.

Fig. (**3**) depicts a flowchart representation of the P&O algorithm for MPPT in PV systems. This flowchart illustrates the decision-making process employed by the algorithm to continuously adjust the PV module's operating voltage and maintain operation near the MPP as environmental conditions fluctuate [12].

Fig. (**4**) exemplifies a photovoltaic system incorporating a Perturb and Observe MPPT algorithm for maximizing power output. The system comprises three key elements:

Solar Panel Module: This component directly converts solar irradiance into electrical energy, generating a DC voltage and current output.

Boost Converter: This circuit raises the DC voltage level of the solar panel module to a level appropriate for the attached load or battery bank. The duty cycle pulse generated by the PWM controller regulates the boost converter's operation.

P&O MPPT Algorithm: This control algorithm continuously monitors the system's performance and modifies the duty cycle. The P&O algorithm indirectly controls the solar module's operating voltage by managing its duty cycle. The adjusted duty cycle pulse is then delivered to the MOSFET switch within the boost converter, dictating its on and off states and ultimately impacting the output voltage. In essence, Fig. (**4**) shows a functional diagram of a PV module with a P&O MPPT approach. The P&O algorithm dynamically adjusts the boost converter's operation to make sure the solar panel module functions near its Maximum Power Point (MPP) under varying environmental conditions, maximizing power generation from the PV system.

- **B. Artificial Neural Networks (ANNS):** The use of artificial neural networks in physical systems has witnessed a significant rise. ANNs share some similarities with how the human brain processes information through interconnected neurons [13 - 15]. Unlike traditional methods that rely on programmed rules, ANNs leverage an expert system and knowledge-discovery approach to learn by identifying patterns and relationships within data [16 - 18].

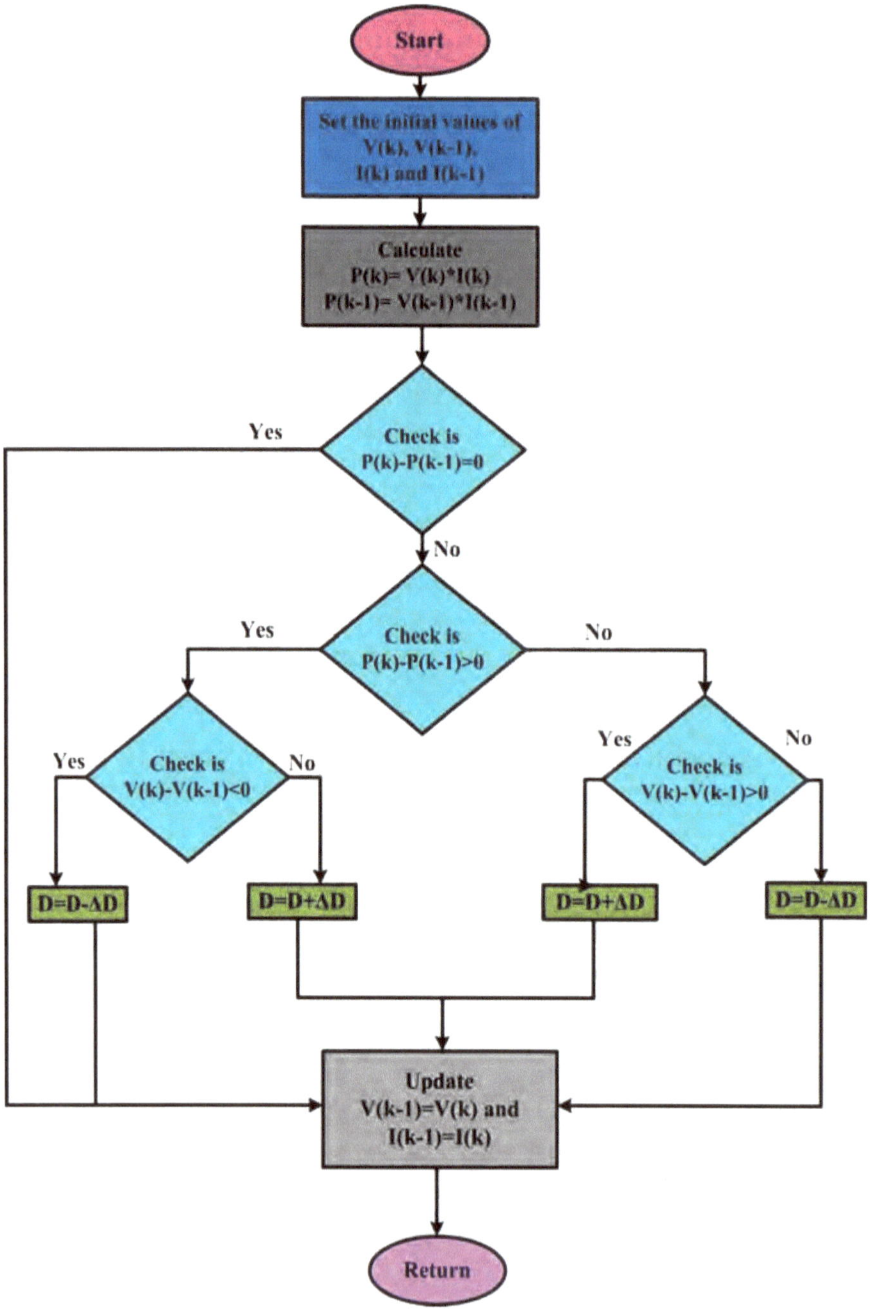

Fig. (3). P&O algorithm.

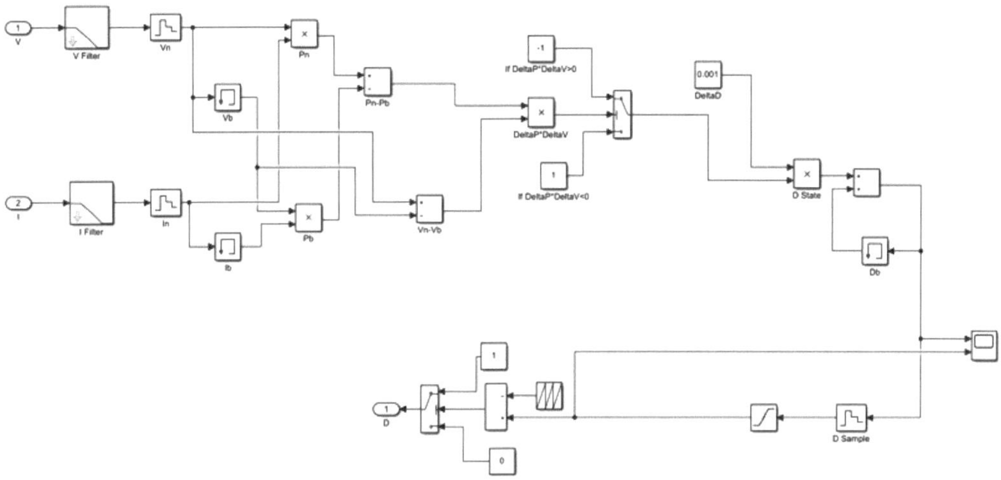

Fig. (4). Simulation Diagram of P&O Algorithm.

These networks consist of interconnected layers containing artificial neurons and associated activation functions. The layers are built upon pre-defined structures and undergo a learning process to improve performance. In the context of solar photovoltaic systems, ANNs are employed for maximum power point tracking. ANNs take various inputs from the PV system, such as voltage and environmental data (temperature, irradiance), to determine the optimal operating point. The system can be trained to produce a specific output, such as duty cycle ratios or other control parameters.

Fig. (**5**) displays a simulation schematic diagram for a photovoltaic system using an artificial neural network-based maximum power point tracking controller.

Simulation Results

The photovoltaic module employed in the simulation is the 1Soltech 1STH-FR--4H-250-M60-BLK model. The specific performance characteristics of this module are included in Table **1**.

Table 1. Solar panel model specification.

Parameter	Value
Maximum Power (W)	248.97
Voltage at maximum power point V_{mp}(V)	30.7
Current at maximum power point I_{mp}(A)	8.11

(Table 1) cont.....

Parameter	Value
Open circuit voltage V_{oc} (V)	38.4
Short-circuit current I_{sc} (A)	8.85
Diode saturation current I_d (A)	2.622e-10
Cells per module (N_{cell})	60

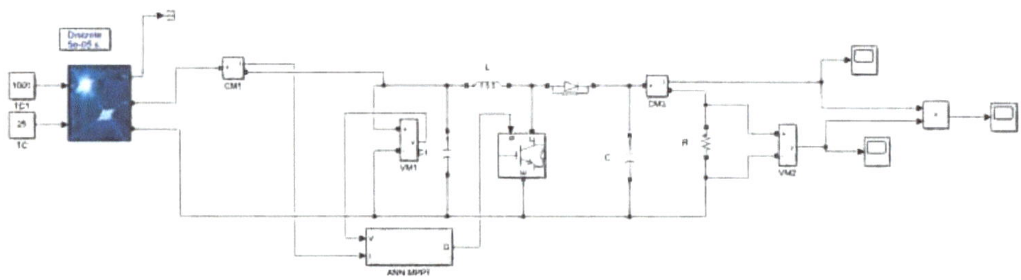

Fig. (5). Simulation diagram of ANN-based MPPT PV system.

Comparison of ANN and P&O Methods at Constant Irradiance

Fig. (**6**) shows the result of maximum power point tracking techniques, which includes an artificial neural network and Perturb and Observe. Notably, the P&O technique returns a lower output power of 238.6 W compared to the ANN, which gives 242.1 W. This performance difference arises from the inherent characteristics of each method. P&O employs a trial-and-error approach, iteratively adjusting voltage to climb the power curve. This can lead to power fluctuations around the maximum power point. But in the case of an ANN, by being trained on historical data, the ANN learns to directly map operating conditions to the optimal operating point by minimizing fluctuations and maximizing power extraction. The comparative results of different MPPT techniques at constant irradiance are given in Table **2**.

Table 2. Comparison of different MPPT techniques at constant irradiance.

Parameter	Artificial Neural Networks (ANN)	Perturb and Observe (P&O)
Output Power (w)	242.1	238.6
Output Voltage(V)	118	117.1
Output Current(A)	2.052	2.037
Data dependency	High	No
Efficiency	Highest	Moderate

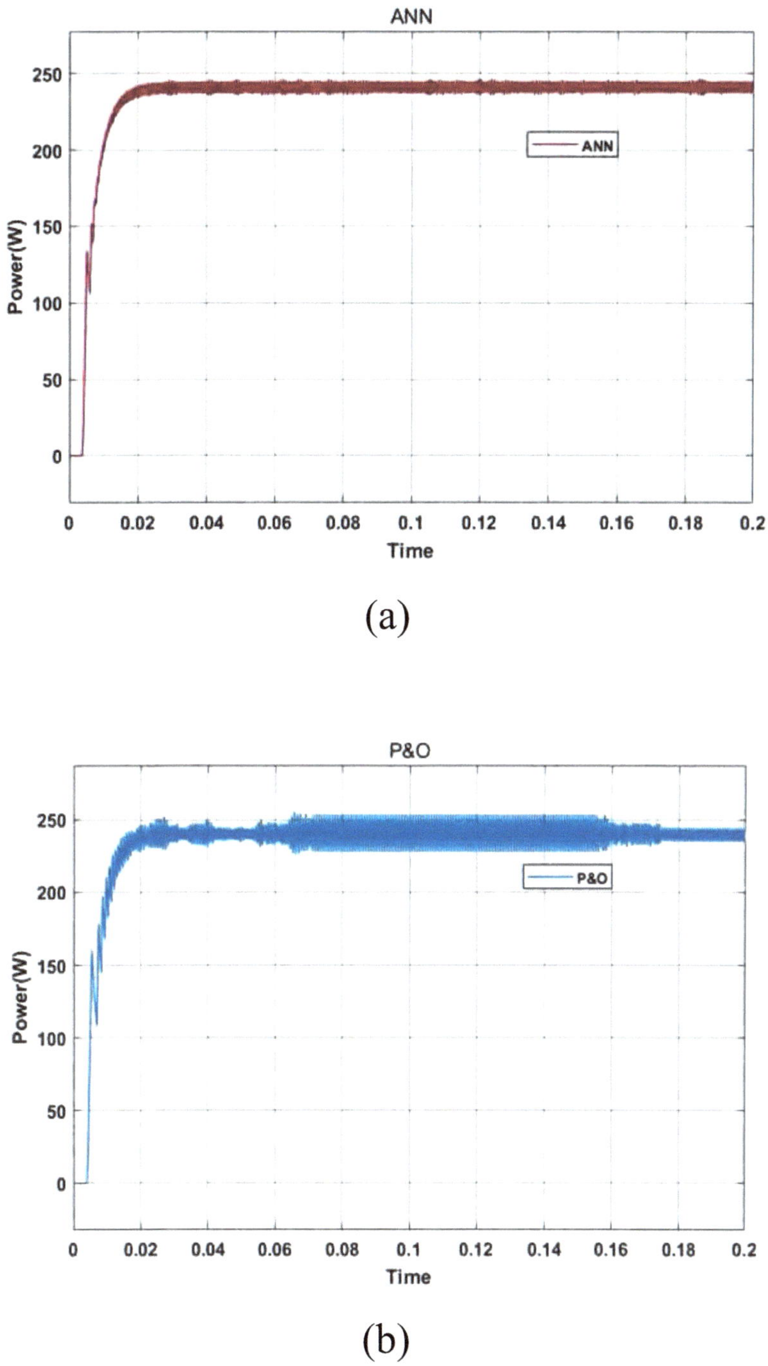

Fig. (6). Comparison of output power generated by (a) ANN MPPT, (b) P&O MPPT under constant irradiance and temperature.

Comparison of ANN and P&O Methods at Variable Irradiance

Fig. (**7**) analyzes the result of perturb and observe and artificial neural network-based MPPT techniques under varying irradiance. At 1000 W/m^2 irradiance, P&O extracts 238.6 W and ANN extracts 242.1 W. Notably, ANN maintains a clear advantage under reduced irradiance (500 W/m^2), by extracting 123.8 W compared to 114.2 W by P&O. This highlights ANN's superior ability to adapt and extract optimal power even with significant irradiance fluctuations. The comparison of both MPPT techniques results at variable irradiance is given in Table **3**.

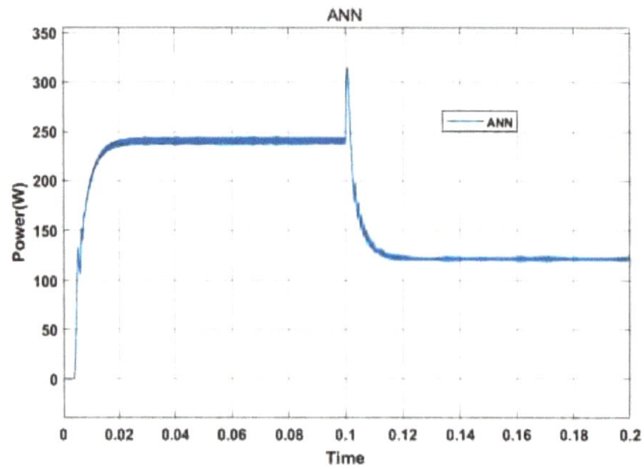

(a)

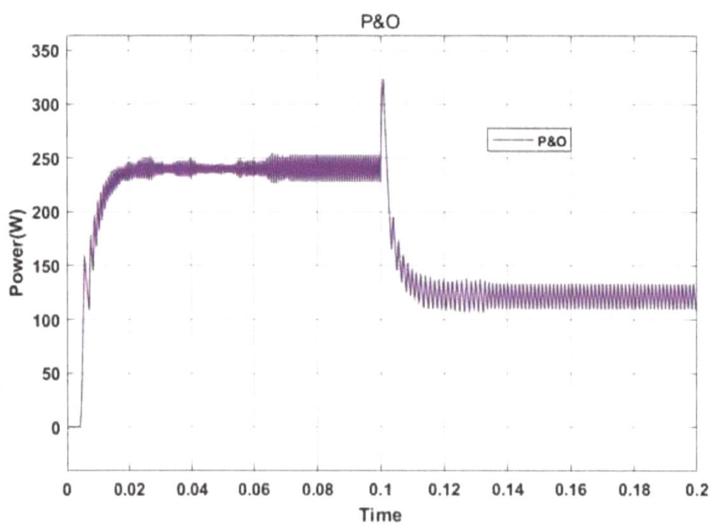

(b)

Fig. (7). Comparison of power generated by (a) ANN MPPT, (b) P&O MPPT under variable irradiance and constant temperature.

Table 3. Comparison of different MPPT techniques at variable irradiance.

Parameter	Artificial Neural Networks Based MPPT	Perturb and Observe Based MPPT
Output power (w) at irradiance(1000W/m^2)	242.1	238.6
Output voltage (V) at irradiance(1000W/m^2)	118	117.1
Output current (A) at irradiance(1000W/m^2)	2.052	2.037
Output power (w) at irradiance(500W/m^2)	123.8	114.2
Output voltage (V) at irradiance(500W/m^2)	84.37	81.04
Output current (A) at irradiance(1000W/m^2)	1.467	1.409

CONCLUSION

This work concludes by discussing the crucial function of MPPT in optimizing PV system power generation. The simple P&O technique offers a basic solution, and its limitations under dynamic conditions necessitate the exploration of more advanced methods. ANN-based MPPT technique holds promise in overcoming these limitations. Through simulations, the comparison of these two MPPT methods, including the MPPT concept, PV module modeling, and DC-DC converter analysis, has been conducted. The results presented in Section V have been analyzed to identify the most effective technique for maximizing solar power extraction under various operating conditions. It can be observed that ANN-based MPPT is 8.7% more efficient than P&O-based MPPT. By providing insights into these advanced MPPT controllers, this work empowers stakeholders to optimize their PV system performance and help create a more sustainable and clean future.

REFERENCES

[1] D.K. Narne, T.A.R. Kumar, and R. Alla, A Brief Review on Conventional and Renewable Power Generation Scenario in India.*Recent Advances in Power Systems. Lecture Notes in Electrical Engineering.,* O.H. Gupta, V.K. Sood, O.P. Malik, Eds., vol. Vol. 812. Springer: Singapore, 2022. [http://dx.doi.org/10.1007/978-981-16-6970-5_47]

[2] K. Obaideen, A.G. Olabi, Y. Al Swailmeen, N. Shehata, M.A. Abdelkareem, A.H. Alami, C. Rodriguez, and E.T. Sayed, "Solar energy: Applications, trends analysis, bibliometric analysis and research contribution to sustainable development goals (SDGs)", *Sustainability,* vol. 15, no. 2, p. 1418, 2023. [http://dx.doi.org/10.3390/su15021418]

[3] D.K. Narne, T.A.R. Kumar, and R.K.R. Alla, "Effect of partial shading on the performance of various 4× 4 PV array configurations", *ECTI Transactions on Electrical Engineering, Electronics, and*

Communications, vol. 20, no. 3, pp. 427-437, 2022.
[http://dx.doi.org/10.37936/ecti-eec.2022203.247518]

[4] R.R. Alla, J.S. Lather, and G.L. Pahuja, "Comparison of PI controller performance for first order systems with time delay", *Journal of Engineering Science and Technology,* vol. 12, no. 4, pp. 1081-1091, 2017.

[5] N. Zwane, H. Tazvinga, C. Botai, M. Murambadoro, J. Botai, J. De Wit, B. Mabasa, S. Daniel, and T. Mabhaudhi, "A bibliometric analysis of solar energy forecasting studies in Africa", *Energies,* vol. 15, no. 15, p. 5520, 2022.
[http://dx.doi.org/10.3390/en15155520]

[6] P.K. Sorte, K.P. Panda, and G. Panda, "Current reference control based MPPT and investigation of power management algorithm for grid-tied solar PV-battery system", *IEEE Syst. J.,* vol. 16, no. 1, pp. 386-396, 2022.
[http://dx.doi.org/10.1109/JSYST.2021.3052959]

[7] S. Jadhav, and R. Harchandani, "Performance Characteristics Analysis for Solar PV Module", *5th Biennial International Conference on Nascent Technologies in Engineering (ICNTE),* 2023pp. 1-5
[http://dx.doi.org/10.1109/ICNTE56631.2023.10146700]

[8] D.K. Narne, T.A. Ramesh Kumar, and R.K.R. Alla, "Evaluation of series-parallel-cross-tied PV array configuration performance with maximum power point tracking techniques under partial shading conditions", *Clean Energy,* vol. 7, no. 3, pp. 620-634, 2023.
[http://dx.doi.org/10.1093/ce/zkad013]

[9] Rama Koteswara Rao Alla, Manoj Venkata Sai Neeli, and Kandipati Rajani, "Artificial intelligence techniques based PID controller for speed control of DC motor", *The Future of Computing: Ubiquitous Applications and Technologies,* vol. 70, 2024..

[10] V. Jha, *Comprehensive Technique for Modeling of PV Module.* Artificial Intelligence for Solar Photovoltaic Systems, 2022, pp. 43-78.
[http://dx.doi.org/10.1201/9781003222286-3]

[11] Rakeshkumar Mahto, and Reshma John, "Modeling of photovoltaic module", *Solar Cells: Theory, Materials and Recent Advances,* vol. 19, 2021.
[http://dx.doi.org/10.5772/intechopen.97082]

[12] R.T. Yadlapalli, A. Kotapati, and R. Kandipati, "Advancements in power conditioning units for electric vehicle applications: a review", *International Journal of Electric and Hybrid Vehicles,* vol. 13, no. 1, pp. 81-115, 2021.
[http://dx.doi.org/10.1504/IJEHV.2021.115198]

[13] R. Alla, R. Kandipati, R.T. Yadlapalli, and S. Vunnam, "Monocrystalline photovoltaic material based symmetrical and unsymmetrical Triple-Series Parallel-Ladder configuration for harvesting maximum power under partial shading conditions", *Results in Optics,* vol. 16, p. 100682, 2024.
[http://dx.doi.org/10.1016/j.rio.2024.100682]

[14] Seungchul Jung, Sang Joon Kim, Junyoung Park, Yoonmyung Lee, and GI Hyungmin, "Boost converter and boost converter cell", *Google Patents,* 2021.

[15] Binti Mahmor Norsa'adah, Norazila Binti, Md Posdzi, and Rasidah Binti Abdul Rani, *Design and develop a boost converter by using matlab simulink simulation,* 2020.

[16] D.K. Narne, T.A.R. Kumar, and R.K.R. Alla, "Effect of Partial Shading on the Performance of Various 4×4 PV Array Configurations", *ECTI Transactions on Electrical Engineering, Electronics, and Communications,* vol. 20, no. 3, pp. 427-437, 2022.
[http://dx.doi.org/10.37936/ecti-eec.2022203.247518]

[17] K. Rajani, and T. Ramesh, "Impact of Wiring Resistance on PV Array Configurations in Harvesting the Maximum Power Under Static and Dynamic Shading Conditions", *J. Inst. Electron. Telecommun. Eng.,* vol. 70, no. 1, pp. 936-964, 2024.

[http://dx.doi.org/10.1080/03772063.2022.2130454]

[18] K. Rajani, and T. Ramesh, "An Automatic Column Wiring Resistance Algorithm for Static Reconfiguration of PV Arrays and Analysis of Reconfigured T-C-T and T-T-C-L Under Dynamic Shading Conditions", *Journal of Control, Automation and Electrical Systems,* vol. 34, no. 3, pp. 637-657, 2023.
[http://dx.doi.org/10.1007/s40313-023-00988-5]

CHAPTER 3

Artificial Intelligence in Curriculum Design: Shaping the Future of Education

Ketanpreet Kaur[1], **Nripinder Kaur**[2] and **Love Singla**[3,*]

[1] *Bahra College of Law, Patiala, Punjab, India*

[2] *Amar Shaheed Baba Ajeet Singh Jujhar Singh Memorial College, College, Bela, Punjab, India*

[3] *Department of Microbiology, Maharaja Agrasen University, Baddi, Himachal Pradesh, India*

Abstract: AI has the potential to revolutionize curriculum design by creating more personalized, flexible, and efficient educational systems. Curriculum development has traditionally been a cumbersome and time-consuming approach of creating curricular content, and has often been unable to tailor quickly to the varied needs of individual learners. AI can revolutionize this process, as it can make use of data analytics and machine learning algorithms to develop dynamic, adaptive curricula that are suited to the individual students' way of learning, their needs, and progress. This allows adjusting content and learning speed based on real-time interactions, which leads to a more student-centered teaching experience. In fact, AI-powered technologies could evaluate millions of pieces of educational information to find knowledge gaps, optimize learning paths, and recommend additional resources. This minimizes the blanket approach to teaching, which further supports differentiated instruction that can meet the needs of learners at different levels of proficiency.

All these together lead to administrative workloads in terms of content generation, assessment generation, and feedback analysis, which AI reduces in a significant way and enhances the curriculum design process. This enables educators to spend more time on mentoring and facilitating learning, as AI takes over repetitive tasks. AI also integrates into curriculum design in a way that can allow for predictive modeling, making it feasible for institutions to forecast trends in job markets and to adapt curricula accordingly. Despite such challenges, ethical issues including data privacy and the risk of excessive dependency on technology, AI's involvement in curriculum design is an exciting development that could transform the future of education.

Keywords: Artificial intelligence (AI), AI in Education, AI-powered tools, Dynamic curriculum, Machine learning (ML), Personalized learning.

* **Corresponding author Love Singla:** Department of Microbiology, Maharaja Agrasen University, Baddi, Himachal Pradesh, India; E-mail: Lsingla04@gmail.com

Shilpa Gupta, Ritika Sharma & Gokana Mohana Rani (Eds.)

INTRODUCTION

With the fast-paced advancement of solo technology, some of the strategies have evolved as well. Artificial Intelligence (AI) is perhaps the most significant technology promoting curriculum innovation among these advancements. With promising potential, AI can be used to build personalized, flexible, and efficient learning plans instead of the traditional, one-size-fits-all systems of education. Historically, curriculum design has been a largely static and labour-intensive process in attempting to deliver a comparison on set of knowledge and skills to all learners. But this system has frequently failed to address the individual needs of students, resulting in failures and inequities in what students learn. AI can bridge this disconnect with its ability to create flexible, personalized learning experiences to meet the specific demands of every student. This chapter addresses AI revolutionizing curriculum design with an emphasis on personalized learning, differentiated instruction, administrative efficiency, and predictive modeling for future-ready learning experiences. We will also examine the ethical considerations of AI in curriculum design, the challenges faced, and potential future directions for AI-assisted curriculum development [1].

AI is changing many sectors, and education is one of the industries undergoing a major transformation. AI technologies are transforming how curriculum design is accomplished, providing educators and institutions with powerful new tools for developing, delivering, and optimizing educational content. Curriculum design has traditionally been a manual and time-consuming process, depending heavily on teachers' experience in designing courses that meet different learning objectives. But now, thanks to AI, this process is becoming much more dynamic, data- and personalisation-driven. Artificial Intelligence (AI) technology is able to comb through great lakes of data, detect trends in student performance, and modify material in real time; is aiding teachers in creating curricula that are more successful and customized to the characteristics of each student. This is ushering in an era of technology-driven transformations that promise to create more equitable, effective, and future-ready education systems, poised to equip students with proficiency across multiple learning pathways to meet the demands of an increasingly complex world [2]. One of the most important aspects of AI in curriculum design is its ability to personalize learning experiences. Traditional curriculum is designed with a one-size-fits-all policy, where all students are assumed to follow the same pace and need to benefit from the same materials. AI, on the other hand, provides an answer to this dilemma with customized learning journeys. Using AI-driven platforms, curricula can be tailored in real-time according to each student's performance, preferences, and knowledge gaps [3]. Such an AI system can detect the way a student interacts with various forms of content, such as videos, quizzes, reading material, etc., and tailor future lessons to focus on the topics around which the student struggled the most. Not only does this provide a more engaging experience for the students, but it also leads to better learning outcomes since each learner is getting what is most relevant and useful for their development [4].

AI is also transforming how curricula are updated and maintained. It is imperative that curricula keep pace with the most current developments in knowledge domains such as technology, science, and engineering, where the rate of knowledge expansion is exponential. In the past, this has been a detail-burning task for teachers, who have to keep on editing course content to accommodate changing data. This is the process where AI can save probably the most time by automating the identification of which content is outdated and what should be updated. From a practical standpoint, AI can sift through academic publications, industry reports, and online resources to identify emerging trends or novel research findings for educators to weave into their curricula with minimal additional effort. This enables more time coverage and ensures students get to know and learn the latest in the field of their study [5, 6]. AI can facilitate educational change from the ground up in several ways: by personalizing and transcription curricula, by modernising the infrastructure and model of education, or by enabling a more bottom-up approach to educational structure. These intelligent, AI-driven systems have the ability to analyze data from thousands of students to determine which types of content and which learning strategies prove effective. Using big data can help teachers implement courses that are more suited for the students to succeed [7]. AI can suggest several topics to educators, for instance, what topics students find most perplexing, what teaching strategies result in the highest retention rates, or which types of assessments give the best picture of whether students understand the material. With this data in hand, educators are in a position to adapt these curricula to better explore pedagogical practices that are conducive to deep and meaningful learning for all students [8].

One of the major benefits of AI in curriculum design is its potential to improve accessibility and inclusivity. Tools powered by AI can help students with different needs to learn better, for example, students with disabilities or students whose first language is not the language of instruction. AI, for example, can automatically translate course materials to multiple languages, increasing accessibility to education for those who are not native speakers. Moreover, similar use of AI can provide auto-generating captioning for video content so students with hearing impairments can engage in online courses in full capacity [9]. Moreover, AI can customize the lesson's pace and format based on students with a learning disability(s) or other special needs, allowing them to enjoy classes without missing out due to a lack of support. AI is aiding in creating a more inclusive education system by making the curricula more accessible, so that all students can be catered [10].

Assessment and feedback are one of the vital parts of curriculum design, and AI plays an important role here, too. Rather than offering a comprehensive perspective of students' comprehension and progress, traditional assessments like various quizzes and exam formats only tend to scratch the surface. On the other hand, AI can provide much higher quality and more purposeful assessment with in-the-moment feedback for students and the educational establishment [11]. For instance, AI can track not only the way a student approaches a question, but also their reason for doing so, then give individual feedback on how you might better your process. The formative assessment allows educators to revise the course when needed based on the exams taken by the students. AI can also streamline repetitive grading processes, allowing teachers to spend time on productive exchanges with students, like offering individualized assistance or crafting novel pedagogical approaches [12, 13]. The impact of artificial intelligence on curriculum design will increase as the technology evolves. One emerging area of development is using AI to generate fully immersive and interactive learning environments. AI can also be fused with Virtual Reality (VR) and Augmented Reality (AR) platforms in order to develop simulations where students can engage with abstract concepts in an interactive manner [14]. For example, in a medical curriculum, the students could experience AI-based VR simulations in which they could practice surgical procedures in a regulated, controlled atmosphere of a VR, and have a slight hand up when the moment of practicing the real procedures comes [15]. For example, AI could help gamify the curriculum in a way that allows learning to take place in a more interactive and engaging fashion, encouraging students to dig deeper into subject matter.

Conversely, challenges accompany the embrace of AI in curriculum development. One of the primary issues is that of bias in AI algorithms. AI systems could learn from the training data and biased data themselves, where some groups will be favored over others or certain stereotypes will be reinforced, ultimately propagating existing inequalities manifest in the education system. This can be done by making sure educators and developers train the AI algorithms on a wide range of data sets and perform regular audits to ensure that the data used is fair and accurate. There is also a need for continued professional development for educators on how to use AI in their teaching and curriculum development. If/when AI does hit the mean estimate for the US in 2028 and the world in 2030, an important thing to note is that whilst it could have a profound impact on education, educators themselves will still be needed to implement these technologies as tools themselves, rather than replacements for their role as mentors and guides [15, 16]. As a result, AI is transforming the future of education by completely changing curriculum design. AI provides powerful tools for educators to create more effective, inclusive, and engaging curricula, from personalizing learning experiences to updating and optimization of content. If we still face challenges like algorithmic bias and the necessity of educator training, the potential benefits of AI in education are huge. With the evolution of AI, it is only going to become more integral to the future of curriculum design and will be the source of innovative solutions that equip students with the skills to thrive in an ever-changing world. Moreover, through the embrace of AI by educators, the ability to develop dynamic and flexible curricula will serve the requirements of today's practitioners while also predicting the needs of the workplace and society of the morrow. Fig. (**1**) shows applications of AI in different sectors of education.

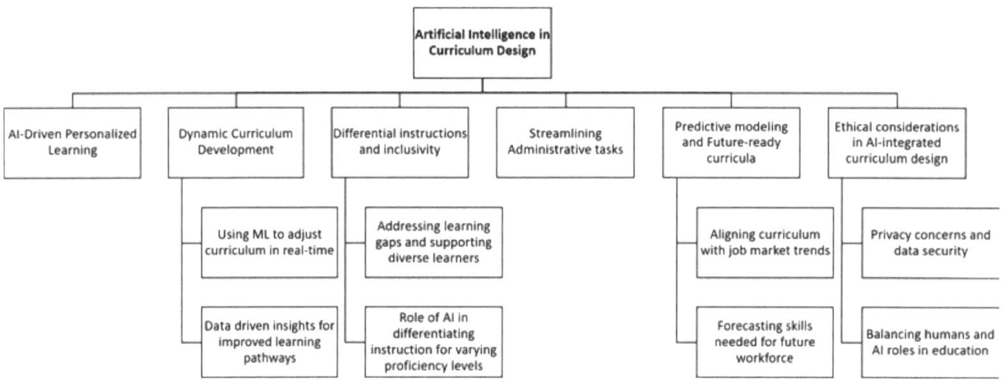

Fig. (1). Application of artificial intelligence in different areas of education.

AI-Driven Personalized Learning

Personalized learning experiences are a really exciting opportunity for AI in education. Individualized learning is the practice in which the learning is tailored to the specific needs and preferences of each learner. The solutions use data to observe learning habits and preferences and provide personalized educational pathways. All students learn at different rates, some retaining information better with visual aids, others through text or kinesthetic activities. Data on how students interact with various forms of content allows AI technology to develop adaptive systems that can tailor what information they show learners, depending on their learning style. This flexibility in addressing different styles is crucial for developing a more effective and engaging learning experience [17]. Moreover, these adaptive learning systems ensure motivation for students as they reinforce and teach them new skills while avoiding frustration or boredom. AI delivers a personalized learning experience that caters to students' current knowledge level and interests, offering content and resources that stimulate engagement [18].

Dynamic Curriculum Development

Traditionally, curriculum development has been an extensive, manual process that tends to create static educational content. AI is revolutionizing this by turning the syllabus development into a living process that never ends. For instance, AI-enabled systems can analyze performance data and accordingly adjust the curriculum in real-time so that it better matches learners' needs.

- **Using Machine Learning to Adjust Curriculum in Real-Time** - AI uses the machine learning algorithm to assess the student's progress and identify the weak points that need to be worked on. This equips educators with real-time data to help them shape the learning pathway. For example, if the student has trouble understanding a certain concept, it can offer extra material or slow down in order to make sure that they understand the material before continuing [19]. This enables any and every student to move forward at their own pace, being challenged as most appropriate for their abilities. Platforms such as Knewton are one such example where it adapts the course content based on a learner's progress that gets re-assessed continuously using AI. Not only does this dynamic nature ensure that students are more effective masters of content, it also gives them a sense of accomplishment, as they seek the benefit of a curriculum that is personally tuned to them [20].
- **Data-Driven Insights for Improved Learning Pathways-** These AI-tailored data have become essential for educators to understand each student's performance, learning style, and level of engagement. This data enables educators to identify where students are doing well and where students are struggling. Data-driven decisions help to identify where instructional strategies need to be adjusted and whether learning objectives are being met. Moreover, by analyzing engagement and performance patterns, AI systems can detect students at risk early in the learning cycle. As a result, timely interventions can be put in place to support educators in overcoming learning issues before they become significant barriers. For example, an AI engine may observe that a student is regularly doing poorly on quizzes related to a particular subject. Using this information, the teacher can provide extra resources or one-on-one support to resolve the issue.

Differentiated Instruction and Inclusivity

Differentiated instruction is one of the most important aspects of inclusive education, which provides the opportunity for every single student, inspite of their needs and abilities, to gain an education. AI rethinks the delivery of differentiated instruction to serve different learners in the same classroom.

- **Addressing Learning Gaps and Supporting Diverse Learners-** The potential for AI to pinpoint and solve learning gaps stands as one of its greatest benefits. These AI-driven systems can identify areas in which students are struggling and provide tailored support to address those specific gaps. In classrooms where students may have a wide range of proficiencies and needs for intervention, this can be especially important. Within an individualized learning framework, AI tools like Edmentum and SMART Learning Suite employ data analytics to monitor student achievement and offer customized resources to reinforce or expand academic knowledge and skills. These systems enable teachers to swiftly identify areas where their students require additional assistance and which concepts have been mastered, making differentiated instruction possible even in large-classroom settings [21]. Ultimately, this all boils down to the fact that AI tools can especially lay the groundwork required to help students with learning disabilities thrive, providing them a more manageable and conducive environment to learn. Text-to-speech, visual assistance, and interactive modules can help build a customized, inclusive curriculum for every student. These give students, whatever their ability, meaningful access to the curriculum through AI.
- **The Role of AI in Differentiating Instruction for Varying Proficiency Levels-** AI adapts, making sure that students at varying levels of proficiency get the materials tailored to their specific learning needs. Students who have an understanding can be shown to advance content, and make students who need further practice with content on fundamental concepts. As an illustration, the AI-powered learning platform Squirrel AI employs adaptive technology to evaluate a learner's abilities and weaknesses and create a customized learning trajectory. Through this method, the system encourages a satisfying learning experience for users, adjusting the difficulty and speed of information based on what the system can tell about each student's progress. Such a model indeed minimizes the gaps in learning, ensuring equity in what an individual takes away from education [22, 23].

Streamlining Administrative Tasks

In addition to personalizing the learning experience, AI can greatly enhance the efficiency of the entire educational process by automating various tasks. AI can also relieve the burden facing educators in areas such as curriculum design, content creation, assessment, and feedback. However, content creation can be incredibly time-consuming for teachers, needing lots of effort to create lesson plan documents, assessments, and additional materials. For instance, CTI and

Quizlet, AI-powered tools, can automate segments of the content creation workflow. CTI, for instance, has created an AI that can generate textbooks by extracting relevant information from multiple digital libraries and formatting it into instructor-student-friendly sample papers. It enables educators to spend less time preparing for classes and more time engaging in teaching [24].

AI is also a vital contributor to assessment and feedback. Platforms like Gradescope and Turnitin use machine learning algorithms to help assess student submissions, give immediate feedback, and even detect plagiarism. Not only does this automation save hours for educators, but it also enables a timely delivery of feedback to students, enhancing their ability to learn from mistakes and master concepts quickly [25]. AI is useful in assessment-driven environments, particularly in larger classrooms where it can feel impossible to provide each student with targeted feedback. This allows educators to provide timely grading and feedback in order to give every student the quality assistance they should get.

Predictive Modeling and Future-Ready Curricula

One other major facet of AI in curriculum design is predictive modeling. Artificial intelligence can contribute to the revolution of education from the lens of what society will need from student populations in the future by pulling data on student performance, engagement, and trends in the job market.

- **Aligning Curriculum with Job Market Trends** -AI systems also enable analysis of large amounts of data related to labor market trends, sectoral needs, and new skillsets. This enables education institutions to tailor their curricula to job market demands, ensuring students gain skills that will be needed in the future. For example, institutions can use AI to analyze emerging trends, such as data science, renewable energy, or digital marketing sectors, and recommend changes to curriculum content to equip students with skills relevant to these sectors [26, 27]. AI can also predict what kinds of skills will be in demand in the future and can help institutions to prepare students for jobs that do not yet exist. This forward-thinking aspect not only prepares students for current roles but also prepares them to be capable of adapting in a constantly evolving job market.
- **Forecasting Skills Needed for Future Workforce** - Predictive modeling can assist educational institutions in utilizing AI to determine which skills may become most important in the upcoming years. Thus, it enables timely changes to the curriculum, ensuring that students are equipped for the workforce. In fields like automation and AI technologies becoming mainstream, skills such as critical thinking, creativity, and emotional intelligence are expected to gain importance. By predicting these trends, educational institutions may prioritize

teaching such skills, ensuring that students are still competitive in the job market [28].

Ethical Considerations in AI-Integrated Curriculum Design

Although AI has much potential in the facilitation of curriculum design, it can also create ethical issues that need to be resolved to allow for ethical applications of AI in society. Then this goes to your new role as a teacher, the challenges of data privacy and interactivity, and reliance on the technology.

- **Privacy Concerns and Data Security -** Artificial Intelligence is based on tons of data to offer better learning experiences for students. The collection, storage, and use of student data, however, have significant privacy implications. This is essential as, for this purpose, institutions must follow data privacy laws that allow companies to avoid data abuse and keep students' personal information secured. It will go a long way in addressing these concerns if data collection and usage are done with transparency and proper consent from students and parents. Making room for users' data compromise is extremely unethical and needs proper prevention; therefore, education institutions must build a better way to secure data and/or join hands with their technology partners who respect data. Security measures such as encryption, securing data storage, and clear policies of data access could help in protecting students [29, 30].
- **Balancing Human and AI Roles in Education -** Another ethical question relates to the balance between AI and human roles in education. AI has the potential to improve the learning experience, but it must be a complement to, not a substitute for, the human experience of learning. Teachers are an integral part of motivating, mentoring, and building meaningful relationships with students, which is something that AI cannot do. The focus should be on using AI as a tool that assists and complements the educator's work rather than replacing it.

CHALLENGES AND LIMITATIONS

Although AI can allow for transformative possibilities in curriculum design, there are challenges and limitations that need to be considered to ensure effective integration. Data privacy and security are one of the chief concerns because AI systems depend on vast quantities of student data for optimal performance. The protection of this data from misuse or a breach is also essential, especially considering the various regulations such as GDPR. Moreover, AI algorithms can also adopt biases from their training data, which can serve to perpetuate existing disparities in education. This bias may result in unfair evaluations or recommendations, especially for underrepresented groups. Another challenge is that it may promote too much reliance on AI, leading to the loss of crucial human interaction that helps in developing aspects like critical thinking in children, creativity, and emotional intelligence. Moreover, the implementation of AI-driven curriculum design systems can be overly no for numerous establishments, especially in underdeveloped sectors, amplifying the digital disparity. The adaptation process can also be a challenge for teachers, who have to be properly trained to introduce AI into their teaching workflows. There's also skepticism about AI's potential to grasp the nuances of human learning at a deeper, particularly emotional and social level. These developments create ethical issues when decisions based on AI start to take precedence over human educators' decisions, effectively transferring control over curriculum design places into the hands of algorithms and tech companies. Varied Standards of AI Tools and Platforms. Due to such a wide variety of AI tools and platforms available, no particular solution can be standardized, which both hindered the adoption. Moreover, the fast pace of development in AI may prompt short-term disruption of educational systems, with continual updates and adaptations needed [31].

The challenge with any form of AI in an educational setting comes with the concept of over-reliance. AI is a great tool, but a tool is not a god. Students and educators' over-dependence on AI may result in students and educators losing their critical thinking skills, and the quality of education may suffer if the AI engines do not evolve as required. With this said, it is important to find a balance between keeping human educators in the loop wherever possible and using AI as a tool to assist in place for a substitute supplement [32]. AI algorithms learn from the past data in which they were trained, and they can be biased by it. In education, this could lead to discriminatory actions towards students or implicit biases in educational resources. In this vein, the creation of assessment AI must be a continuous and iterative process to refine the algorithms and remove biases. To mitigate these biases, it is important to use diverse and representative data to develop models that accurately reflect the population under consideration in order to promote fair outcomes for all learners [33 - 35].

CONCLUSION

Curriculum design is being redefined by AI, paving the way for personalized learning, range-finding and personalized curriculum, adaptive instruction, and preparation for the next chapters. AI brings many benefits that can improve both teaching and learning experiences through streamlining administrative tasks, providing data-driven insights, and powering predictive modeling. Yet the use of AI also poses major ethical and practical challenges, such as concerns about data privacy and potential biases, not to mention the need to strike a balance between human and AI roles.

We must navigate these challenges and leverage the opportunities AI presents to us in the future. This way, the educational organizations can cultivate a more inclusive, adaptive, and future-oriented learning environment that equips students for the challenges of the contemporary world. AI in curriculum design is not only a technology advancement but a paradigm shift towards a more student-centered and responsive education system.

REFERENCES

[1] H.G. Zhao, X.Z. Li, and X. Kang, "Development of an artificial intelligence curriculum design for children in Taiwan and its impact on learning outcomes", *Humanities and Social Sciences Communications,* vol. 11, no. 1, p. 1339, 2024. [http://dx.doi.org/10.1057/s41599-024-03839-z]

[2] Q. Cao, "Curriculum Design of Art Higher Vocational Education Based on Artificial Intelligence Assisted Virtual Reality Technology", *Secur. Commun. Netw.,* vol. 2022, no. 1, pp. 1-9, 2022. [http://dx.doi.org/10.1155/2022/3535068]

[3] R. Ahuja, D. Khan, S. Tahir, M. Wang, D. Symonette, S. Pan, and S. Stacey, "Machine Learning and Student Performance in Teams", in Artificial Intelligence in Education, I. Bittencourt, M. Cukurova, K. Muldner, R. Luckin, and E. Millán, Eds., Lecture Notes in Computer Science, vol. 12164, Cham: Springer, 2020, pp. 301–305 [http://dx.doi.org/10.1007/978-3-030-52240-7_55]

[4] F.A. Oliehoek, R. Savani, E. Adderton, X. Cui, D. Jackson, P. Jimmieson, J. C. Jones, K. Kennedy, B. Mason, A. Plumbley, and L. Dawson, "LiftUpp: Support to Develop Learner Performance", in Artificial Intelligence in Education, E. André, R. Baker, X. Hu, M. Rodrigo, and B. du Boulay, Eds., Lecture Notes in Computer Science, vol. 10331, Cham: Springer, 2017, pp. 553–556. [http://dx.doi.org/10.1007/978-3-319-61425-0_62]

[5] M.B. Garcia, "Using AI Tools in Writing Peer Review Reports: Should Academic Journals Embrace the Use of ChatGPT?", *Ann. Biomed. Eng.,* vol. 52, no. 2, pp. 139-140, 2024. [http://dx.doi.org/10.1007/s10439-023-03299-7] [PMID: 37368125]

[6] N. Ahmed, M. Wahed, and N.C. Thompson, "The growing influence of industry in AI research", Science, vol. 379, pp. 884–886, 2023. [http://dx.doi.org/10.1126/science.ade2420]

[7] R.I. Popescu, O.M. Sabie, and M.I. Trușcă, "The Contribution of Artificial Intelligence to Stimulating the Innovation of Educational Services and University Programs in Public Administration", *Transylv. Rev. Adm. Sci.,* vol. 19, no. 70 E, pp. 85-108, 2023. [http://dx.doi.org/10.24193/tras.70E.5]

[8] A. Gogoberidze, I. Kalabina, and L. Savinova, "Modern Educational Programs for the Training of Preschool Teachers: Experience in the Implementation and Assessment of Educational Results of Students", *Education & Self Development,* vol. 16, no. 3, pp. 230-237, 2021. [http://dx.doi.org/10.26907/esd.16.3.19]

[9] M. Keech, and A. Goel, "Why Are Some Online Educational Programs Successful? Student Cognition and Success", arXiv preprint arXiv:2209.05462.

[10] G. Rees, and L. Schutte, "Advancing Digital Health Equity: An Interdisciplinary Educational Approach to Digital Health Access and Inclusivity", *Stud. Health Technol. Inform.,* vol. 315, pp. 511-514, 2024.

[http://dx.doi.org/10.3233/SHTI240201] [PMID: 39049311]

[11] A.V. Ryabko, O.V. Zaika, R.P. Kukharchuk, T.A. Vakaliuk, and V.V. Osadchyi, "Methods for predicting the assessment of the quality of educational programs and educational activities using a neuro-fuzzy approach", *CTE Workshop Proceedings,* vol. 9, 2022 pp. 154-169. [http://dx.doi.org/10.55056/cte.112]

[12] A.I. Pisica, T. Edu, R.M. Zaharia, and R. Zaharia, "Implementing artificial intelligence in higher education: Pros and cons from the perspectives of academics", *Societies (Basel),* vol. 13, no. 5, p. 118, 2023. [http://dx.doi.org/10.3390/soc13050118]

[13] B.D. Wale, and B.D. Wale, "Artificial intelligence in education: Effects of using integrative automated writing evaluation programs on honing academic writing instruction", *Jurnal Cakrawala Pendidikan,* vol. 43, no. 1, pp. 273-287, 2024. [http://dx.doi.org/10.21831/cp.v43i1.67715]

[14] M. Puggioni, E. Frontoni, M. Paolanti, and R. Pierdicca, "ScoolAR: An Educational Platform to Improve Students' Learning Through Virtual Reality", *IEEE Access,* vol. 9, pp. 21059-21070, 2021. [http://dx.doi.org/10.1109/ACCESS.2021.3051275]

[15] M.H. Akhtar, M. Anderson, and T. Cochrane, "Implementing Augmented Reality and Virtual Reality for authentic healthcare education", *Pacific Journal of Technology Enhanced Learning,* vol. 6, no. 1, pp. 2-3, 2024. [http://dx.doi.org/10.24135/pjtel.v6i1.177]

[16] T.K.F. Chiu, Q. Xia, X. Zhou, C.S. Chai, and M. Cheng, "Systematic literature review on opportunities, challenges, and future research recommendations of artificial intelligence in education", *Computers and Education: Artificial Intelligence,* vol. 4, p. 100118, 2023. [http://dx.doi.org/10.1016/j.caeai.2022.100118]

[17] A. Mishra, "Enhancing Personalized Learning with Artificial Intelligence: Opportunities and Challenges", *RESEARCH REVIEW International Journal of Multidisciplinary,* vol. 8, no. 8, pp. 73-80, 2023. [http://dx.doi.org/10.31305/rrijm.2023.v08.n08.014]

[18] M. Chauhan, "Investigating Personalized Learning Paths to Address Educational Disparities Using Advanced Artificial Intelligence Systems", *International Conference on E-Mobility, Power Control and Smart Systems: Futuristic Technologies for Sustainable Solutions, ICEMPS 2024,* 2024. [http://dx.doi.org/10.1109/ICEMPS60684.2024.10559339]

[19] J. Heland, J.C. Ortega, A.C. Lagman, R.M. de Angel, H.D.A. Balmeo, A.J.M. Rubio, and J.P. Lazaro, "Designing student's study plan: Decision-based recommendation system towards program completion using forward chaining algorithm", in Proc. 2023 IEEE 15th Int. Conf. Humanoid, Nanotechnol., Inf. Technol., Commun. Control, Environ., Manage. (HNICEM), Coron, Palawan, Philippines, 2023, pp. 1–6. [http://dx.doi.org/10.1109/HNICEM60674.2023.10589118]

[20] E.M. Recalde Drouet, D.M. Tello Salazar, T.L. Charro Domínguez, and P.J. Catota Pinthsa, "Analysis of the repercussions of Artificial Intelligence in the Personalization of the Virtual Educational Process in Higher Education Programs", *Data and Metadata,* vol. 3, pp. 386-386, 2024. [http://dx.doi.org/10.56294/dm2024386]

[21] A.F. Salazar-Gomez, A. Bagiati, N. Minicucci, K. D. Kennedy, X. Du and C. Breazeal, "Designing and implementing an AI education program for learners with diverse background at scale", 2022 IEEE Frontiers in Education Conference (FIE), Uppsala, Sweden, 2022, pp. 1-8. [http://dx.doi.org/10.1109/FIE56618.2022.9962632]

[22] Impact of Artificial Intelligence (AI) on Lecturers' Proficiency Levels in English Teaching and Library Practice in Nigerian Universities," International Journal of Research and Innovation in Social Science, vol. VIII, no. IIIS, pp. 2217–2235, 2024, doi: 10.47772/IJRISS.2024.803161S.

[23] E.A. Tomas, "Science Process Skills and Proficiency Levels among the Junior and Senior High School Science Teachers", *Int. Multidiscip. Res. J.,* vol. 5, no. 3, 2023. [http://dx.doi.org/10.54476/ioer-imrj/231565]

[24] D. Aggarwal, D. Sharma, and A.B. Saxena, "Adoption of Artificial Intelligence (AI) For Development of Smart Education as the Future of a Sustainable Education System", *Journal of Artificial Intelligence, Machine Learning and Neural Network,* vol. 3, no. 36, pp. 23-28, 2023. [http://dx.doi.org/10.55529/jaimlnn.36.23.28]

[25] A. Bewersdorff, "“Taking the Next Step with Generative Artificial Intelligence: The Transformative Role of Multimodal Large Language Models in Science Education,” vol. 1", arXiv: 2401.00832. https://arxiv.org/abs/2401.00832v3

[26] A.E. Yahya, W.M.S. Yafooz, and A. Gharbi, "Mapping Graduate Skills to Market Demands: A Holistic Examination of Curriculum Development and Employment Trends", *Engineering, Technology & Applied Science Research,* vol. 14, no. 4, pp. 14793-14800, 2024. [http://dx.doi.org/10.48084/etasr.7454]

[27] S. Prihhartini and E.S. Priyatna, "Analyzing market trends in the automation era for the development of independent campus curriculum", Makna: Jurnal Kajian Komunikasi, Bahasa dan Budaya, vol. 10, no. 1, pp. 31-49, 2022. [http://dx.doi.org/10.33558/makna.v10i1.3232]

[28] M. Johnson, R. Jain, P. Brennan-Tonetta, E. Swartz, D. Silver, J. Paolini, S. Mamonov, and C. Hill, "Impact of Big Data and Artificial Intelligence on Industry: Developing a Workforce Roadmap for a Data Driven Economy", *Global J. Flex. Syst. Manag.,* vol. 22, no. 3, pp. 197-217, 2021. [http://dx.doi.org/10.1007/s40171-021-00272-y]

[29] L. Huang, "Ethics of Artificial Intelligence in Education: Student Privacy and Data Protection", *Science Insights Education Frontiers,* vol. 16, no. 2, pp. 2577-2587, 2023. [http://dx.doi.org/10.15354/sief.23.re202]

[30] C. Wang, Z. Yuan, P. Zhou, Z. Xu, R. Li, and D.O. Wu, "The Security and Privacy of Mobile-Edge Computing: An Artificial Intelligence Perspective", *IEEE Internet Things J.,* vol. 10, no. 24, pp. 22008-22032, 2023. [http://dx.doi.org/10.1109/JIOT.2023.3304318]

[31] C. Preiksaitis, and C. Rose, "Opportunities, Challenges, and Future Directions of Generative Artificial Intelligence in Medical Education: Scoping Review", *JMIR Med. Educ.,* vol. 9, no. 1, p. e48785, 2023. [http://dx.doi.org/10.2196/48785] [PMID: 37862079]

[32] X. Wang, and X.Q. Liu, "Potential and limitations of ChatGPT and generative artificial intelligence in medical safety education", *World J. Clin. Cases,* vol. 11, no. 32, pp. 7935-7939, 2023. [http://dx.doi.org/10.12998/wjcc.v11.i32.7935] [PMID: 38073698]

[33] N. Levantis, and A. Sgora, "Algorithmic Decision Making in Education: Challenges and Opportunities", *IEEE Global Engineering Education Conference, EDUCON,* 2024. [http://dx.doi.org/10.1109/EDUCON60312.2024.10578645]

[34] R. Sharma, and V. Mehan, "Skin Disease Detection Using Image Processing and Soft Computing", *ECS Trans.,* vol. 107, no. 1, pp. 17051-17061, 2022. [http://dx.doi.org/10.1149/10701.17051ecst]

[35] R. Sharma, S. K. Bansal, A. Verma, G. Goyal, and M. Singla, "Multi-class deep learning-based enhanced image segmentation and feature extraction technique for early classification of skin diseases", *Commun. Appl. Nonlinear Anal,* 2024.

CHAPTER 4

Artificial Intelligence Aided Optimization Techniques for Microstrip Antenna Design

Bimal Raj Dutta[1,*]

[1] *Department of Electronics and Communication Engineering. Chandigarh University, Chandigarh, Punjab, India*

Abstract: Artificial intelligence can be used in many walks of life; one such use is in designing and optimizing various antennas. The microstrip patch antenna uses AI for the same reason. In today's techno world, the various aspects of micro-patch antenna design and optimization can be performed using Artificial Intelligence (AI). Micro-patch antennas are compact, planar antennas and are mostly used in wireless communication systems. AI techniques can optimize the design of micro-patch antennas to enhance their performance. The designing of microstrip patch antennas, and specifically the antennas used in wireless communication and mobile phones, is challenging due to the presence of various physical limits. This chapter specializes in the usage of Artificial Neural Networks (ANN) and gadgets getting to know Machine Learning (ML) based on regression. Using ML and ANN, the challenges faced in the design of microstrip patch antennas are addressed, and solutions are provided for the analysis and synthesis of these antennas. The study is mainly focused on the calculation of resonant frequency, although the synthesis focuses on the mathematical geometrical dimensions of the antenna. These are two substantial processes that one will need for the precise designing of antennas, since these are mutually dependent. MATLAB and its graphical user interface have been used. Also, in order to minimize time duration and inaccuracy, the back-propagation technique has been used. In comparison with the standard simulation platforms and tools, this method provides a higher level of precision in calculating the geometric dimensions, along with minimizing the time required to calculate the dimensions. Usage of high-priced and prolonged software is not required along with the usage of the ANN method. ANN helps in achieving design attribute determination and parameter retrieval easily. The best performance of the Gaussian Process Regression model helps in determining the physical and electrical attributes. A prototype antenna is designed whose performance is close to the expected design, and with this prototype, the GPR model is verified.

Keywords: Artificial Intelligence, Microstip Antenna Design, Neural Networks, SADEA Algorithm.

* **Corresponding author Bimal Raj Dutta**: Department of Electronics and Communication Engineering. Chandigarh University, Chandigarh, Punjab, India; E-mail: brajdutta@gmail.com

Shilpa Gupta, Ritika Sharma & Gokana Mohana Rani (Eds.)

INTRODUCTION

AI is a tool used for the performance of different machine tasks that are human intelligence-oriented. AI is performing various steps like reasoning, problem-solving, understanding language, recognizing objects, and making decisions for the accomplishment of the task. The task is performed automatically by AI systems due to learning data and providing new inputs accordingly. AI tools are able to handle problems ranging from rule-based modest systems to more sophisticated models [1 - 6].

Types of AI

• **Narrow AI (Weak AI):** Minor tasks like internet surfing or face detection are performed by this type of AI system. Different analogous attendants, for example, Siri and Alexa of the present day, are falling into this group.

• **General AI (Strong AI):** This category of AI systems is speculative and needs universal cognitive capabilities, the same as human intelligence. This system is in a position to complete different complex tasks that can be performed by humans. Presently, this type of AI system is in the exploration and theoretical stage.

Applications in Telecommunications

• **Network Optimization:** To estimate the traffic of a network in real time, automated structures and optimized networks of telecommunication are provided by AI systems. This system is useful for the recognition of bottlenecks and future failures. It also regulates the data flow of the network [7 - 11].

• **Periodical Maintenance:** The network equipment failure forecast can be done by an AI system after examining the equipment data. It also provides the reduction of failure time and costs of operation through periodical maintenance.

• **Customer Support Automation:** The AI machine regulates extraordinary customer services like chatbots and digital assistants, offering 24/7 customer support, answering ordinary questions, processing requests, and escalating complex problems to human marketers.

• **Intelligent Antenna Design:** Different antenna designs can be optimized after automation of typical parametric results using AI algorithms. The AI system is helping in the efficient and quick design of antennas.

• **Machine Learning (ML):** A subset of AI systems used for preparing machines from data is known as machine learning. For knowing the patterns from huge datasets, the ML system applies algorithms. It also uses these patterns for making forecasts or preferences without being explicitly programmed. A better forecast of the system relies on a large amount of data processing, as its model is regularly refined [12 - 14].

Types of Machine Learning

• **Supervised Learning:** When the algorithm training on a designated dataset is performed for each input with a corresponding output in an ML system, it is called supervised learning. The learning model of mapping inputs to outputs of these examples is used in this system. This system is mostly used in functions such as categorization (spam detection) and regression (as in forecasting prices of houses).

• **Unsupervised Learning:** In unsupervised learning, data is supplied to the model without specific tags, and the search for concealed designs and correlations in the data depends on the algorithm. The normal uses of unsupervised learning are assembling (grouping analogous elements) and exception exposure (ruling out outliers).

• **Reinforcement Learning:** A model determined by cooperation of its atmosphere and admitting guidance in the shape of rewards or punishments is known as reinforcement learning. This gadget is often applied in programs such as recreational gambling (e.g., AlphaGo), robotics, and self-sufficient structures.

Applications in Antenna Design

• **Parameter Prediction:** Unique ML fashions as aid Vector Machines (SVM) and Artificial Neural Networks (ANN), are given to analyze distinct antenna traits, like resonant frequency, bandwidth, and impedance, determined by training data from the preceding designs of antennas [15 - 18].

• **Optimization:** To enhance execution, different machine learning algorithms are used for improving different parameters of the antenna. The encircling parameters are minimizing size while maintaining or enhancing efficiency, enlarging bandwidth, and enhancing the radiation pattern.

• **Automation of Design Processes:** Different ML algorithms can be applied for the dimensions' calculation of an antenna automatically. This system of calculation leads to an exceptionally reduction in the duration and effort required in manual calculation.

Advantages in Telecommunications

• **Data-driven Insights:** The network execution can be enhanced by the use of ML algorithms. These algorithms give useful perceptions due to the exploration of a large amount of network data.

• **Fraud Detection:** Diagnosis of distrustful actions of network traffic that may result in deception or reliability warnings can be done by machine learning models.

• **Deep Learning (DL):** A subset system of ML using many layers for modelling composite sequences in data is known as deep learning. In this system of Deep Neural Networks (DNN), each layer derives attributes from the data; more outline attributes derive from deeper layers. In the image recognition example, edges are identified by primary layers and faces, and objects are identified by deeper layers. For training data in the deep learning models, huge data with considerable computational resources are required, but they perform well at working with unregulated data (like images, audio, and text) after training. Here, the human brain design has been considered by these models due to the neuron connections and combinations to develop intelligence.

Key Elements

• **Neural Networks:** A neural community includes nodes (neurons) arranged in layers. Every neuron gets inputs, processes them (by way of applying weights and activation capabilities), and passes the end result to the following layer. This structure allows the network to study complicated relationships in records.

• **Convolutional Neural Networks (CNNs):** CNN networks are applied for image perception; they reveal natural sequences as edges and textures, and further, by applying filters to the input data.

• **Recurrent Neural Networks (RNNs):** This community is carried out to procession-based assignments as natural language processing (NLP) or time series forecasting. RNNs transform inputs sectionally and are directed to recollect preceding information through observation loops.

Applications in Antenna Design

• **Complex Antenna Structures:** DLL models are especially effective for forecasting and optimizing complicated antenna architectures, such as fractal and multi-band antennas. DLL is used to model complications of antenna architectures; these result in different parameters and nonlinear associations more accurately.

• **Impedance Bandwidth Prediction:** Microstrip antenna design appearances as impedance matching bandwidths can be forecasted by deep learning, serving designers to optimize execution promptly.

• **Miniaturization of Antennas:** Consolidated designs of antennas, which are mandatory for applications such as mobile devices and satellites with space restrictions, can be examined by deep neural networks.

Broader Applications in Telecommunications

• **Network Traffic Prediction:** To interpret classical network traffic and forecast forthcoming bottleneck points, deep learning models can be used. These models are permitting operators to designate resources more effectively.

• **Speech and Text Processing:** The virtual assistants and speech recognition systems applied in telecommunication services can be executed by deep learning. For providing further induction to users, these systems are deducing and measuring the natural language.

• **Image Recognition for Maintenance:** To evaluate images or video feeds from network equipment for the identification of defects or issues, AI-powered image recognition systems can be used. These systems are estimating the examination and preservation procedure.

The Significance of Intelligence in the Design of IoT Antennas

The rapid expansion of the Internet of Things (IoT) requires advances in antenna technology to meet the demand for increased connectivity, small applications, and electricity usage. Although effective, traditional antenna designs often underperform in dynamic and complex IoT environments. This research aims to fill this gap by integrating Artificial Intelligence (AI) technology into the antenna design process, making antennas smarter and more flexible. Antennas play an important role in IoT systems by enabling wireless communication between IoT devices and the network. They transmit and receive electromagnetic waves and facilitate the exchange of information. Given the promise and limitations of IoT devices, antennas must be designed to be efficient, compact, and capable of operating at the specific frequencies required for various IoT applications [19 - 24]. The Internet of Things (IoT) is rapidly developing as a technological revolution that includes various devices and systems that facilitate the exchange of information and technology. The Internet of Things is inherently wireless and uses wireless communication and communication principles and requires wireless components such as antennas, antenna supports, legacy devices, gateways, and nurseries. These devices are essential for the design and deployment of IoT networks. IoT nodes and sensors are generally small and have limited capabilities, which places special demands on the design of wireless devices. Antennas are important components of IoT devices and need to be customized according to the specific requirements of different IoT applications, and provide good performance in confined spaces. This requires a careful balance between miniaturization, efficiency, and functionality. Recent advances in Artificial Intelligence (AI) offer great opportunities for advanced antenna design and optimization. Artificial intelligence technologies, especially device learning algorithms, have an awesome capacity to enhance performance indicators consisting of profit, efficiency, and overall performance standards. By incorporating artificial intelligence, antennas can be designed to adapt to dynamic environments and provide the repeatability needed for robust IoT operations.

This looks at objectives to discover the combination of artificial intelligence within the layout and optimization of antennas for IoT packages. This chapter proposes a clever antenna that uses device learning to enhance key performance indicators. The study chapter contains a theoretical framework that demonstrates a significant improvement in antenna performance, supported by simulations and experimental validations. In addition, it addresses the architectural challenges of large and small IoT deployments and provides insight into the use of antenna technologies with artificial intelligence. The outcomes of this study demonstrate the capacity of synthetic intelligence to transform IoT antenna layout and pave the way for more efficient, bendy, and intelligent IoT networks. As the Internet of Things continues to expand, integrating wireless device design expertise will help meet connectivity, reliability, and performance requirements.

The role of intelligence in IoT antenna design, as shown in Fig. (**1**), provides insights into optimization, adaptation, design automation, and predictive functionality. AI, however, improves the optimization of antennas through machine learning algorithms. Machine learning models can identify optimal parameters, such as gain, performance, and power models, by analyzing large amounts of performance data. The data-driven approach can be fine-tuned to maximize antenna efficiency while meeting the limitations of IoT devices. One of the advantages of AI is that antennas can be configured on the fly. IoT devices operate in dynamic environments, and conditions such as interference, signal congestion, and motion can impact performance. AI algorithms can continuously monitor these conditions and adjust antenna faults to ensure efficient and reliable communication. AI accelerates the antenna design process through advanced simulation and modeling. Prototyping is often time-consuming and requires a lot of trial and error. AI-powered design automation greatly reduces this time by predicting the outcome of various design options and guiding engineers to the most consistent configurations. This not only speeds up development but also

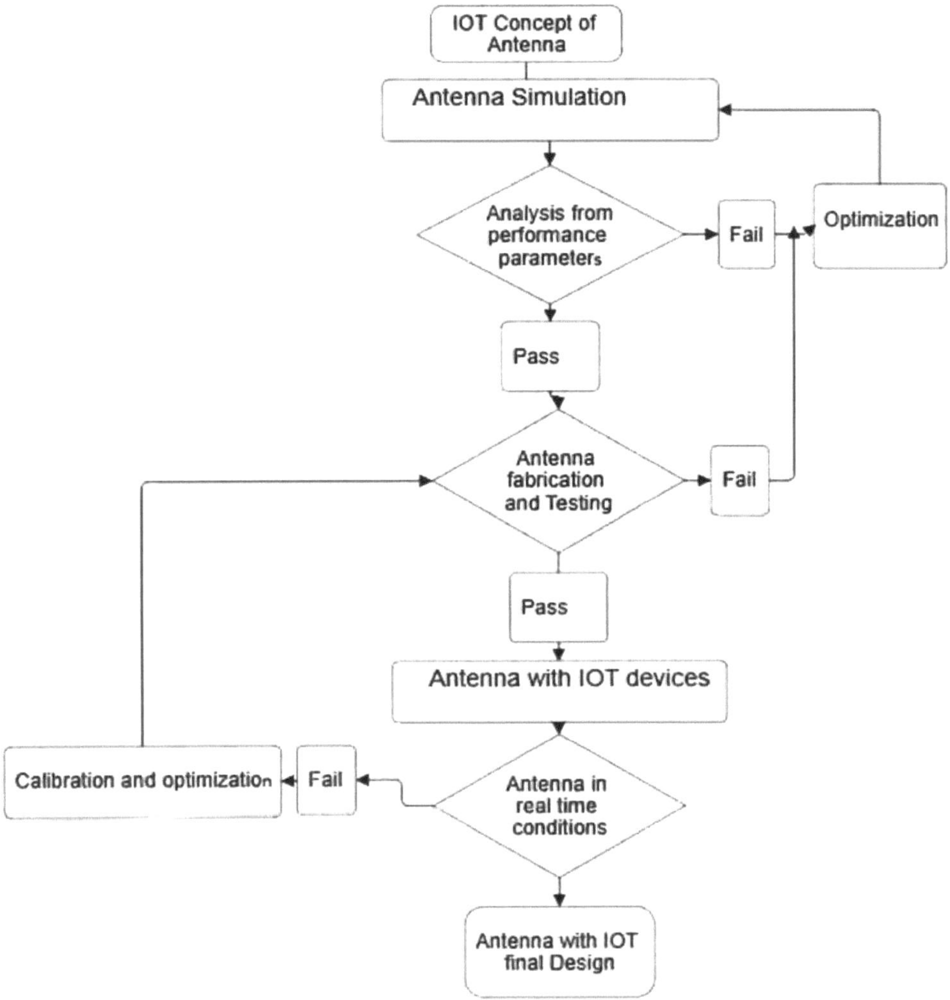

Fig. (1). IoT antenna design framework.

leads to innovation and profitability. Performance prediction is key to good antenna design. Intelligent models trained on historical performance data can predict how an antenna will perform under different conditions. This agreement allows designers to make changes early in development, reducing the need for expensive products and physical models. The AI model is trained using data on antenna performance measurements, including gain, efficiency, and power models in a variety of environments. The improved design provides a 20% increase in performance and a 15% increase in gain over the original design. In addition, the antenna can strongly adapt to changes in the working environment and maintain high performance in different conditions. Integrating AI into IoT antenna design can provide many benefits, including advanced design, fast transition, layer design standard speed, and predictive performance. Using AI, such as large limitations, engineers can design antennas that are efficient, flexible, and can meet the stringent requirements of IoT device applications. AI provides powerful tools to improve antenna performance, flexibility, and design efficiency through machine learning and predictive modeling. As the Internet of Things continues to expand, the role of AI in the design of wireless communication devices, driving innovation, and overall improving the functionality of IoT networks will become increasingly [25 - 30].

Integration of Artificial Intelligence into Micro Patch Antenna Design

In the overall performance plane, missile and satellite programs, the need for antennas may be taken into consideration by thinking about the dimensions, weight, price, performance, ease of installation, and aerodynamic boundaries. Today, there are many important programs and corporations with similar commands, together with radio broadcasting and wireless communication. Microstrip antennas in Fig. (**2**) can be used to fulfill those necessities. These antennas are small in length and suitable for both planar and non-planar surfaces, clean and inexpensive to create using current printers, mechanically robust while installed in narrow spaces, can exceed MMIC layout, and are to be had in unique shapes and selected types. There is a wide variety of them in terms of resonant frequency, polarization, structure, and impedance. Reconfigurable antennas, *etc.* Antennas do not change continuously, which makes antenna design difficult, tedious, and time-consuming since long analysis and design cycles must be used to calculate the limits. The review of many articles shows that the neural network model is widely used in wireless communication today; this eliminates complex and time-consuming mathematical methods, such as time in antenna manufacturing. Rectangle, triangle, *etc* [31 - 33].

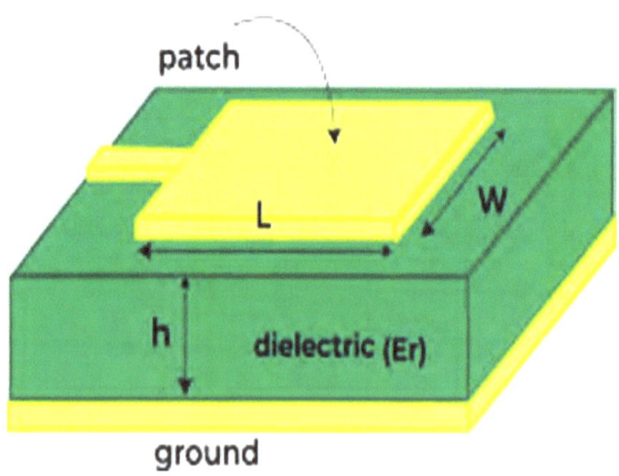

Fig. (2). Layout of microstrip antenna.

Microstrip Antenna Research

An ANN model was developed in Fig. (**3**) to determine the frequency of microstrip patches of various shapes. Many designs have been proposed using ANN techniques and backpropagation-based learning algorithms. The present study focuses on the use of RBF neural networks in the field of microstrip antenna design. When there are many variable input parameters. Based on the test data, consider the placement of the microstrip antenna as it is related to the decision of many parameters and justifies the use of an ANN in its design. Therefore, this observation establishes an ANN version, as per Fig. (**4**) offers the microstrip antenna design for the preferred frequencies of 3.5 GHz and 5.5 GHz.

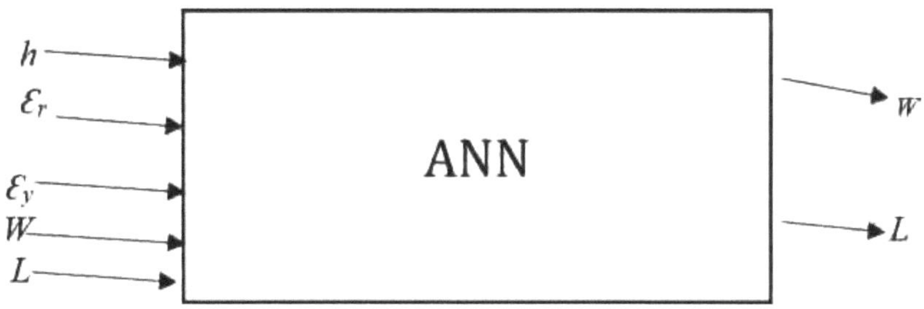

Fig. (3). Formulation of Microstrip Patch using ANN [11].

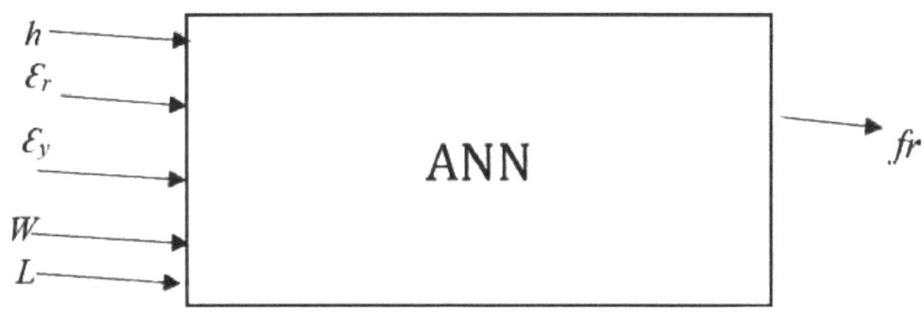

Fig. (4). Assessment of Microstrip Patch with ANN [11].

Optimization is widely used in antenna design and is based primarily on gradient-based algorithms and manual modifications. The needs of today's antennas are often overlooked when designing these systems. Part of this review will examine the difficulties and limitations inherent in the optimization process. Examples from the literature will be used to illustrate the cases where these strategies are effective and inadequate, as shown in Fig. (**5**). Genetic algorithms (GAS) have gained importance due to their ability to explore large solution spaces and discover patterns by following evolutionary processes. This bankruptcy discusses using genetic algorithms (GAS) in antenna layout. It will overview of the large literature and recent research displaying that gases can improve antenna performance. A full assessment may be made to decide the benefits and downsides of this technique to gain the specified antenna. Particle swarm optimization has been successfully implemented in electromagnetic programs. Particle Swarm Optimization (PSO) is an effective algorithm inspired by the conduct of animals, along with birds, found in nature. This chapter covers the theoretical perspective of Population Swarm Optimization (PSO) and its application to various problems in electromagnetic design.

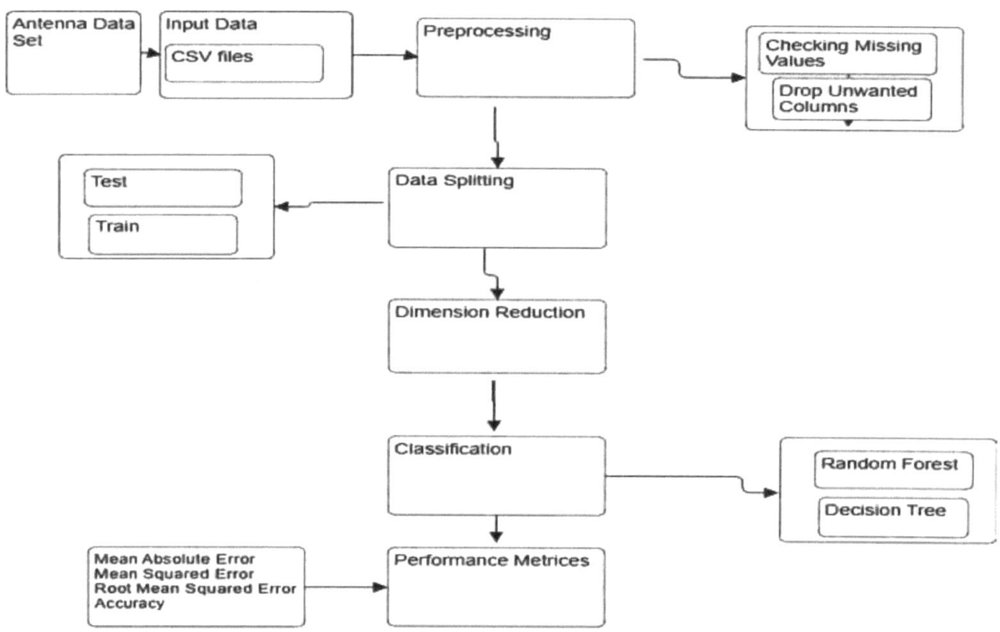

Fig. (5). Predictive Optimization Model for Microstrip Patch Antenna.

It will show areas where PSO performs better than other methods. Presentations will include comparative studies focusing on performance, efficient solutions, and general applications in antenna design [11, 34, 35].

Evolution of Microstrip Antenna Design: Deep Learning (DL) has revolutionized many engineering fields, including antenna design. This section discusses deep learning techniques suitable for antenna development, such as neural networks. It's going to also become aware of progress made on this system that has decreased design time and improved predictive overall performance, as per Fig. (**6**). This speech will describe the evolution of Deep Learning (DL) to revolutionize antenna layout. Gaining deep knowledge of studying statistics and making predictions facilitates creating a nice antenna design. In spite of a few developments, there are great gaps in the subject of AI antenna design research work. The final part of the literature evaluation turned into discovering gaps by analyzing the principal troubles and barriers of the modern approach. It additionally identifies potential areas for further research, consisting of the mixing of hybrid AI models and the testing of recent computational strategies, as per Fig. (7). Those efforts have the capacity to improve the design and performance of microstrip antennas. This section provides an overview of the main issues in antenna design, focusing on achieving high electrical performance while considering physical limitations [14].

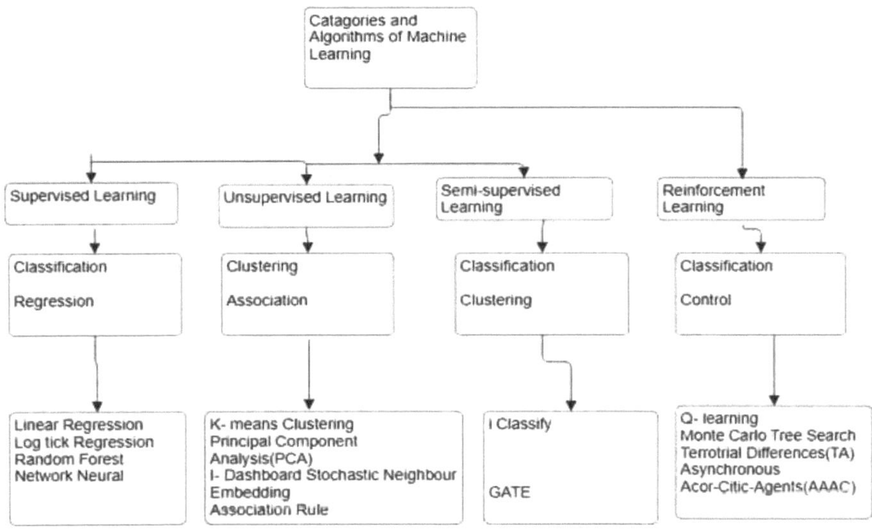

Fig. (6). Machine learning approaches and methods.

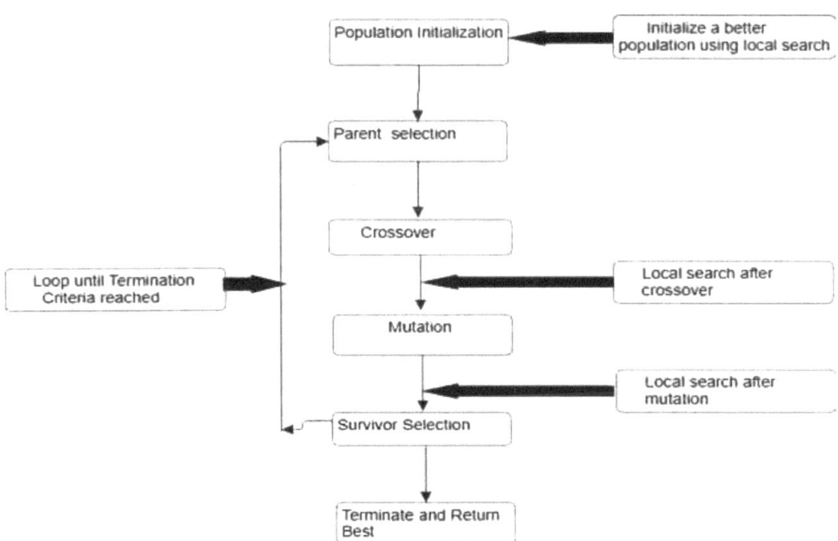

Fig. (7). Workflow of genetic algorithm [16].

Challenges in Antenna Design

The resonant frequency of a microstrip antenna may be calculated using the simple equation 1:

$$Fr = 2L\mathcal{E}rc \quad \textbf{(1)}$$

The resonant frequency c, the period of the antenna L, and the relative permittivity of the substrate Ɛr are the primary elements that have an effect on numerous design aspects.

Genetic Algorithms (GA): The GA optimization process is defined by using a health feature that is generally used to maximize or minimize antenna parameters. For instance, the health feature for optimizing the gain and bandwidth will be expressed as in equation 2

$$F(x) = w1.x + w2.\ Bandwidth(x) \quad \textbf{(2)}$$

in which w1 and w2 are weights that suggest the importance of every parameter in the normal layout. Genetic Algorithms (GA): The method of GA optimization is described by using a fitness function, which is generally used to maximize or minimize antenna parameters.

In Particle Swarm Optimization (PSO), the updates that control the particle speed and position are important to determine the convergence behavior and can be expressed mathematically as equation 3:

$$vi+1 = w.\ vi+c1.r1.\ (pbest-xi) + c2.r2.\ (best-xi) \quad \textbf{(3)}$$

v is the particle speed, x is the instantaneous position right here, pbest is the known position of the particle, and gbest is the best recognized position of every acknowledged position. r1 and r2 are random numbers, and cl and c2 are the situation.

Deep learning (DL) model: In deep learning, the negative function used in the training phase can reduce the difference between the antennas, which can be expressed as equation 4:

$$Loss=Nl\ \mathcal{E}i =lN(yi-yi\hat{}2) \quad \textbf{(4)}$$

N is the number of education samples, Where yi is the actual fee and yi^ is the predicted value of the version

This file gives details on specialized software, like HFSS or CST Studio, which can correctly observe the necessary equations and strategies for electromagnetic simulations. The mathematical formulas used to assess antenna overall performance, which includes advantage, are represented *via* advantage = 10logl0. (input electricity 4x radiated strength) This component measures the performance of an antenna in changing electricity into radio waves along a certain route. The steps for making use of those equations, measuring the results, and confirming the effectiveness of the optimized designs are described. The design, as shown in Fig. (**8**), includes manipulative experiments and predetermined parameters to carefully compare the effectiveness of various techniques [14].

Evaluation Metrics for Antenna Performance

This phase explores the mathematical concepts of how every antenna layout technique adapts to the complexities of antenna engineering. One manner to evaluate the effectiveness of GA is to use an optimization function as in equation 5.

$$\text{Minimize } f(x) = -(\text{Gain}(x) + \lambda x \text{Bandwidth}(x)) \quad \textbf{(5)}$$

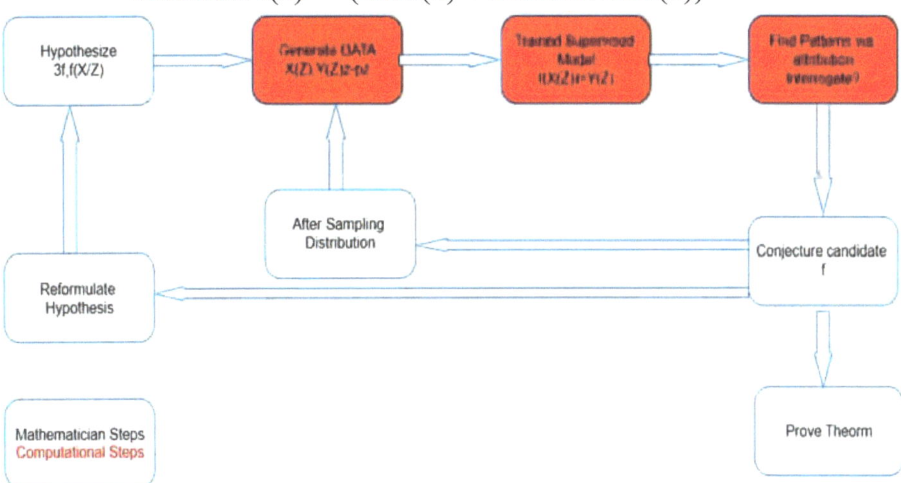

Fig. (8). Framework process chart.

The miles represent a factor that weighs the significance of bandwidth in terms of earnings. This system allows assessing the capacity of GA to simultaneously optimize multiple conflicting parameters. The section illustrates the practical implications of the findings. This communication makes a specialty of the sensible implications of integrating Artificial Intelligence (AI) into antenna design processes, highlighting the benefits of economic systems and improved performance. A cost savings equation may include variables like decreased design time and more suitable resource utilization, as per equation 6.

$$\text{Cost Savings} = \text{Old Cost} - \text{New Cost} = \text{Old Timex Rate} - \text{New Timex Rate} \quad \textbf{(6)}$$

This equation illustrates the explicit financial benefits of making use of superior artificial intelligence techniques. Through incorporating equations that explain the principles at the back of each method, a deeper understanding of their strengths and weaknesses can be achieved. As an example, the system of updating in PSO may be expressed mathematically as per equation 7:

$$vi+l = \omega vi+\varphi g(gbest-xi)\ xi+l=xi+vi+l \quad \textbf{(7)}$$

Here, the inertia weight and cognitive social coefficients are represented by way of the symbols ro and q, respectively. This enables making a clear PSO equilibrium by conducting a global search (exploring different regions) and focusing on local search (exploring unique areas).

Benefits: It defines a more efficient and more powerful computer. It introduces an enhanced and contemporary interface for human interaction. It provides a novel approach to address distinctive challenges. It handles the data more efficiently than humans. The expense of implementing AI is quite substantial. The fee for implementing AI is considerably elevated. The challenges with software program development for the implementation of AI are that the development of software is high-priced and time-consuming. An artificial intelligence robot is one of the ways that companies are replacing jobs and starting to provide employment opportunities. Machines can easily cause destruction if they are misused by individuals with malicious intent. The consequences can be extremely dangerous for human beings. To estimate the likelihood of future research, one can suggest modifications to existing equations or suggest the development of new formulas. For example, a hybrid artificial intelligence version should utilize a combined optimization function as per equation 8:

$$fhybrid(x)=\alpha fGA(x)+\beta fPSO(x)+\gamma fDL(x) \quad \textbf{(8)}$$

The coefficients α, β, and γ determine the effect of each technique. This equation can be used as a theoretical basis for creating more superior and complete optimization methods.

Execution and consequences: The preliminary implementation of genetic algorithms concerned careful planning and employer-defined primary parameters, including population size, crossover fee, and mutation fee, as well as the specific hardware and software used. The effects were carefully analyzed, and performance signs such as convergence speed and computation time have been provided through numerous visual representations. The findings highlighted the benefits and disadvantages of genetic algorithms in solving complex optimization problems. Eventually, the Particle Swarm Optimization (PSO) technique was applied with cautious consideration of essential parameters such as particle number and coefficients to improve performance [36, 37].

Recommendations for Future Research and Applications

The consequences obtained from PSO provide essential information about the performance of the set of rules and their ability to remedy the trouble. Those findings are confirmed by using statistical analysis and a visual illustration of the records. The complete analysis in Fig. (**9**) allows us to understand PSO behavior and overall performance styles in distinct computing environments. The outcomes received from PSO offer critical data approximately the overall performance of the set of rules and its capacity to remedy the problem. Those findings are validated by using statistical evaluation and visualization of consultant facts. This comprehensive analysis helps to apprehend PSO behavior and performance patterns in extraordinary computing environments. Make comparisons using visual equipment, including tables and graphs. The section concludes with a discussion of the comparison results and recommendations for specific applications, providing useful suggestions for choosing the best optimization method based on the observed results.

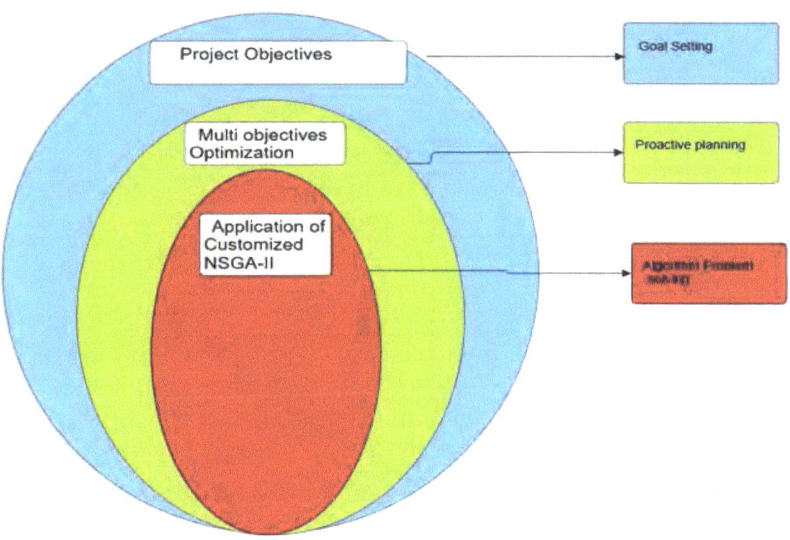

Fig. (9). Key Layers of Resilient and Proactive Scheduling in Construction Projects [16].

This study presents the use and comparison of various computational tools, including genetic techniques, optimization, and deep learning models. The technology is specifically designed to improve the manufacturing process of complex antennas. Genetic algorithms have been shown to be effective in controlling the optimization process, but have limitations in special environments with pressure constraints. Particle Swarm Optimization (PSO) has been shown to be useful in solving dynamic problems by demonstrating the efficiency of many computational tasks [16]. Deep Learning strategies together with Convolutional Neural Networks (CNN) and Long Short-Term Memory (LSTM) models have proven first-rate success in studying and mastering massive datasets. They offer extraordinary accuracy in modeling and predicting antenna characteristics. The results of this observation are very important for antenna layout, accuracy, and performance. Studies show the use of this technology to create higher and greater green antennas. Alternatively, gaining deep knowledge of models can enhance the antenna to meet the necessities. This generalization not only handily improves the design manner but also reduces the production time and price of the antenna. The ability of AI to process large amounts of data and offer insights from models could make antenna management extra efficient and flexible. Those systems can regulate and optimize their overall performance in keeping with the desires of the environment and the community. Further, the mixing of AI with future technology, which includes the Internet of Things (IoT) and 5G networks, has the capability to create smarter, more efficient, and higher communication for these days' communications [38, 39].

SADEA Algorithm for Antenna Optimization

Sadea is an optimization algorithm, shown in Fig. (**10**), that utilizes strategies in designing an antenna that are better by way of artificial intelligence, or AI. This algorithm is developed using device mastering concepts and continuously improving calculation techniques, with the blessings of optimization, superiority, effectiveness, simplification, and weight. Sadea makes use of Differential Evolution (DE) because the exploration system and Gaussian Process (GP) mechanism scheme for replacement demonstrate method [14].

The DE method is a metaheuristic algorithm that is used to solve optimization problems. It is based on the concept of differential evolution, which involves combining the best solutions from a population of candidate solutions to create new solutions. The GP mechanism is a method for generating new candidate solutions based on the current best solution. The Gaussian process is based on the idea that random functions represent the stochastic process proposed by Gauss. The generalization of the results to new cases can be predicted from the arguments. Estimates of the estimated values and uncertainties for new arguments are given, and the analysis can use them to identify new participants, leading to a clear evaluation. It also outperforms other products in terms of good resolution and optimized connection speed in permanent locations. Different workers are used to generate new solutions, while the peer-to-peer competition system also allows a competitive selection process for new participants. This approach and the upgrades it offers are extensively used in the layout and analysis of antennas. The antenna is pleasantly tuned to the use of MATLAB optimization equipment to optimize the gain and impedance bandwidth. A distressing algorithm is used. This algorithm is discussed intensively. Determine 3 shows the operation of this set of rules. To improve the antenna performance, dimensions such as patch length, width, and amplitude were adjusted to ensure that the S11 value was less than -10 dB. In a research article, it was found that a wide leaf improved the recovery. The values determined by the lower and upper limits are given by equations 1 and 2. Among the many research articles on microstrip antenna design, this article presents some of the research. Sharma and Pandey (2021) [40] proposed a method using the Gaussian Process Regression machine learning algorithm and an artificial neural network to calculate the square patch length, the square patch difference length, and other parameters of a Compact Microstrip Antenna (CMA). The resonant frequency of the primary mode is planned as a 7.8476 GHz band. The Gaussian Process Regression (GPR) model is evaluated with the aid of layout and deployment. Antenna prototype. The performance of the fabricated antenna is similar to the conventional antenna, and the Gaussian regression technique is used to predict the outcomes. It gives a lower prediction. Gao et al. proposed a semi-integrated training method using a Gaussian Process (GP) and a Support Vector Machine (SVM) for Yagi Microstrip Antenna (YMA) and GPS-Beidou dual-mode microstrip antenna message (GPS-BMMA). Use a custom configuration to train the preliminary SVM model and the preliminary GP technique. The education community changed to evaluating using the nice design MSA and GPS Beidou twin-mode microstrip antennas with high performance.

The predictive strength of the set of rules is drastically higher compared to traditional learning control techniques. The effectiveness of the collaborative education system has lead to the usage of real-time simulation software for prediction. It offers high root suggest square errors. The researcher delivered a bendy MSA that can be tuned to perform at 28 GHz and consists of liquid crystal structures. The fabrication manner becomes developed through the usage of a warm press to shape a thin layer with a thickness of 0.13 to 0.25 mm. The antenna's three-layer design was created to accommodate a liquid crystal layer. This design reveals a circuit board where the lower trace of the upper layer makes direct contact with the liquid crystal.

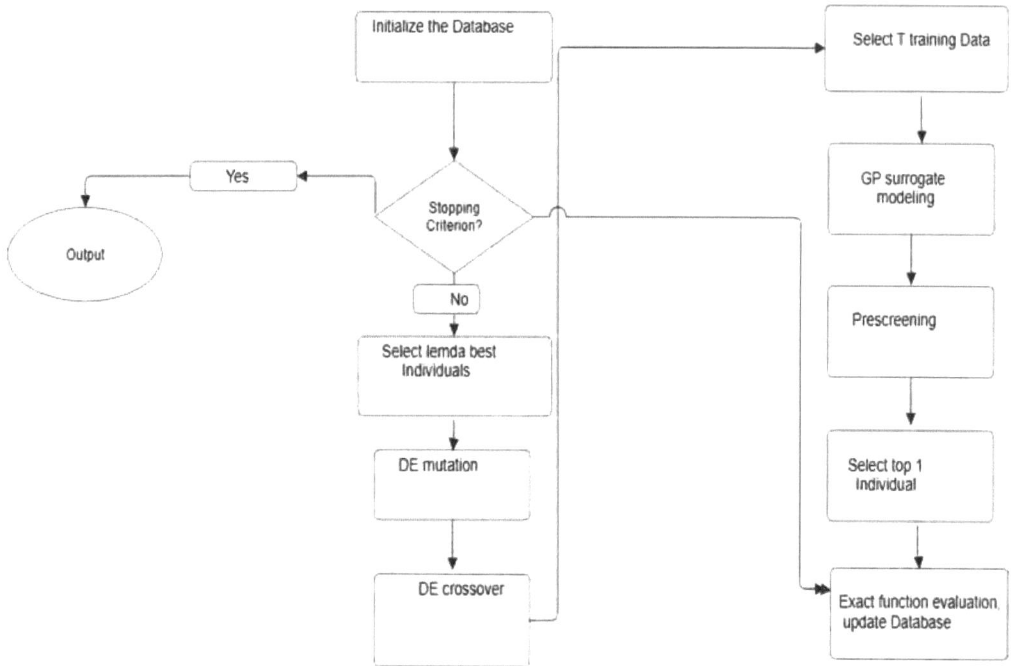

Fig. (10). SEDEA Methodology [14].

This leads to a higher average error. A Researcher introduced a method to determine the MSA resonance frequency using the deep learning method. The process of obtaining the train model using labels in the full-wave electromagnetic simulation software is time-consuming, especially after the electromagnetic equipment is optimized and activated better than before. The nuclear learning model, combined with the particle swarm optimization algorithm, proposed a multi-layer nonlinear mapping DKL technology. The overall performance of the DKL version is evaluated using the resonant frequency of two microstrip Yagi antennas and the necessities of the deep learning technique. High-strength line yields, researchers proposed a modified ground aid structure (DGS) that simultaneously constrains the E-aircraft and H-plane coupling in a 2 × 2 MSA array at 2.45 GHz. Based on magnetic flux and modal concept, the DGS is developed and analyzed. In addition, machine learning is also utilized to suit the parameters of the weak building in the constraints and optimize them to acquire the first-rate layout, specifically lowering the development time of the weak construction.

To verify the effectiveness of the scheme, 2 MSA antennas were used for transmission. Therefore, the simulation and size results show that the poor floor call can have an effect on the discount of the E-aircraft and H-couplings. Considering the general scope, Jacobs (2021) points out that there are special problems in modeling pixelated MSAs because their geometry cannot be easily parameterized compared to antenna geometries in image models. A method for dual-band pixelated MSA associated with CNN regression is proposed for the L2 resonance frequency model, which will use the entire pixelated surface represented by the antenna as input. The prediction performance of CNNs with shallow (as well as deep) normal neural networks is analyzed. Identify the hyperparameters of models and subjects using Bayesian optimization. It gives a lower estimate.

CONCLUSION

AI calculations can empower a versatile microstrip antenna that can powerfully alter its setup based on changing natural conditions or client necessities. This may be accomplished through methods like reconfigurable patches, beam-forming, or tunable materials controlled by AI calculations. It is vital to note that the fruitful usage of AI in microstrip antenna plans requires precise preparation information, appropriate approval, and a profound understanding of the electromagnetic theory and radio wire plan standards. Also, a multidisciplinary approach, including mastery in receiving wire plans, machine learning, and electromagnetic reenactments, is regularly essential for compelling integration of AI procedures into micro-patch radio wire advancement. A neural network-based CAD show should be created for the plan and investigation of a rectangular microstrip antenna, which is strong in terms of computation and exactness. An unmistakable advantage of neurocomputing is that, after appropriate preparation, a neural arrangement totally bypasses the rehashed use of complex iterative forms for unused cases presented to it. The single arranged structure can anticipate the outcomes for fixed radio wire, given that input values are within the space of preparing values. This work may be of potential application for planned receiving wire creators in arranging to finalize plan parameters for achieving ideal execution. Introducing this optimization of the technology will establsih the way to demonstrate India as one of the finest innovatively creating nations in the world.

REFERENCES

[1] D.M. Pozar, *Microwave Engineering.* John Wiley & Sons, 2011.

[2] S. Raudys, and A.K. Jain, "Small sample size effects in statistical pattern recognition: Recommendations for handling small datasets in Aldriven antenna design", *Pattern Recognit. Lett.*, vol. 12, no. 5, pp. 297-307, 1991.

[3] C.M. Bishop, *Pattern Recognition and Machine Learning.* Springer, 2006.

[4] C.A. Balanis, *Antenna Theory: Analysis and Design.* Wiley, 2016.

[5] R. Chaudhury, and B.R. Dutta, "Advanced ultrawideband patch antenna for wearable and WBAN applications", *Telecommun. Radio Eng.,* vol. 83, no. 6, pp. 39-65, 2024.

[6] A. Alhammadi, I. Shayea, A.A. El-Saleh, M.H. Azmi, Z.H. Ismail, L. Kouhalvandi, and S.A. Saad, "Art.ificial Intelligence in 6G Wireless Networks: Opportlmities, Applications, and Challenges", *Int. J. Intell. Syst.,* vol. 2024, no. 1, p. 8845070, 2024.

[7] B.R. Dutta, and B. Biswas, *"Review of Synergistic Integration of Microstrip patch Antennas in Biomedical and Artificial Intelligence domains" Springer Communications in Computer and Information Science book series.* vol. 2000. CCIS, 2024, pp. 65-81. [http://dx.doi.org/10.1007/978-3-031-54162-9_5]

[8] R. Chaudhury, and B.R. Dutta, "Advanced ultrawideband patch antenna for wearable and WBAN applications", *Telecommun. Radio Eng.,* vol. 83, no. 6, pp. 39-65, 2024. [http://dx.doi.org/10.1615/TelecomRadEng.2024051936]

[9] M.M. Islam, H. Yang, and J. Zhou, "An overview of artificial intelligence techniques for 5G wireless communication systems", *IEEE Access,* vol. 8, pp. 88073-88087, 2020.

[10] X. Sun, and Y. Li, "Application of machine learning in antenna design: A review", *IEEE Access,* vol. 8, pp. 155714-155726, 2020.

[11] R. Sharma, S. Gupta, and A. Rao, "Practical implementation of Al-optimized antennas for loT", *Int. J. Wirel. Inf. Netw.,* vol. 26, no. 3, pp. 282-294, 2019.

[12] Y. Huang, X. Wang, and Y. Liu, "Real-time reconfigurable antennas using Al techniques", *IEEE Trans. Antenn. Propag.,* vol. 68, no. 11, pp. 8442-8455, 2020.

[13] J. Chen, J. Huang, and T. Zhang, "Al-driven optimization of reconfigurable antennas for loT applications", *IEEE Trans. Antenn. Propag.,* vol. 69, no. 2, pp. 899-911, 2021.

[14] L. Aluigi, G. Orecchini, and L. Larcher, "A 28 GHz scalable beamforming system for 5G automotive connectivity: An integrated patch antenna and power amplifier solution", in Proc. 2018 IEEE MTT-S Int. Microw. Workshop Series 5G Hardw. Syst. Technol. (IMWS-5G), Dublin, Ireland, 2018, pp. 1–3. [http://dx.doi.org/10.1109/IMWS-5G.2018.8484325]

[15] X. Li, H. Sun, and Z. Zhou, "Al-enhanced antenna design for loT applications: A case study", *IEEE Internet Things J.,* vol. 8, no. 9, pp. 7557-7567, 2021.

[16] Swapna Mudey, "AI-Enhanced Optimization Techniques for MicroStrip Antenna Design: A Comparative Study", *Intemational Journal of Intelligent Systems and Applications in Engineering.,* vol. 12, no. 22s, pp. 298-306, 2024.

[17] P. Kumar, A. Singh, and S. Roy, "Enhancing loT antenna performance through machine learning algorithms", *Sensors (Basel),* vol. 22, no. 5, p. 1473, 2022.

[18] T. Taha, M.J. Al-ani, and A.A. Al-shawi, "The role of artificial intelligence in wireless communications", in Proc. 2018 IEEE Int. Conf. Inf. Commun. Technol. (ICICT), 2018, pp. 1–5.

[19] J. Wang, R. Li, J. Wang, Y. Ge, and W. Shi, "Artificial intelligence and wireless communications, *Frontiers of Information Technology & Electronic Engineering*, vol. 21, pp. 1413–1425, 2020.

[20] F. Hu, X. Wen, and K. Wu, "Al-based beamforming and power allocation for NOMA- enabled wireless powered communication networks", *IEEE Trans. Vehicular Technol.,* vol. 70, no. 3, pp. 3140-3151, 2021.

[21] Y. Xie, and Y. Peng, "Artificial intelligence for next-generation wireless communication systems: A comprehensive survey", *IEEE Access,* vol. 7, pp. 10127-10151, 2019.

[22] D. Guha, Y.M. Antar, Ed., *Microstrip and printed antennas: new trends, techniques and applications.* John Wiley & Sons, 2011.

[23] S. Koziel, and A. Bekasiewicz, *Multiobjective design of antennas using surrogate models.* World Scientific, 2016.

[24] M.S.I. Sagar, H. Ouassal, A.I. Omi, A. Wisniewska, H.M. Jalajamony, R.E. Fernandez, and P.K. Sekhar, "Application of machine learning in electromagnetics: Mini-review", *Electronics (Basel),* vol. 10, no. 22, p. 2752, 2021.
[http://dx.doi.org/10.3390/electronics10222752]

[25] B. Liu, H. Aliakbarian, Z. Ma, G.A.E. Vandenbosch, G. Gielen, and P. Excell, "An efficient method for antenna design optimization based on evolutionary computation and machine learning techniques", *IEEE Trans. Antenn. Propag.,* vol. 62, no. 1, pp. 7-18, 2014.
[http://dx.doi.org/10.1109/TAP.2013.2283605]

[26] S. Singh, G. Sethi, and J.S. Khinda, "A Historical Development and Futuristic trends of Microstrip Antennas", *International Journal of Computing and Digital Systems,* vol. 12, no. 1, pp. 187-204, 2022.
[http://dx.doi.org/10.12785/ijcds/1201017]

[27] A. Pietrenko-Dabrowska, and S. Koziel, "Expedited gradient-based design closure of antennas using variable-resolution simulations and sparse sensitivity updates", *IEEE Trans. Antenn. Propag.,* vol. 70, no. 6, pp. 4925-4930, 2022.
[http://dx.doi.org/10.1109/TAP.2021.3138487]

[28] J. Mietzner, R. Schober, L. Lampe, W.H. Gerstacker, and P.A. Hoeher, "Multiple-antenna techniques for communications-a comprehensive survey", *IEEE Commun. Surv. Tutor.,* vol. 11, no. 2, pp. 87-105, 2009.
[http://dx.doi.org/10.1109/SURV.2009.090207]

[29] B. Ozpoyraz, A.T. Dogukan, Y. Gevez, U. Altun, and E. Basar, "Deep learning-aided 6G wireless networks: A comprehensive survey of revolutionary PHY architectures", *IEEE Open J. Commun. Soc.,* vol. 3, pp. 1749-1809, 2022.
[http://dx.doi.org/10.1109/OJCOMS.2022.3210648]

[30] A. Abdulla, B. Wang, F. Qian, T. Kee, A. Blasiak, Y.H. Ong, L. Hooi, F. Parekh, R. Soriano, G.G. Olinger, J. Keppo, C.L. Hardesty, E.K. Chow, D. Ho, and X. Ding, "Project IDentif. AI: harnessing artificial intelligence to rapidly optimize combination therapy development for infectious disease intervention", *Adv. Ther. (Weinh.),* vol. 3, no. 7, p. 2000034, 2020.
[http://dx.doi.org/10.1002/adtp.202000034] [PMID: 32838027]

[31] K. Gopalakrishnan, A. Adhikari, N. Pallipamu, M. Singh, T. Nusrat, S. Gaddam, P. Samaddar, A. Rajagopal, A.S.S. Cherukuri, A. Yadav, S.S. Manga, D.N. Damani, S. Shivaram, S. Dey, S. Roy, D. Mitra, and S.P. Arunachalam, "Applications of Microwaves in Medicine Leveraging Artificial Intelligence: Future Perspectives", *Electronics (Basel),* vol. 12, no. 5, p. 1101, 2023.
[http://dx.doi.org/10.3390/electronics12051101]

[32] F.M. Isa, W.N.M. Ariffin, M.S. Jusoh, and E.P. Putri, "A Review of Genetic Algorithm: Operations and Applications", *Journal of Advanced Research in Applied Sciences and Engineering Technology,* vol. 40, no. 1, pp. 1-34, 2024.

[33] B.R. Dutta, R. Chaudhury, A. Tripathi, and B. Biswas, "Advance T-shaped microstrip patch antenna for improved radio frequency energy harvesting", *Telecommunications and Radio Engineering,* vol. 83, no. 1, pp. 1-16, 2024.
[http://dx.doi.org/10.1615/TelecomRadEng.2023049976]

[34] A. Essien, and C. Giannetti, "A deep learning model for smart manufach1ring using convolutional LSTM neural network autoencoders", *IEEE Trans. Industr. Inform.,* vol. 16, no. 9, pp. 6069-6078, 2020.
[http://dx.doi.org/10.1109/TII.2020.2967556]

[35] S.G. Franzblau, M.A. DeGroote, S.H. Cho, K. Andries, E. Nuermberger, I.M. Orme, K. Mdluli, I. Angulo-Barturen, T. Dick, V. Dartois, and A.J. Lenaerts, "Comprehensive analysis of methods used for the evaluation of compounds against Mycobacterium tuberculosis", *Tuberculosis (Edinb.),* vol. 92, no. 6, pp. 453-488, 2012.
[http://dx.doi.org/10.1016/j.tube.2012.07.003] [PMID: 22940006]

[36] I.J. Bahl, and P. Bhartia, *Microstrip Antennas.* Artech House: Dedham, MA, 1980.

[37] Q.J. Zhang, and K.C. Gupta, *Neural Networks for RF and Microwave Design.* Artech House Publishers: USA, 2000.

[38] K.Sharma, and G.P. Pandey. Efficient modelling of compact microstrip antenna using machine learning, *AEU-Int. J. Electron. Commun.* vol. 135. 153739, 2021. [http://dx.doi.org/10.1016/j.aeue.2021.153739]

[39] R. Chaudhary and B. R. Dutta, “Advance antenna array design for Sub-6GHz 5G applications,” in *Proc. 14th Int. Conf. Comput. Commun. Netw. Technol. (ICCCNT)*, 2023. [http://dx.doi.org/10.1109/ICCCNT56998.2023.10308217]

[40] D. Elhani, A.C. Megherbi, A. Zitouni, F. Dornaika, S. Sbaa, and A. Taleb-Ahmed, "Optimizing convolutional neural networks architecture using a modified particle swarm optimization for image classification", *Expert Syst. Appl.,* vol. 229, p. 120411, 2023. [http://dx.doi.org/10.1016/j.eswa.2023.120411]

CHAPTER 5

Revolutionizing Heart Disease Prediction: A Review of Machine Learning Techniques and Challenges

Shifa Shah[1], **Madhu Bala**[2,*], **Aashima**[2], **Anjum Rouf**[2] and **Tabassum Rahim**[1]

[1] *Department of Computer Science and Engineering, National Institute of Technology, Srinagar, Jammu & Kashmir, India*

[2] *Department of Computer Science and Engineering, Lovely Professional University, Phagwara, Punjab, India*

Abstract: Cardiovascular diseases (CVD) are the foremost cause of death worldwide, leading to extensive research in prediction models for early prognosis and intervention. This study presents a comprehensive overview of Machine Learning (ML) approaches in predicting ischemic cardiovascular diseases, synthesizing insights from various studies. Key themes include dataset diversity, rigorous preprocessing, and the exploration of various ML algorithms like logistic regression, random forests, decision trees, and various deep learning models. Challenges such as data imbalance and model interpretability are addressed, with future directions emphasizing multimodal data integration and novel ML architectures. Overall, ML-based approaches offer significant potential to revolutionize heart disease prediction and management, driving improved risk assessment, treatment strategies, and patient outcomes in cardiovascular care.

Keywords: Cardiovascular Diseases, Heart Disease Prediction, Ischemic Cardiovascular Diseases, Machine Learning, Predictive Models.

INTRODUCTION

Heart disease, medically termed as cardiovascular disease, stands as a primary cause of mortality across the globe. Recent findings from the World Heart Federation reveal that one in every three fatalities is attributed to CVD [1]. Projections by the World Health Organization (WHO) suggest that by 2030, over 23.6 million individuals might succumb to CVD, predominantly due to strokes and heart failure. Various factors contribute to the onset of CVD, including stress,

* **Corresponding author Madhu Bala:** Department of Computer Science and Engineering, Lovely Professional University, Phagwara, Punjab, India; E-mail: madhucse0105@gmail.com

Shilpa Gupta, Ritika Sharma & Gokana Mohana Rani (Eds.)

alcohol consumption, smoking, poor dietary habits, sedentary lifestyle, and underlying health conditions such as hypertension or diabetes. However, early detection significantly enhances the chances of complete recovery from most CVD-related ailments [2]. Hence, there's a critical need for healthcare providers to prioritize the diagnosis and anticipation of heart failure. Advanced data analysis techniques applied to patients' health records can improve early CVD diagnosis [3]. Analysis of health status is done as a precaution against different fatalities, determining major anomalies and, therefore, arriving at a precise diagnosis (Fig. **1**). Establishing a diagnosis can be with genetic predispositions, socio-medical conditions, environmental situations, and personal lifestyle selection. Modern medical approaches rely more on risk assessment and factor analysis to

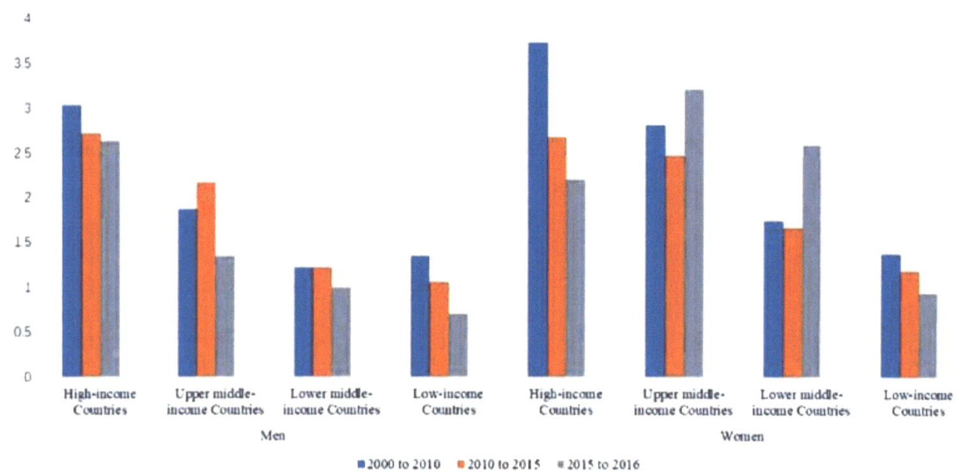

Fig. (1). Percentage decline in premature CVD deaths (2000–2016) by gender and national income group [5].

prevent conditions from deteriorating to acute stages, contributing to enhanced health results [4]. This raises the concern for developing an accurate clinical data examination system concerning HD to identify the extent of heart failure [4]. Many studies have used the ML approach for predicting CVD using clinical databases. However, these datasets are challenging due to class imbalances and high dimensionality. Failure to overcome these barriers undermines the effectiveness and reliability of ML techniques. Some earlier studies have focused on FS techniques and applied several ML systems for CVD prediction. For example, Long *et al.* [5] developed a CVD decision system combining Rough Sets (RS) with the Chaos Firefly algorithm (CFARS-AR) to identify optimal features, followed by the use of a type-2 fuzzy logic system for HD detection, which had an accuracy of 88.3%. Similarly, Dwivedi combined RS with a backpropagation neural network (BPNN) for CVD prediction, while Haq *et al.*

performed a comparative study on FS methods integrated with different ML models, highlighting the significance of feature retention for optimal model performance.

Amin *et al.* [6] worked on different ML models, and one hybrid model with feature identification, reporting the hybrid model's superior accuracy of 87.41%. Furthermore, efforts have also been made to improve the precision of prediction through hybrid models such as RF with a linear model (HRFLM), and new optimization techniques, for instance, those presented by Vijayashree *et al.* [7], demonstrating better CVD prediction techniques.

Cardiovascular diseases are one of the most serious global health crises, causing millions of mortalities every year and posing significant challenges to healthcare systems worldwide. According to the World Health Organization (WHO), there is a concern to underline the imperative to work on CVD, such as heart attacks and stroke, which cause a substantial portion of deaths in any given country. Scarily enough, it has been estimated that one person dies from cardiovascular disease every 34 seconds in the United States, and therefore, there is an ongoing need for more effective and earlier interventions to prevent this aspect [8].

Though there has been advancement in medical science, late diagnosis and limited monitoring of the ailment continue to hinder precise and actual management of CVD, exacerbating its impact on public health. To resolve this challenge, there has been a growing trend of leveraging Machine Learning (ML) techniques to develop accurate and useful models for predicting fatal diseases, including heart disease and stroke. By utilizing ML algorithms to analyze diverse patient data, encompassing factors such as sex, age, cholesterol levels, and blood pressure, researchers aim to improve risk management and facilitate timely interventions, thereby improving patient outcomes and reducing the load on the healthcare system [9]. Hybrid models integrated with the different ML techniques have also been shown to have better performance in predicting CVD. HRFLM has achieved up to 88.4% accuracy by incorporating Random Forest with a linear model [10]. Besides, novel strategies, such as the SVM using a novel PSO fitness function, have gained importance and provided accuracies up to 84.36% [11]. Some studies have proven the versatility of ML-based prediction models for detecting risky individuals and devising targeted treatment protocols. These advancements have led to the creation of powerful frameworks that outshine traditional methodologies, offering valuable insights into disease detection and prognosis. Moreover, with the proliferation of electronic health records and advancements in ML techniques, the prospects for developing efficient AI models for disease detection have never been more promising [12]. In this study, we explore the advanced ML-based approaches for predicting cardiovascular diseases. This study aims to bring a comprehensive overview of the existing methodologies and comparison with the ML approach and seeks to provide progress toward efficient risk assessment, optimized treatment strategies, and better patient outcomes against fatal CVD.

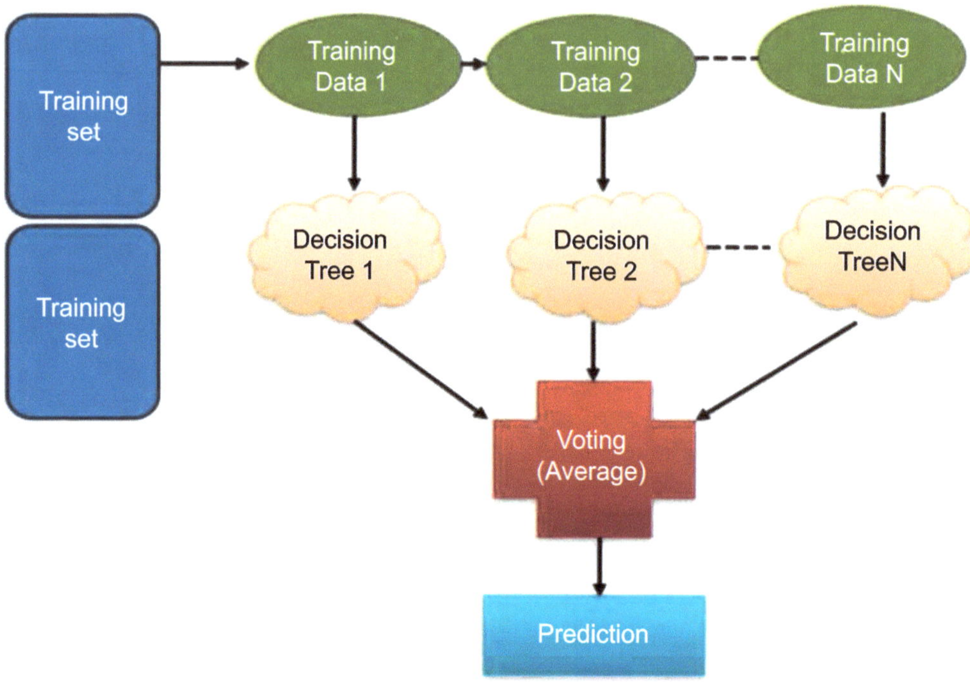

Fig. (2). Procedure of using decision trees in Random Forest.

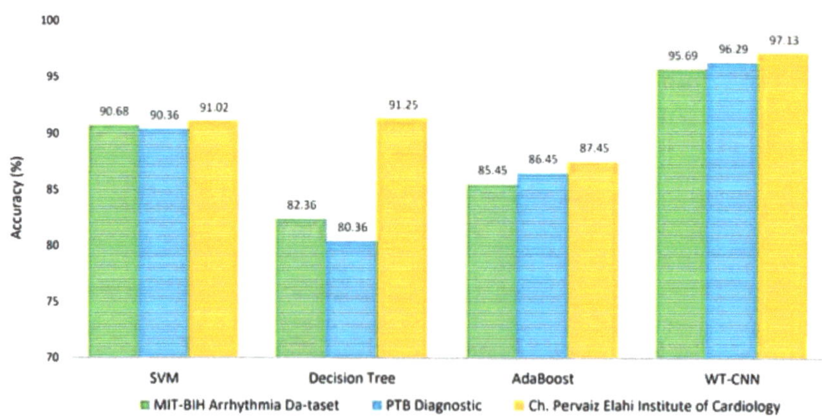

Fig. (3). Graph comparing the accuracy of various algorithms [44].

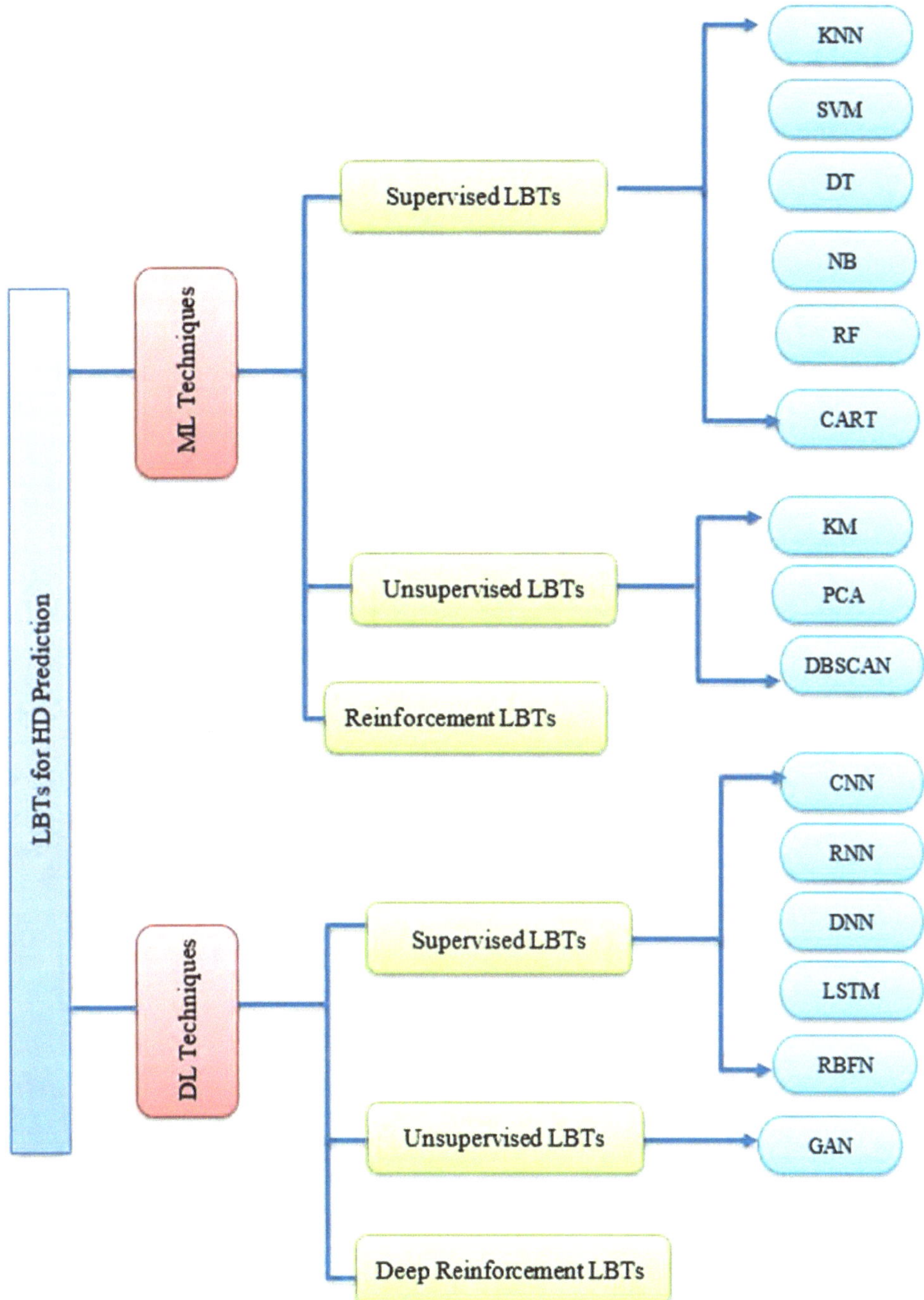

Fig. (4). Different LBTs [10].

RELATED WORK

The current chapter explains the key factors for predicting heart disease, highlighting its importance as a major cause of death worldwide. Utilizing advancements in Artificial Intelligence (AI), particularly through ensemble learning techniques such as Random Forest (RF) (depicted in Fig. (**2**)) and Support Vector Machines (SVM), the research addresses persistent challenges in achieving accurate predictions. In response to limitations in existing methodologies, the study introduces an innovative self-attention-based transformer model specifically designed for heart disease prediction.

This pioneering model not only demonstrates remarkable accuracy but also exhibits adaptability across various risk prediction tasks, potentially transforming personalized risk assessment in healthcare. By exploring previously unknown risk factors and meticulously evaluating demographic categories, the study offers invaluable insights to enhance patient outcomes and refine predictive methodologies. Through analysis of bio-clinical variables and applying ten standard classification models, the research identifies significant predictors of heart disease, with the support vector machine emerging as the most effective classifier. This effectiveness is confirmed through tenfold cross-validation on the Statlog data, highlighting the robustness of the proposed approach.

The progress of Machine Learning (ML) methods in forecasting Heart Disease (HD) has notably enhanced the precision and effectiveness of diagnosis and prognosis. Through the utilization of supervised, unsupervised, and deep learning techniques, scientists have gained valuable insights from intricate medical datasets, resulting in more tailored and efficient patient treatments. Comparison of various algorithms is shown in Fig. (**3**), and it can be noted that deep neural networks are giving better results as compared to machine learning algorithms.

Nonetheless, there are various challenges and prospects that await in this domain. Despite the promising results of Machine Learning (ML) models in research settings, integrating them seamlessly into clinical practice poses a significant challenge. Their real-world applicability and usability need further evaluation and validation, addressing concerns such as interpretability, scalability, and reliability. It is crucial to ensure that healthcare professionals can trust and effectively utilize these predictive models in decision-making processes. Additionally, the availability and quality of medical data remain a hurdle despite increasing digitization of healthcare systems and the widespread use of Electronic Health Records (EHRs). Enhancing data interoperability, privacy protection, and data quality assurance are essential to fully harnessing the potential of ML in predicting and diagnosing Heart Disease (HD). Furthermore, developing robust and generalizable ML algorithms necessitates interdisciplinary collaboration among computer scientists, statisticians, healthcare professionals, and domain experts. Integrating domain-specific knowledge and expertise into algorithmic design and evaluation can lead to the creation of more accurate and clinically relevant predictive models.

Future perspectives of integration of various data sources, such as genetic, imaging, and clinical data, have the potential to increase the accuracy of heart disease prediction. It will allow for a better understanding of the mechanisms of diseases and risk factors, which in turn can be used for personalizing and accurate prediction models. Advancements in techniques such as GNNs offer promising prospects in modeling complex relationships between various items in medical data. Two other approaches- recurrent neural networks and transformers have indeed shown good results in figuring out sequential data like longitudinal patient records and electrocardiograms. Approaches based on machine learning are new, powerful tools for the prediction and diagnosis of heart disease; potentially, they will completely revolutionize healthcare delivery and patient outcome improvement. However, addressing current concerns and analyzing upcoming technology aim to be key to fully realizing the effects of ML in the prognosis of cardiovascular care. In the realm of heart disease prediction with machine learning techniques, a number of studies have contributed significantly toward improving the accuracy and efficiency of diagnostic systems. Nilashi *et al.* [13] took their approach to the task in order to improve the accuracy, which involved SVM along with some imputation methods and noise reduction techniques. Their method involved combining fuzzy SVM analysis in an attempt to further refine their predictive results. Karthikeyan *et al.* [14] demonstrated that a deep learning network study reached great accuracy levels, hence providing the capabilities of deep learning techniques in disease detection.

Agrawal *et al.* [15] resolved the issue of missing entries in various datasets of heart disease by using various machine learning classifiers like the random forest, decision trees, support vector machines, k-nearest neighbors, and logistic regression. They obtained considerable improvements in accuracy using ensemble techniques in their study, like boosting and bagging, which emphasizes the significance of preprocessing data for better disease prediction. A few researchers [16] created a new approach using GSOM with PSO for cluster information, showing promising performance in the classification of diseases.

Sridevi *et al.* [17] investigated the utilization of Kohonen networks in the classification of heart disease. In this case, feature selection methods to identify relevant and irrelevant features were stressed. Their research proved that Self-Organizing Maps (SOM) effectively optimize the feature extraction. Baccouche *et al.* [18] developed a hybrid model with integration of BiLSTM or BiGRU models with CNN for precise heart disease detection. Their hybrid model has shown tremendous results in terms of accuracy, showing the robust use of a deep learning approach in disease diagnosis. This research in itself adds very important findings to the realm of predicting heart disease by machine learning. From the preprocessing approach to applying classification algorithms, all these contribute to filling gaps in diagnostic systems while improving accuracy and efficiency. Thereby, future developments can further bridge existing methodologies' flaws and help with better prediction and management of heart disease with time.

Ayesha Noor *et al.* [19] explored a new stacking model called PaRSEL to develop an early prediction method for heart disease, addressing its global health impact. It is designed using four types of base classifiers and LogitBoost that predict heart disease at a very early stage of its occurrence. The challenges of the data are reduced and balanced in order to carry out the experimentation process. PaRSEL outperforms the other methods with 97% accuracy, 80% of F1-score, and high precision. The internals of the model have been explained through Shapley additive explanations (SHAP). In summary, PaRSEL results in efficient prediction of heart disease compared to various classifiers.

Subhash Mondal *et al.* [20] work addresses the alarming problem of mortality across the globe due to cardiovascular diseases (CVDs) with a novel two-stage stacked machine learning model to predict heart disease risks efficiently. The researchers have used five classifiers on a dataset containing 1190 patients with an improvement in performance *via* cross-validation and hyperparameter tuning validation and hyperparameter tuning. The stacking model achieves an impressive 96% accuracy, 0.98 recall, and 0.96 ROC-AUC score, with fewer than 1% false negatives, demonstrating its accuracy and reliability. When tested on a comparable dataset, it consistently achieves 96.88% accuracy, underscoring its potential for timely and precise heart disease diagnosis to contribute to global efforts in reducing fatalities. In the realm of improving prognostic accuracy for ischemic cardiovascular disease using Machine Learning (ML) algorithms, previous studies have mainly concentrated on methodologies and techniques with limited datasets, often relying on sources like the UCI repository, which typically contains 303 instances. However, this review paper discusses a fresh approach introduced by Muhammad *et al.* [21], which utilizes a substantial dataset comprising over 918 observations obtained from Kaggle. The study incorporates 12 essential features crucial for predicting ischemic disease. It assesses the performance of six ML-based algorithms, including K-Nearest Neighbors (KNN), Random Forest (RF), Logistic Regression (LR), Support Vector Machine (SVM), Gaussian Naïve Bayes (GNB), and Decision Trees (DT), employing Convolutional Neural Networks (CNN) along with Deep Belief Networks (DBN).

Abdellatif *et al.* [22] introduced an innovative approach that integrates the Synthetic Minority Oversampling Technique (SMOTE) to address data imbalance, six machine learning classifiers, and Hyperparameter Optimization (HPO) to improve model performance. Their study, supported by the Ministry of Higher Education, yields superior results, achieving 99.2% and 98.52% accuracy in CVD detection using SMOTE and Extra Trees optimized with hyperband. Additionally, the model achieves a 95.73% convergence rate in severity classification using the Cleveland dataset, providing a valuable tool for early disease detection and prevention of heart-related mortality. The use of various ML and DL-based techniques used by the researchers is shown in Fig. (**4**), and basic steps to be followed for the prediction of heart diseases are represented in Fig. (**5**).

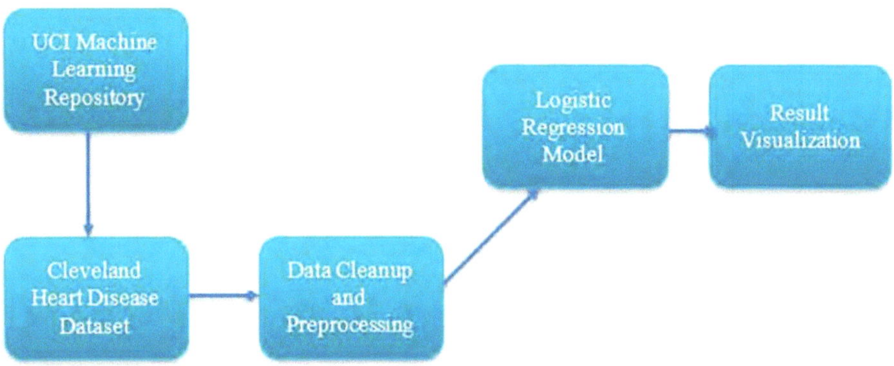

Fig. (5). Heart disease probability analysis flow.

In the realm of biomedical applications, the integration of Machine Learning (ML) techniques holds significant promise, despite challenges in algorithm selection and parameter tuning. Manduchi *et al.* [23] explore the applicability of the Tree-based Pipeline Optimization Tool (TPOT), an Automated ML (AutoML) method, in the genetic analysis of Coronary Artery Disease (CAD). Leveraging public functional genomic resources, the researchers intelligently group Single-Nucleotide Polymorphisms (SNPs) into biologically meaningful sets for TPOT selection, focusing on genes with high potential as CAD drug targets. Utilizing data from the U.K. Biobank, the study reveals a recurrent signal from a group of 28 SNPs, demonstrating their functional relevance to genes associated with CAD in existing literature and resources. The incorporation of game-theory-based metrics not only assesses the importance of these SNPs in TPOT predictions but also identifies distinct clusters of well-predicted CAD cases, offering a promising avenue towards precision medicine in the realm of coronary artery disease. Firouzi *et al.* [24] explored the collective impact of Smart and Connected Health technologies—IoT, AI, Robotics, and Blockchain—in addressing the COVID-19 pandemic. Their collaborative study highlights the significant roles these technologies play, including IoT's role in tracking and remote monitoring, AI's applications in diagnosis and risk prediction, and Robotics' use in surveillance and essential supply delivery. The study also discussed how blockchain and distributed ledger technologies can complement other tools in the fight against COVID-19.

TECHNIQUES USED

Machine learning algorithms are giving significant results in healthcare due to their capacity to analyze intricate data [25 - 27]. This results in assistance of disease diagnosis, prognosis, planning, and treatment. The present research utilized various machine learning approaches to construct a well-defined model trained for assessing the risk of heart disease. Through the application of data-centric methodologies, our objective was to elevate current clinical practices and enhance patient outcomes by facilitating early detection and intervention strategies.

Data Collection and Preprocessing

Data collection and preprocessing are important steps that need to be performed before passing the data to the model [28 - 31]. For the current work, an extensive dataset was compiled from Kaggle, consisting of patient records that include a diverse array of demographic, clinical, and lifestyle characteristics. Before initiating model training, rigorous preprocessing procedures were conducted on the dataset to guarantee data integrity and suitability for ML algorithms. The data cleaning step is performed, where all the missing values and inaccurate values have been rectified by applying feature engineering. It was observed that there is a huge mismatch between the values of different parameters. Hence, scaling is applied to those attributes to alleviate potential algorithmic biases. Various datasets are available for heart disease detection, and some of them are mentioned below:

Hungarian Heart Disease Dataset: This dataset is widely utilized by researchers in the field of cardiovascular research and has been referenced in various studies. It contains information about patients with heart disease. A number of features, such as age, sex, chest pain type, cholesterol levels, and more, are present in this dataset.

Switzerland Heart Disease Dataset: This dataset provides data on various risk factors associated with heart disease. It includes features like blood pressure, cholesterol levels, and electrocardiogram results. Researchers and clinicians analyse this dataset to identify patterns and build predictive models for heart disease diagnosis and prevention.

Cleveland Heart Disease Dataset: The Cleveland dataset is one of the most popular for heart disease prediction. It contains 303 instances with features such as age, sex, chest pain type, and ECG results. Data scientists use this dataset to create classification models that predict whether a patient has heart disease or not.

Long Beach Heart Disease Dataset: The Long Beach dataset includes information on risk factors like cholesterol levels, blood pressure, and exercise-induced angina. It also has missing values in some features.

Heart Disease Prediction Dataset on Kaggle: This dataset is available on Kaggle and is specifically designed for predicting the probability of heart disease. It includes various features related to patients' health, such as age, sex, chest pain type, cholesterol levels, and more. Researchers and data scientists can use this dataset to develop and evaluate machine learning models for heart disease prediction. It's valuable for building predictive models that assist in early diagnosis and risk assessment.

Heart Disease Dataset: This comprehensive dataset combines data from five different heart disease datasets: Cleveland, Hungarian, Switzerland, Long Beach, and VA Statlog (Heart). It includes a total of 11 common features related to heart health. Researchers and practitioners can use this extensive dataset to explore heart disease patterns, develop robust prediction models, and gain insights into risk factors. It's particularly useful for comparative studies and benchmarking.

Machine Learning–Based Heart Disease Prediction System for Indian Patients: This study focuses on predicting heart diseases using machine learning techniques. It utilizes data from major health factors relevant to Indian patients. Healthcare professionals and researchers can apply the classification methods demonstrated in this study (such as Multilayer Perceptron, Support Vector Machine, Random Forest, and Naïve Bayes) to build accurate prediction models for heart disease in the Indian population.

Source: PubMed Central - Machine Learning–Based Heart Disease Prediction System for Indian Patients.

Feature Engineering

Feature engineering plays a pivotal role in predictive modelling, particularly within healthcare sectors where the choice of relevant features significantly influences model performance and interpretability. Leveraging expertise from cardiovascular specialists and insights gleaned from previous studies, a comprehensive array of features customized for assessing heart disease risk [32 - 34] is crafted. These features spanned across demographic variables (such as age and gender), clinical metrics (including blood pressure and cholesterol levels), and lifestyle factors (such as smoking habits and physical activity levels), capturing a wide spectrum of cardiovascular health indicators and disease risk factors.

Machine Learning Algorithms

A diverse range of machine learning algorithms to construct robust predictive models for heart disease has been explored. Each model offers unique strengths in handling various data types and learning patterns [35]. The algorithms are mentioned below:

- Logistic Regression: Ideal for binary classification tasks, logistic regression yields interpretable outcomes and can effectively model intricate relationships between predictors and outcomes.
- Decision Trees and Random Forests: These ensemble learning methods excel at capturing nonlinear relationships and interactions among predictors, making them highly suitable for intricate datasets with diverse features.
- Support Vector Machines (SVM): SVMs demonstrate proficiency in segregating classes within high-dimensional feature spaces, rendering them valuable for tasks involving small to moderate-sized datasets and non-linear decision boundaries.
- Artificial Neural Networks (ANN): Deep learning models like ANNs offer unparalleled adaptability in discerning complex patterns from raw data, albeit at the expense of heightened computational complexity and potential overfitting.

Model Training

The chosen ML algorithms were trained on the pre-processed dataset using a meticulously planned training protocol. This protocol included dividing the dataset into training (Fig. **6**), validation, and test sets to aid in model selection and performance assessment [36, 37]. To fine-tune model hyperparameters and mitigate overfitting, methods such as grid search, random search, and cross-validation were employed. Furthermore, to tackle class imbalance within the heart disease dataset, strategies such as oversampling minority classes and applying class weights during training were implemented to ensure fair model learning across various outcome classes [38].

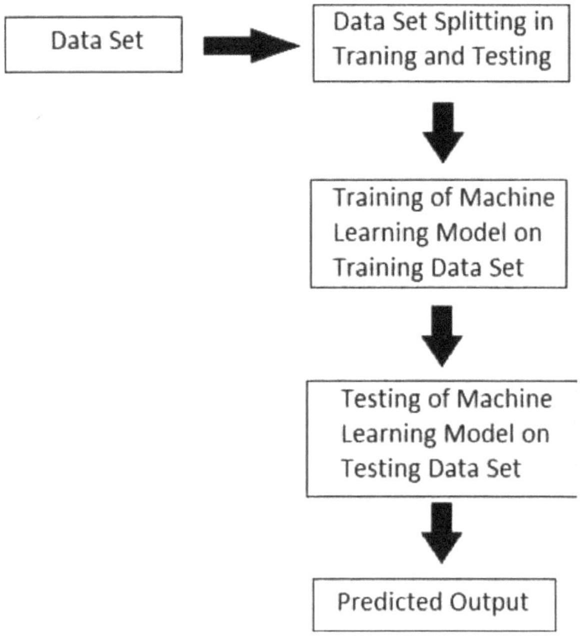

Fig. (6). Proposed model for heart disease prediction.

Evaluation Metrics

To evaluate the predictive performance of the developed models, we utilized a comprehensive set of evaluation metrics tailored specifically for binary classification tasks [39 - 41]. These metrics comprised:

Accuracy: Reflecting the percentage of correctly classified instances out of the total.

Precision: Representing the ratio of true positive predictions to the total number of positive predictions, indicating the model's capability to minimize false positives.

Recall (Sensitivity): Describing the ratio of true positive predictions to the total number of actual positives, demonstrating the model's effectiveness in capturing all positive instances.

F1-score: Calculated as the harmonic mean of precision and recall, providing a balanced assessment of the model's overall performance.

Area under the Receiver Operating Characteristic curve (AUC-ROC): Offering a graphical measure of the model's discriminatory ability between positive and negative instances across various decision thresholds.

Area under the Precision-Recall curve (AUC-PR): Serving as a summary measure of the model's precision-recall trade-off, particularly valuable for datasets with imbalanced classes.

Validation and Testing

To guarantee the reliability and applicability of the trained models, we executed thorough validation and testing protocols. This encompassed conducting stratified cross-validation on the training set to evaluate the models' performance across diverse folds and conducting holdout validation on an independent test set to gauge their ability to generalize to unseen data. By adhering to stringent validation procedures, our objective was to minimize the risk of overfitting and obtain trustworthy estimates of the models' performance in real-world scenarios [42, 43].

COMPARATIVE ANALYSIS

A comparative analysis (shown in Table **1**) was undertaken to assess the relative effectiveness of various ML algorithms in predicting the risk of heart disease. This analysis encompassed evaluating the models' performance using diverse evaluation metrics, identifying the specific strengths and weaknesses of each algorithm, and elucidating the factors that influence the selection and application of models in clinical practice. Through a systematic comparison of predictive capabilities, our aim was to offer insights into the most efficient methods for assessing heart disease risk and to guide future research endeavours in this domain.

Table 1. Accuracy achieved by different models.

Algorithm	True Positive Rate (TPR)	False Positive Rate (FPR)	True Negative Rate(TNR)	False Negative Rate	Accuracy
Logistic Regression	0.85	0.15	0.75	0.25	0.80
Support Vector Machine	0.90	0.10	0.80	0.20	0.85
Random Forest	0.92	0.08	0.82	0.18	0.88
k-Nearest Neighbor	0.88	0.12	0.78	0.22	0.83
Neural Network	0.91	0.09	0.81	0.19	0.87

DISCUSSION

The quick expansion of big data in various areas calls for researchers to engage in the active advancement of new Machine Learning (ML) methods that are suitable for the task. A lot of machine learning methods have been developed in the recent past that are meant to take care of differing aspects of data in terms of its variety or its complexity. In Table **1**, logistic regression has 0.85 TPR, indicating that 85% of actual positive cases are correctly identified. While this shows a reasonably good sensitivity, the FPR is 0.15, meaning 15% of negative cases are incorrectly classified as positive. The overall accuracy stands at 80%, which is respectable but lower compared to more advanced models. With an accuracy of 85%, SVM offers a solid balance between precision and recall, making it a suitable candidate for applications requiring higher reliability in classification. KNN is showing 83% accuracy, but it may not be the top choice when high precision or sensitivity is critical. However, its simplicity and effectiveness in small to medium datasets still make it a valuable tool in certain contexts. Neural Networks show a strong performance profile with a TPR of 0.91 and a FPR of 0.09, closest to Random Forest. The TNR is 0.81, and the FNR is 0.19, both indicators of a highly capable model in classifying both positive and negative instances. Its accuracy of 87% further reinforces its reliability.

In particular, future research should develop the organization of management and treatment of patients suffering from severe heart disease by adding deeper and broader datasets and using deep learning on such data. The combination of enhancement of meaningful technologies with these activities has the potential to improve the quality of care provided to the patients. Enhancements to application functionalities could encompass features such as alerting family members of users experiencing a heart attack and transmitting pertinent information in real-time to the nearest medical facility. Collaborating with nearby healthcare providers to facilitate online consultations with doctors could also yield benefits. It's noteworthy that the application of ML [45, 46] extends beyond disease prediction and diagnosis, encompassing various medical domains such as electronics, bioinformatics, and medical diagnostics. Future studies may explore automatic method selection to supplant manual processes and delve into additional ML and deep learning models for integration into a comprehensive diagnostic framework, potentially enhancing heart disease diagnosis performance.

CONCLUSION

The current study highlights the transformative role of ML techniques in heart disease prediction and management. The progress shown with predictive modelling, data preprocessing, and algorithmic approaches is all towards improving the accuracy and efficiency of the diagnosis of cardiovascular diseases (CVDs), of which heart disease is an important one. A key takeaway from this analysis is the variety of ML algorithms used for heart disease prediction, ranging from logistic regression to artificial neural networks. Each of these algorithms has its own strengths and contributes to the development of robust predictive models. Moreover, the review emphasizes the critical role of rigorous data collection, preprocessing, and feature engineering in optimizing model performance. By utilizing detailed data sets and extracting useful predictors, risk assessment, as well as patient outcomes, has significantly improved. Even so, problems like data imbalance and model interpretability have become significant issues, necessitating interdisciplinary collaboration and new methodological developments. Diversity in data sources and advances in deep learning hold good promises for further enhancing the predictive accuracy. ML-based methods have made immense progress so far in the prediction of heart disease. Further studies and research remain essential in ensuring that this progress goes down to the clinics. Further with the powers of the technique of ML, service providers in health care should ensure early diagnosis, a method of giving a treatment, and reducing cardiovascular diseases globally.

REFERENCES

[1] A. K. Singh and S. Singh, "Predicting Cardiac Diseases Using Machine Learning: A Review," 2021 *5th International Conference on Information Systems and Computer Networks (ISCON)*, Mathura, India, 2021, pp. 1-6. [http://dx.doi.org/10.1109/ISCON52037.2021.9701501]

[2] T. Obasi, and M.O. Shafiq, "Comparison of Machine Learning Models for Heart Disease Prediction", *Proceedings of the 2023 IEEE 13th Annual Computing and Communication Workshop and Conference (CCWC),* 2023pp. 983-985 [http://dx.doi.org/10.1109/CCWC57344.2023.10099294]

[3] *International Conference on Computer Communication and Informatics (ICCCI 2021)* 2021; pp. 1-10. [http://dx.doi.org/10.1109/ICCCI50826.2021.9402653]

[4] A. Noor, "Heart Disease Prediction Using Stacking Model", *J. Med. Artif. Intell.,* vol. 11, no. 3, pp. 116026-116028, 2023.

[5] J. Zhang, P Jin, N. Li, and Z-J. Zheng, " Global Gender Disparities in Premature Death from Cardiovascular Disease, and Their Associations with Country Capacity for Noncommunicable Disease Prevention and Control", *Int. J. Environ. Res. Public Health.,* vol. 18, no. 19, p. 10389, 2021. [http://dx.doi.org/10.3390/ijerph181910389]

[6] M.S. Amin, Y.K. Chiam, and K.D. Varathan, "Identification of significant features and data mining techniques in predicting heart disease", *Telemat. Inform.,* vol. 36, pp. 82-93, 2019. [http://dx.doi.org/10.1016/j.tele.2018.11.007]

[7] J. Vijayashree, and N.C.S. NarayanaIyengar, "Heart Disease Prediction System Using Data Mining and Hybrid Intelligent Techniques: A Review", *International Journal of Bio-Science and Bio-Technology,* vol. 8, no. 4, pp. 139-148, 2016. [http://dx.doi.org/10.14257/ijbsbt.2016.8.4.16]

[8] E. Manduchi, T.T. Le, W. Fu, and J.H. Moore, "Genetic Analysis of Coronary Artery Disease Using Tree-Based Automated Machine Learning Informed By Biology-Based Feature Selection", *IEEE/ACM Trans. Comput. Biol. Bioinformatics,* vol. 19, no. 3, pp. 1379-1386, 2022. [http://dx.doi.org/10.1109/TCBB.2021.3099068] [PMID: 34310318]

[9] F. Firouzi, B. Farahani, M. Daneshmand, K. Grise, J. Song, R. Saracco, L.L. Wang, K. Lo, P. Angelov, E. Soares, P.S. Loh, Z. Talebpour, R. Moradi, M. Goodarzi, H. Ashraf, M. Talebpour, A. Talebpour, L. Romeo, R. Das, H. Heidari, D. Pasquale, J. Moody, C. Woods, E.S. Huang, P. Barnaghi,

M. Sarrafzadeh, R. Li, K.L. Beck, O. Isayev, N. Sung, and A. Luo, "Harnessing the Power of Smart and Connected Health to Tackle COVID-19: IoT, AI, Robotics, and Blockchain for a Better World", *IEEE Internet Things J.,* vol. 8, no. 16, pp. 12826-12846, 2021. [http://dx.doi.org/10.1109/JIOT.2021.3073904] [PMID: 35782886]

[10] M Bala, and S Bansal, "Review—Unveiling the power of deep learning in plant pathology: A review on leaf disease detection", ECS J. Solid State Sci. Technol., vol. 13, no. 4, p. 047003, 2024. [http://dx.doi.org/10.1149/2162-8777/ad3981]

[11] E.A. Ogundepo, and W.B. Yahya, "Performance analysis of supervised classification models on heart disease prediction", *J. Big Data,* pp. 1-16, 2023. [http://dx.doi.org/10.1186/s40537-022-00626-y]

[12] P.C. Bizimana, Z. Zhang, M. Asim, A.A.A. El-Latif, and M. Hammad, "RETRACTED ARTICLE: Learning-based techniques for heart disease prediction: a survey of models and performance metrics", *Multimedia Tools Appl.,* vol. 83, no. 13, pp. 39867-39921, 2023. [http://dx.doi.org/10.1007/s11042-023-17051-9]

[13] M. Nilashi, and R.A. Abumalloh, "Heart Disease and Stroke Statistics", *Journal of Soft Computing and Decision Support Systems,* vol. 10, no. 5, pp. 1-2, 2023.

[14] G. Karthikeyan, N. Devasenapathy, L. Zühlke, M.E. Engel, S. Rangarajan, K.K. Teo, B.M. Mayosi, and S. Yusuf, "Digoxin and clinical outcomes in the global rheumatic heart disease registry", *Heart,* vol. 105, no. 5, pp. 363-369, 2019. [PMID: 30209123]

[15] R. Aggarwal and S. Kumar, "Classification model for meticulous presaging of heart disease detection through SDA and NCA using machine learning: CMSDANCA," *Int. J. Recent Innov. Trends Comput. Commun.*, vol. 10, no. 1s, pp. 217-224, 2022. [http://dx.doi.org/10.17762/ijritcc.v10i1s.5827]

[16] S. Y. Hera, M. Amjad, and M. K. Saba, "Improving heart disease prediction using multi-tier ensemble model," *Netw. Model. Anal. Health Inform. Bioinform.*, vol. 11, no. 41, 2022. [http://dx.doi.org/10.1007/s13721-022-00381-3]

[17] R. Sridevi, P. Dinadayalan, and S. Bastin Britto, "An appropriate feature classification model using Kohonen network", *Int. J. Comput. Eng. Technol.,* vol. 10, no. 2, pp. 148-159, 2019. [http://dx.doi.org/10.34218/IJCET.10.2.2019.016]

[18] Asma Baccouche, "Ensemble deep learning models for heart disease classification: A case study from Mexico", *Inf.,* vol. 11, no. 4, p. 207, 2020. [http://dx.doi.org/10.3390/info11040207]

[19] A. Noor, N. Javaid, N. Alrajeh, B. Mansoor, A. Khaqan, and S.H. Bouk, "Heart disease prediction using stacking model with balancing techniques and dimensionality reduction", *IEEE Access,* vol. 11, pp. 116026-116045, 2023. [http://dx.doi.org/10.1109/ACCESS.2023.3325681]

[20] S. Mondal, R. Maity, Y. Omo, S. Ghosh, and A. Nag, "An Efficient Computational Risk Prediction Model of Heart Diseases Based on Dual-Stage Stacked Machine Learning Approaches", *IEEE Access,* vol. 12, pp. 7255-7270, 2024. [http://dx.doi.org/10.1109/ACCESS.2024.3350996]

[21] Y Muhammad, M. Tahir, M. Hayat, "Early and accurate detection and diagnosis of heart disease using intelligent computational model", *Sci. Rep.,* vol. 10, p. 19747, 2020. [http://dx.doi.org/10.1038/s41598-020-76635-9]

[22] A. Abdellatif, H. Abdellatef, J. Kanesan, C.-O. Chow, J. H. Chuah, and H. M. Gheni, "An effective heart disease detection and severity level classification model using machine learning and hyperparameter optimization methods," *IEEE Access*, vol. 10, pp. 79974–79985, 2022. [http://dx.doi.org/10.1109/ACCESS.2022.3191669]

[23] E. Manduchi, D. Hemerich, J. van Setten, V. Tragante, M. Harakalova, J. Pei, S.M. Williams, P. van der Harst, F.W. Asselbergs, and J.H. Moore, "A comparison of two workflows for regulome and transcriptome□based prioritization of genetic variants associated with myocardial mass", *Genet. Epidemiol.,* vol. 43, no. 6, pp. 717-726, 2019.
[http://dx.doi.org/10.1002/gepi.22215] [PMID: 31145509]

[24] Z. Noroozi, A. Orooji, and L. Erfannia, "Analyzing the impact of feature selection methods on machine learning algorithms for heart disease prediction," *Sci. Rep.*, vol. 13, no. 1, p. 22588, 2023.
[http://dx.doi.org/10.1038/s41598-023-49962-w] [PMID: 38114600] [PMCID: PMC10730875]

[25] K. Rahmani, R. Thapa, P. Tsou, S. Casie Chetty, G. Barnes, C. Lam, and C. Foon Tso, "Assessing the effects of data drift on the performance of machine learning models used in clinical sepsis prediction", *Int. J. Med. Inform.,* vol. 173, no. May, p. 104930, 2023.
[http://dx.doi.org/10.1016/j.ijmedinf.2022.104930] [PMID: 36893656]

[26] S. Mohapatra, S. Maneesha, S. Mohanty, P.K. Patra, S.K. Bhoi, K.S. Sahoo, and A.H. Gandomi, "A stacking classifiers model for detecting heart irregularities and predicting Cardiovascular Disease", *Healthcare Analytics,* vol. 3, no. Nov, p. 100133, 2023.
[http://dx.doi.org/10.1016/j.health.2022.100133]

[27] Pamir, N. Javaid, M. Akbar, A. Aldegheishem, N. Alrajeh, and E.A. Mohammed, "Employing a machine learning boosting classifiers based stacking ensemble model for detecting non technical losses in smart grids", *IEEE Access,* vol. 10, pp. 121886-121899, 2022.
[http://dx.doi.org/10.1109/ACCESS.2022.3222883]

[28] A. Jain, A. Chandra Sekhara Rao, P. Kumar Jain, and Y.C. Hu, "Optimized levy flight model for heart disease prediction using CNN framework in big data application", *Expert Syst. Appl.,* vol. 223, no. Aug, p. 119859, 2023.
[http://dx.doi.org/10.1016/j.eswa.2023.119859]

[29] R. Sawhney, A. Malik, S. Sharma, and V. Narayan, "A comparative assessment of artificial intelligence models used for early prediction and evaluation of chronic kidney disease", *Decision Analytics Journal,* vol. 6, no. Mar, p. 100169, 2023.
[http://dx.doi.org/10.1016/j.dajour.2023.100169]

[30] Y. Shen, J. Zhu, Z. Deng, W. Lu, and H. Wang, ""EnsDeepDP: An ensemble deep learning approach for disease prediction through metagenomics," IEEE/ACM Trans", *IEEE/ACM Trans. Comput. Biol. Bioinformatics,* vol. 20, no. 2, pp. 986-998, 2023.
[http://dx.doi.org/10.1109/TCBB.2022.3201295] [PMID: 36001521]

[31] A.U. Haq, J. Li, M. H. Memon, M. Hunain Memon, J. Khan and S. M. Marium, "Heart Disease Prediction System Using Model Of Machine Learning and Sequential Backward Selection Algorithm for Features Selection", 2019 IEEE 5th International Conference for Convergence in Technology (I2CT), Bombay, India, 2019, pp. 1-4.
[http://dx.doi.org/10.1109/I2CT45611.2019.9033683]

[32] A. Pati, M. Parhi, and B.K. Pattanayak, "IDMS: An Integrated Decision Making System for Heart Disease Prediction", 2021 1st Odisha International Conference on Electrical Power Engineering, Communication and Computing Technology (ODICON), Bhubaneswar, India, 2021, pp. 1-6.
[http://dx.doi.org/10.1109/ODICON50556.2021.9428958]

[33] G.T. Reddy, M.P.K. Reddy, K. Lakshmanna, R. Kaluri, D.S. Rajput, G. Srivastava, and T. Baker, "Analysis of dimensionality reduction techniques on big data", *IEEE Access,* vol. 8, pp. 54776-54788, 2020.
[http://dx.doi.org/10.1109/ACCESS.2020.2980942]

[34] V. Chaurasia, and A. Chaurasia, "Novel method of characterization of heart disease prediction using sequential feature selection-based ensemble technique", *Biomedical Materials & Devices,* vol. 1, no. 2, pp. 932-941, 2023.
[http://dx.doi.org/10.1007/s44174-022-00060-x]

[35] J. Wang, C. Liu, L. Li, W. Li, L. Yao, H. Li, and H. Zhang, "A stacking-based model for non-invasive detection of coronary heart disease", *IEEE Access,* vol. 8, pp. 37124-37133, 2020. [http://dx.doi.org/10.1109/ACCESS.2020.2975377]

[36] M. Bala, and S.K. Bansal, "Investigating a Spectrum of Machine Learning Methods for Leaf Disease Detection in Pepper, Potato, and Tomato", *ECS J. Solid State Sci. Technol.,* vol. 13, no. 10, p. 107003, 2024. [http://dx.doi.org/10.1149/2162-8777/ad83f2]

[37] M. Trigka, and E. Dritsas, "Long-term coronary artery disease risk prediction with machine learning models", *Sensors (Basel),* vol. 23, no. 3, p. 1193, 2023. [http://dx.doi.org/10.3390/s23031193] [PMID: 36772237]

[38] D. Hassan, H.I. Hussein, and M.M. Hassan, "Heart disease prediction based on pre-trained deep neural networks combined with principal component analysis", *Biomed. Signal Process. Control,* vol. 79, no. Jan, p. 104019, 2023. [http://dx.doi.org/10.1016/j.bspc.2022.104019]

[39] S. Bej, N. Davtyan, M. Wolfien, M. Nassar, and O. Wolkenhauer, "LoRAS: an oversampling approach for imbalanced datasets", *Mach. Learn.,* vol. 110, no. 2, pp. 279-301, 2021. [http://dx.doi.org/10.1007/s10994-020-05913-4]

[40] D.K. Choi, "Data-driven materials modeling with XGBoost algorithm and statistical inference analysis for prediction of fatigue strength of steels", *Int. J. Precis. Eng. Manuf.,* vol. 20, no. 1, pp. 129-138, 2019. [http://dx.doi.org/10.1007/s12541-019-00048-6]

[41] M Bala, and V Mehan, "Metaheuristic techniques for classification used in identification of plant diseases", *ECS Trans.,* vol. 107, no. 1, p. 13473, 2022. [http://dx.doi.org/10.1149/10701.13473ecst]

[42] A.H. Gonsalves, F. Thabtah, R. M. A. Mohammad, and G. Singh, "Prediction of coronary heart disease using machine learning: An experimental analysis", in Proc. 3rd Int. Conf. Deep Learn. Technol. (ICDLT), New York, NY, USA, 2019, pp. 51–56. [http://dx.doi.org/10.1145/3342999.3343015]

[43] F. Mohammad, and S. Al-Ahmadi, "WT-CNN: A Hybrid Machine Learning Model for Heart Disease Prediction", *Mathematics,* vol. 11, no. 22, p. 4681, 2023. [http://dx.doi.org/10.3390/math11224681]

[44] R. Sharma, and V. Mehan, "Skin Disease Detection Using Image Processing and Soft Computing", *ECS Trans.,* vol. 107, no. 1, pp. 17051-17061, 2022. [http://dx.doi.org/10.1149/10701.17051ecst]

[45] R. Sharma, S.K. Bansal, A. Verma, G. Goyal, and M. Singla, "Multi-class deep learning-based enhanced image segmentation and feature extraction technique for early classification of skin diseases", *Commun. Appl. Nonlinear Anal.,* 2024.

[46] M. Woodward, "Cardiovascular disease and the female disadvantage," *Int. J. Environ. Res. Public Health*, vol. 16, p. 1165, 2019. [http://dx.doi.org/10.3390/ijerph16071165]

CHAPTER 6

Advanced Gait Analysis Leveraging Machine Learning and Artificial Intelligence: A Comprehensive Approach to Biomechanical Assessment and Predictive Health Monitoring

Routhu Shanmukh[1,*], **Rama Devi Gude**[2], **G. Madhavi**[3] and **Routhu Daswanta Kumar**[1]

[1] *Department of Computer Science and Engineering, Centurion University of Technology and Management, Vizianagaram, Andhra Pradesh, India*

[2] *Computer Science and Systems Engineering, Lendi institute of Engineering and Technology, Jonnada, Andhra Pradesh, India*

[3] *Mahatma Gandhi Institute of Technology (Autonomous) affiliated with Jawaharlal Nehru Technological University, Hyderabad (JNTUH) Hyderabad, Telangana, India*

Abstract: Biomechanical Evaluation and health monitoring can be done by using gait analysis along with ML and AI. Using Artificial Intelligence (AI) and Machine Learning (ML) will enable us to analyze the anomalies and identify minute changes in the patterns, so that it can be helpful in real-world applications as well. It can identify minute variations and anomalies that standard techniques would overlook. The chapter examines potential artificial intelligence (AI)-powered algorithms that may diagnose diseases like Parkinson's disorder, evaluate flexibility, forecast damaging risks, along with offering prompt treatment techniques. It also helps to identify some diseases like Parkinson's Disease, and Forecast Damage Risks, and also to provide early intervention techniques. Combining Artificial Intelligence and sensors improves healthcare outcomes through patient monitoring. Implementing these techniques can be a better approach and can provide well-insulated healthcare.

Keywords: Artificial intelligence, Gait analysis, Machine learning, Medical diagnosis.

INTRODUCTION

A thorough evaluation of the body's mechanics, joint motions, as well as contractions of muscles during locomotion, is part of "gait analysis," the methodi-

* **Corresponding author Routhu Shanmukh:** Department of Computer Science and Engineering, Centurion University of Technology and Management, Vizianagaram, Andhra Pradesh, India;
E-mail: routhushanmukh2002@gmail.com

cal study of someone's movement patterns along with motions. In the past, gait analysis has been widely employed in the domains of biomechanics, sports science, and promoting clinical health to identify anomalies, identify diseases, and improve athletic performance [1]. However, the potential applications of gait analysis have increased, and new study avenues have been made possible by the development of machine learning, also known as ML, and Artificial Intelligence (AI) technologies. By offering a real-time, remarkably precise understanding of a person's movement patterns and spotting subtle variations that the human eye or outdated mathematical instruments would miss, the marriage of AI and ML has revolutionized traditional methodologies.

Previously, gait analysis was restricted to laboratory environments and relied mostly on visual observation and basic mechanical devices such as force plates, motion-capturing cameras, and pressure sensors [2]. Despite such techniques helping obtain motion or gait data, they had some limitations, such as the demand for sophisticated apparatus, the need for expert interpretation, and the fact that the normal gait of a person during chores or daily work could not be assessed [3]. The increased popularity of smart portable gadgets and respective AI integrations has solved some of these problems in a way that allows for effective gait tracking in different environments without much stress on the subjects being observed. With the advancement of wearable technologies, AI algorithms capable of processing the large amount of information generated by these devices have emerged. Consequently, gait assessment can be applied in more clinical or non clinical activities in the present quality of life [4].

AI's Role in Gait Analysis

One of the areas that has benefited greatly from the advent of AI technology is gait analysis. AI allows AI models to more accurately identify and elaborate on the movements of people, more so than any human can comprehend. Depending on factors like musculoskeletal or neurological disorders or aging factors, these models, through AI, can anticipate possible alterations in a person's gait. The ability of AI models to identify a gait anomaly has led to AI-powered solutions being able to help in the early diagnosis of Parkinson's. Parkinson's disease is a disorder that has been noticed to affect one's gait even before one starts to notice any apparent symptoms. These changes are more so identified by machine learning models that have been trained with large-scale gait datasets. This makes it possible to detect and administer treatment at earlier stages, which the conventional methods would not have made possible. Gait analysis has been transformed by artificial intelligence, enabling a more comprehensive and precise evaluation of human motion. Models driven by Artificial Intelligence (AI) can spot subtle variations in gait patterns that may be signs of a variety of illnesses, including neurological abnormalities, musculoskeletal ailments, and even early aging. The early diagnosis of Parkinson's disease is one of the most significant advancements made possible by AI-based gait analysis. Long before more obvious symptoms show up, Parkinson's disease, a neurological condition, can produce subtle alterations in walking patterns. These alterations can be identified by AI algorithms that have been trained on enormous amounts of gait data. This enables early detection and treatment, which was previously unattainable using conventional techniques. Furthermore, these AI and ML models' immediate time capacities allow for continuous surveillance, which helps doctors keep tabs on a patient's progress as time goes on. When the system notices a worsening of the prerequisites or a higher risk of adverse effects, the course of therapy can be quickly adjusted. This dynamic, continuous input loop encourages prompt treatment along with more individualized care, both of which greatly improve patient results [5].

Predictive Powers of Machine Learning

Machine learning is a branch of artificial intelligence that enhances the predictive capabilities of gait analysis by using historical gait records to identify trends and correlate them with potential impact on health in the future. Clinically, this ability to predict is key in preventive medicine. For instance, the computing strength of machine learning algorithms and the ability to constantly record and optimize a patient's gait may allow the algorithms to predict possibilities of osteoarthritis and the chances of a patient falling in aged people [6].

Wearable Sensors for AI and Constant Monitoring

Combining wearable sensors with artificial intelligence is another ground-breaking advancement in modern gait analysis. Wearable technology has made it simple to collect information about activity across the day, including wristwatches, health monitors, and sensor-equipped shoes. AI algorithms then analyze this data to find patterns, make recommendations, and provide insight into an individual's stride. Because the effectiveness of therapy depends on continuous monitoring, this method is particularly helpful in managing the course of chronic disorders [7].

EXPERIMENTAL WORK

In order to identify latent connections that may be utilized for damage mitigation, efficiency enhancement, and early medical condition detection, machine learning algorithms examine gait data, which comprises a range of variables such as walking velocity, component viewpoints, stride width, including body orientation. Considering Machine Learning (ML) techniques rapidly analyse large amounts of data, find intricate patterns, and produce anticipated breakthroughs that are not achievable with older methods, they are therefore crucial to the improvement of gait analysis.

Logistic Regression is one of the widely used algorithms for binary classification problems. Coming to the Gait Analysis, it will be useful as the fundamental algorithm that will predict binary outcomes; likewise, if any value error in the given parameters identifies a disease in a patient based on the dependent values. The model calculates the input values and the output predicted values, like dependent and independent variables. Variables or Parameters like length, stride, etc. The logistic regression function is used to convert anticipated results into a probabilistic number ranging from 0 to 1. A threshold measurement, usually set at 0.5, is then used to classify the data into whichever of these categories. Logistic regression equations make it simple for researchers to grasp the various elements that influence the outcome. Furthermore, the representation is suitable for immediate fashion peripheral technologies due to its performance.

In an experimental environment, logistic regression can be used as a baseline model to assess how well more complex algorithms work. Although they demonstrate how predictably proficient it is in recognizing various movement structures, parameters, including accuracy, precision, recall, and F1-score, are commonly employed to evaluate its abilities.

Random Forest plays a crucial role in Gait Analysis data from predicted data to the training and testing of the data based on the given inputs. It can handle high-dimensional data without necessitating extensive feature selection. Fig. (**1**) defines the working of the proposed Random Forest algorithm in relation to the Gait Analysis. It can be utilized to foresee ailments such as degenerative diseases and fall risks. Every single tree in the forest casts an overwhelming vote that decides the final forecast and the categorization result. As academics identify which gait data are most suggestive of specific health conditions, this technique improves precision and provides information on feature significance.

Random Forest is particularly helpful when the dataset is large and complex since it can handle large amounts of data without additionally requiring a lot of feature selection. By classifying individuals based on their gait patterns, Random Forest can be used in research to anticipate problems such as degenerative conditions and hazards of falling. Cross-validation and contrasts with simpler models are commonly used to demonstrate the robustness of the measurement of performance.

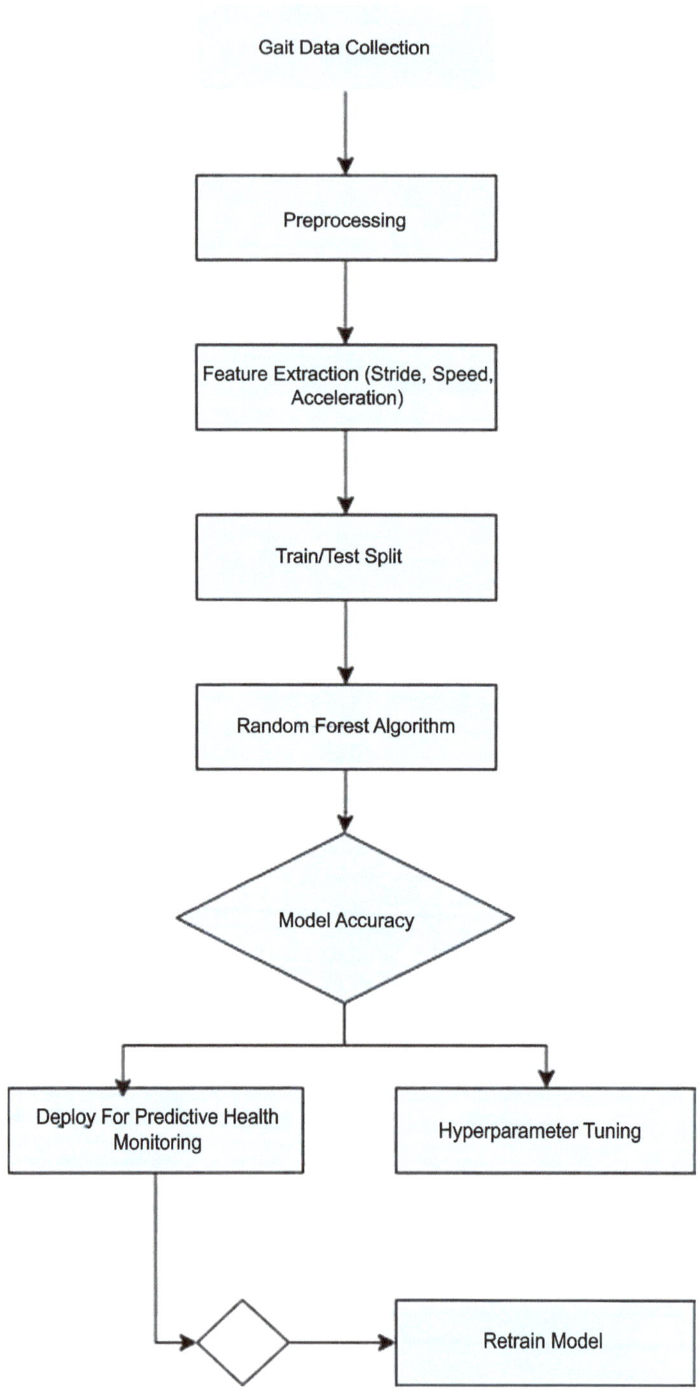

Fig. (1). Work flow of the random forest algorithm.

Support Vector Machine can be useful in gait analysis, one of the popular supervised learning algorithms that helps in high-dimensional data by using the optimal hyperplane that maximizes the range between one class to another class. It can classify the healthy and sick gait patterns depending on the parameters. The Support Vector Machine (SVM) is a widely used supervised learning method for classification tasks. It operates by locating the best hyperspace in a space with many dimensions that maximizes the margin between classes. As shown in Fig. (**2**), the proposed working model, Support Vector Machine, plays a key role in Gait Analysis in identifying the Normal vs Abnormal Healthy Conditions. Because Support Vector Machines (SVM) are capable of extraction parameters to be used from biomechanical and dynamical data, computers can be an invaluable instrument in gait analysis in order to differentiate between optimal and sick gait patterns. SVM can be used to model intricate decision limits using kernel functions and is resistant to overfitting, particularly in high-dimensional fields. For gait analysis, Radial Basis Feature (RBF) kernels can be very helpful since they enable Support Vector Machines (SVMs) to identify nonlinear interactions in the data.

KNN-K Nearest Neighbour is one of the machine learning algorithms, which is an instance-based method, like grouping the data points with the other points based on the feature space. KKN can be used to recognize the gait patterns in gait analysis by comparing the previous observations with the present observations, with the help of historical data points that represent different medical conditions. A straightforward and efficient instance-based learning technique called K-Nearest Neighbours (k-NN) arranges data points according to how close they are to other data points in feature space. Fig. (**3**) describes the working model of the proposed K Nearest Neighbour to help the patterns in grouping the features together for the better identification of the risk factors. By correlating the most recent findings with past data points that indicate various medical conditions, k-NN can be utilized to categorize patterns of walking in the analysis of gait.

K-NN's interpretability and ease of use are just two of its numerous advantages. It relies on assumptions based on the vast majority of the categories of the nearest neighbors with k and does not require a training phase. Instead, it saves the learning data. The success of the method is determined by the value of k and the distance metric, which is commonly known as the distance represented by Euclidean geometry.

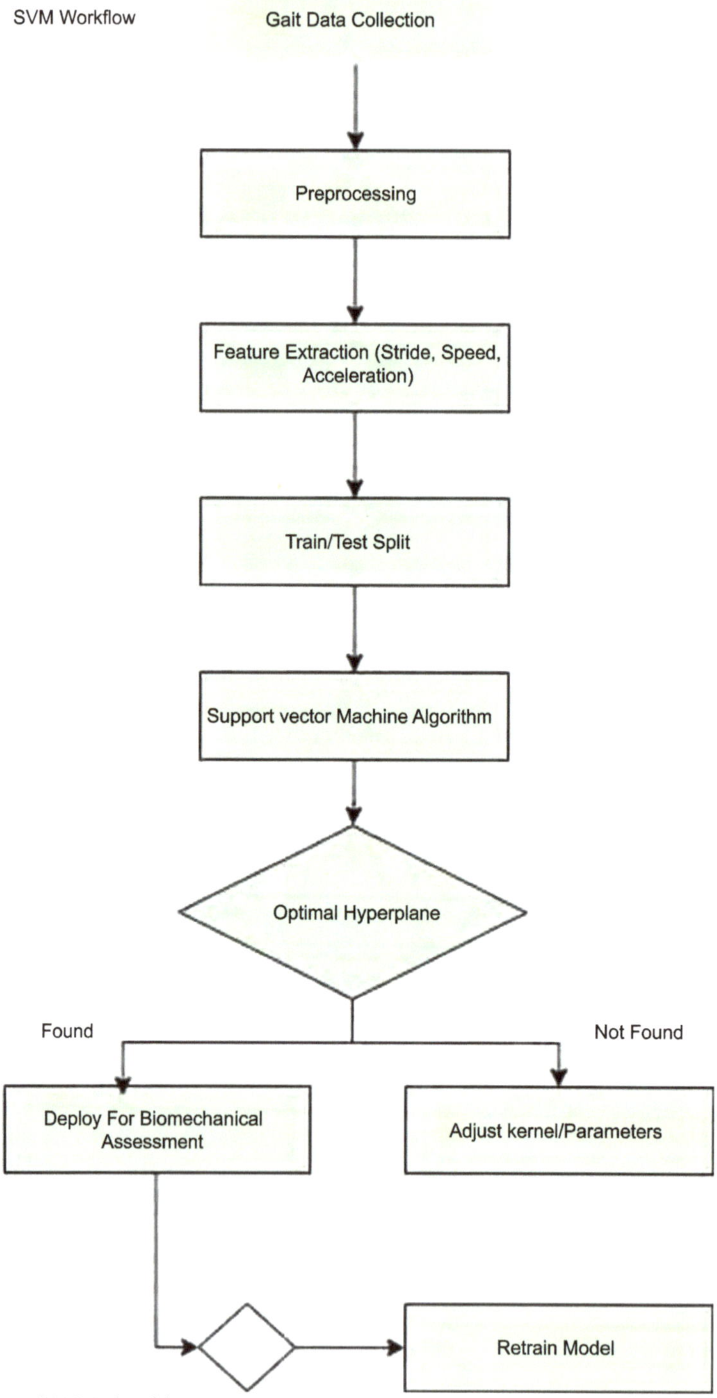

Fig. (2). Work flow of SVM algorithm.

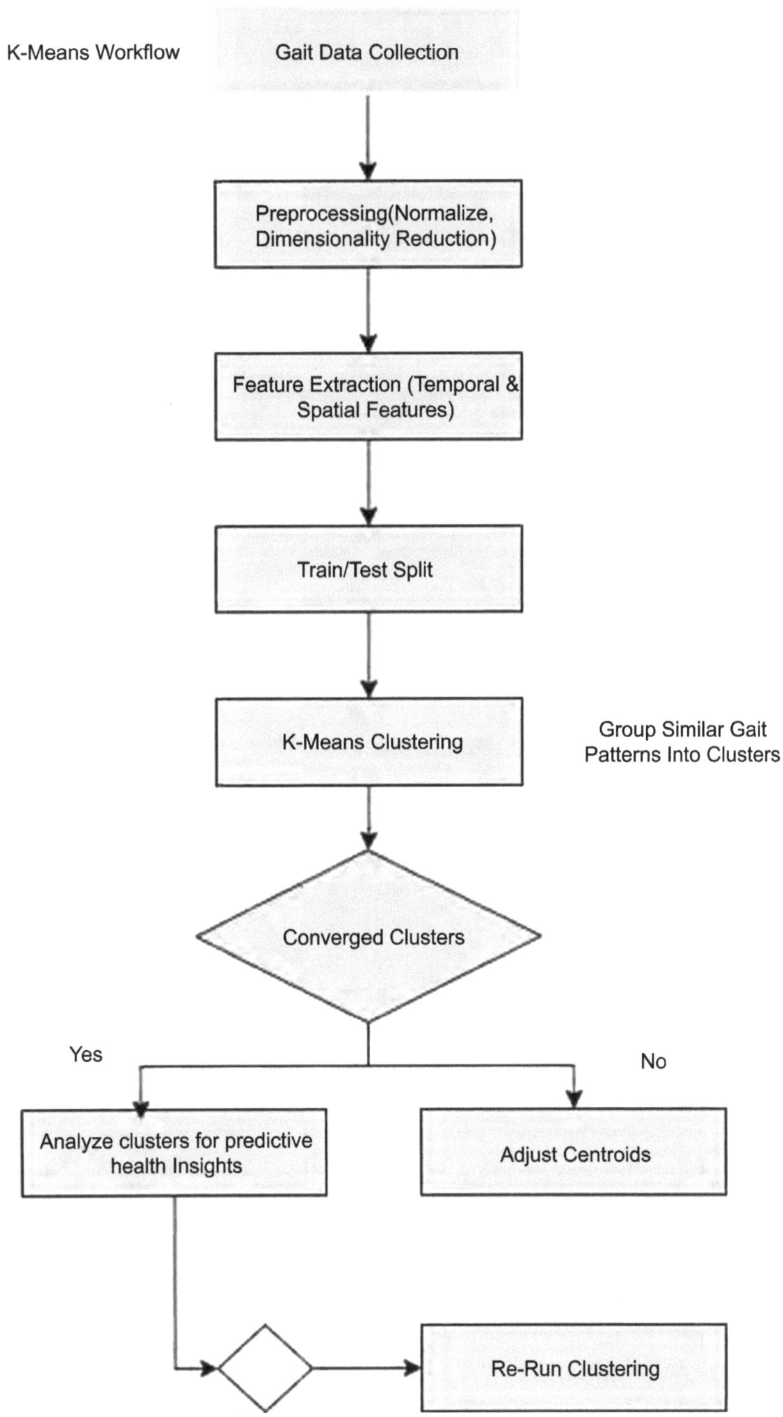

Fig. (3). Work flow of K means algorithm.

Gradient Boosting is one of the best advanced ensemble strategy algorithms that builds the model sequentially with the new model. Gradient boosting is one type of ensemble method that successively builds models in a stack, where each new model is added to improve on the errors made by the previous one. This is possible because gradient boosting offers flexibility as a tuning parameter, where one can fine-tune the performance of the model by varying the learning rate, the tree depth, and the number of estimators. In experimental use cases, the model's enhanced predictive function in biomechanical measurements is established by comparing it with other models and through the utility of cross-validation procedures. Gait analysis has become a crucial tool in the domains of biomechanical evaluation and wellness tracking due to its essential findings about people's movement patterns. With the development of Machine Learning (ML), Artificial Intelligence (AI), and more algorithms for image processing, gait analysis has a far greater chance of becoming highly precise and practical. The combination of Artificial Intelligence (AI) and Machine Learning (ML) with gait analysis enables real-time inspection, anomaly identification, and predictive modelling, all crucial for medical diagnosis, sporting event improvement, and preventative healthcare.

LITERATURE SURVEY

Gait analysis has become a crucial tool in the domains of biomechanical evaluation and wellness tracking due to its essential findings about people's movement patterns [8]. With the development of Machine Learning (ML), Artificial Intelligence (AI), and more algorithms for image processing, gait analysis has a far greater chance of becoming highly precise and practical [9]. Artificial Intelligence in Gait Analysis will be much more helpful and useful in various scenarios to detect abnormalities in sports persons and Parkinson's Disease [10]. Training the historical data with machine learning supervised algorithms and unsupervised algorithms can be a better approach for patient care, as well as individuals using the AI reconsigned patterns, and all will be helpful both for better diagnosis and treatment therapy, and to detect the abnormalities will be a somewhat better vehicle compared to before. The combination of Artificial Intelligence (AI) and Machine Learning (ML) with gait analysis enables real-time inspection, anomaly identification, and predictive modelling, all crucial for medical diagnosis, sporting event improvement, and preventative healthcare [11]. Predict analysis of the Gait Analysis based on the historical records that help machine learning to analyze the previous data patterns and trends to predict the given raw data. It will be helpful in various aspects depending on the parameters [12]. An artificial intelligence gait analysis approach begins with the collection of motion information using cameras or sensors. Gait patterns, including coordinated motion angles as spatiotemporal and spatial properties, are discovered by machine learning approaches after these raw data have been analysed [13]. The application of machine learning methods, specifically deep learning models such as Convolutional Neural Networks (CNNs), is necessary to analyze those trends. Along with Machine Learning and Deep Learning, IoT also helps in various aspects to track the sensor data that can be retrieved through the database, and can give the data to the machine learning algorithms, and can be split into supervised and unsupervised algorithms [14]. Deep Learning data can be used to visualize the data based on the captured images to analyze the patterns or abnormalities by training the data with normal and abnormal images [15]. Using Artificial Intelligence techniques can lead to the identification of various injuries in various sports, along with Parkinson's disease [16]. ML might be used in certain situations according to the goal [17]. These techniques can enhance the efficacy and performance of the models, which will make anomaly detection easier [18]. By employing these techniques, all patient-centered care will be enhanced, resulting in better patient performance and accuracy as well as simpler gait pattern identification [19]. AI is essential to its medical diagnosis and improved performance, making it more useful for the identification of gait analysis [20].

APPLICATIONS

It can be used in the Tracking of Early Neurological Disorder Diagnosis. By training the AI models with accurate data, they can be useful in various scenarios at different aspects, which provides better approaches along with effective outputs.AI models can be helpful in a variety of situations and at different aspects by being trained with reliable data, which leads to improved methods and efficient results. Depending on the situation, machine learning can also be used. With these techniques, the models can perform better and more effectively, making it easier to identify abnormalities.

Early Neurological Disorder Diagnosis

The early detection of diseases of the brain, including Multiple Sclerosis (MS), Parkinson's disease, and Alzheimer's disease, is one of the most significant uses of artificial intelligence assessment of gait. The earliest indications of these diseases are frequently minor irregularities in someone's gait, such as short strides, less room between their feet, or strange walking patterns. Even while AI models programmed to identify such anomalies can provide warning signals, traditional diagnostic techniques can overlook these early indications.

For example, by examining both time and the spatial properties of patient gait data, artificial intelligence techniques search for unique patterns associated with Parkinson's disease. The course of neurological illness may be stopped by prompt interventions and individualized treatment programs made possible by early identification using gait analysis.

Sports Performance Enhancement

Each competitor is searching for strategies to improve their performance while reducing the likelihood of harm. To properly evaluate a competitor's bio mechanics, artificial intelligence-based measurement of gait can be utilized, which also provides information on improving your posture, articulation points of view, ground responsive forces, and momentum cost effectiveness. Machine learning techniques evaluate video records and external measurements to identify biomechanical anomalies or unproductive fluctuations and might adversely impact or hinder effectiveness.

In running sports, for instance, AI models may evaluate stroke length, a rhythm, and impact characteristics to determine the best running style for a certain athlete. If an athlete shows signs of excessive exercise or bad spinal alignment, the coaching staff may recommend remedial measures, such as adjusting frequency of training as well as technique.

Monitoring of Rehab

A very helpful rehabilitation therapy for people recovering from conditions that restrict their capacity of motion, including surgeries for orthopedic issues, is gait analysis. Patients receive real-time status updates from machine learning algorithms that track their walking movements throughout medication. In reaction to objective, data-driven conclusions, rehabilitation professionals and other medical professionals can now adjust their therapy approaches.

People who experienced knee or hip surgery, for example, could walk strangely, staggering perhaps, distributing their muscle mass unevenly. Machine learning algorithms assist patients in improving their gait and accelerating their rehabilitation by detecting these abnormalities and providing feedback. Permanent surveillance ensures that deviations from the expected treatment course are quickly identified and corrected, leading to better outcomes.

- **Evolution of Fall Risk in Elderly Populations.** Accurate data can be used to train AI models, which can then be applied to a variety of situations and elements, leading to improved methods and efficient results. In certain situations, ML can also be added depending on the objectives. With these techniques, the models can perform better and more effectively, making it easier to identify abnormalities, which can be used in real-time applications.

- It can also be used in **Individualized Health Tracking,** which is one of the best benefits, so that it can be a better approach for health and patient care in different aspects. Accurate data can be used to train AI models, which can then be applied to a variety of situations and elements, leading to improved methods and efficient results. In certain situations, ML can also be added depending on the objectives. With these techniques, the models can perform better and more effectively, making it easier to identify abnormalities.
- Variations in the walking patterns may point to musculoskeletal illness or any other cardiovascular disease, for instance. AI models can be used in a range of contexts and domains when they are trained with accurate data, producing better techniques and effective outcomes. Additionally, depending on the objective, ML may be included in specific circumstances. These methods can improve the models' performance and effectiveness, which will make it simpler to spot anomalies.

AI APPROACHES IN VARIOUS ASPECTS

Artificial Intelligence for Pattern Recognition

AI models can be used in a range of contexts and domains when they are trained with accurate data, producing better techniques and effective outcomes. Additionally, depending on the objective, ML may be included in specific circumstances. These methods can improve the models' performance and effectiveness, which will make it simplcr to spot anomalies.

Algorithms for Machine Learning (ML): Using ML Algorithms to analyze the data or to predict the data based on the historical context, and ML can be a better approach.

Deep Learning: Coming to Deep Learning, the images of the walking pattern can be obtained, which can be analyzed and can go for the model preparation so that it can be predicted even on a given image. The CNN, ANN, and RNN algorithms can be used for the analysis of images or the prediction of walking styles.

AI FUTURE ENHANCEMENT

Combining Multiple Data Modes

By using these strategies, all patient-centered treatment will be improved, improving accuracy and performance for the patients and making it easier to identify the gait patterns.

Improved Personalization

AI models can be used in a range of scenarios and elements after being trained on accurate data, which can result in better techniques and more effective outcomes. Depending on the objective, ML may also be introduced in some circumstances. These methods enable the models to function more efficiently and effectively, which facilitates the detection of anomalies. The patients will benefit from improved accuracy and performance, as well as easier identification of the gait patterns, thanks to these procedures and all the individualized treatment.

Combining Robotics and AI

AI-powered robots may help with mobility support and gait therapy in the future. With the help of sophisticated AI algorithms, these robots will be able to correct patients' motions, guide them through rehabilitation activities, and modify their degree of support in real time depending on gait data. This will create new avenues for the therapy of motor impairments and the healing process following surgery. As shown in the Fig (**4**), the applied machine learning plays a crucial role in gait Analysis with various parameters.

RESULTS AND DISCUSSION

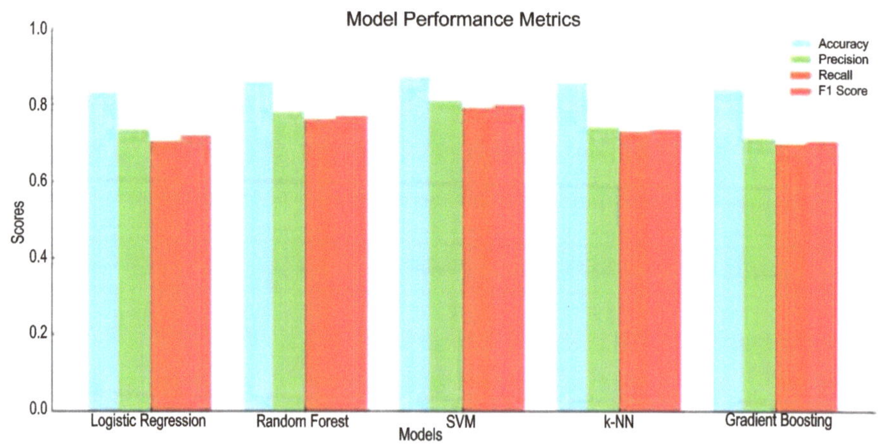

Fig. (4). Performance metrics of the algorithms.

Table 1. Performs metrics of the applied algorithms.

S. No	Algorithm	Accuracy	Precision	F1-Score	Recall
1	Random forest	0.8616	0.7800	0.7708	0.7618
2	Logistic Regression	0.8332	0.7352	0.7197	0.7050
3	SVM	0.8731	0.8102	0.8017	0. 7925

(Table 1) cont.....

S. No	Algorithm	Accuracy	Precision	F1-Score	Recall
4	k-NN	0.8572	0.7423	0.7363	0.7304
5	Gradient Boosting	0.8433	0.7121	0.7056	0.6993

CONCLUSION

Advanced Gait Analysis, which is combined with both AI and ML, can be helpful in health monitoring and biomechanical assessments, as shown in the Table **1**. ML algorithms can calculate the gait patterns in real-time with better accuracy. It can help in early diagnosis and treatment of conditions like sports injuries and Parkinson's Disease. These ML algorithms help detect inequalities and forecast health issues in every individual. In the future, it can develop much more by training the data with real-world applications for better approaches toward medical diagnosis.

REFERENCES

[1] Y. Kharroubi, and A.F. Sari, "Artificial Intelligence in Gait Analysis: A Survey", *J. Health Monit.,* vol. 12, no. 2, pp. 30-39, 2020.

[2] T. Alhussain, "Machine Learning in Predictive Health Monitoring: A Comprehensive Review", *BioMed Res. Int.,* pp. 22-27, 2019.

[3] K. Taira, and S. Ogawa, "Deep Learning and Gait Analysis: A Review", *J. Neural Eng.,* vol. 18, no. 5, pp. 20-25, 2021.

[4] B. Wen, and R. Lin, "Image Processing Techniques in Medical and Gait Analysis", *IEEE Trans. Biomed. Eng.,* vol. 25, no. 3, pp. 33-40, 2018.

[5] C. Zhao, and M. Gao, "Convolutional Neural Networks in Gait Analysis: A Data Processing Approach", *Journal of Applied Science and Engineering,* vol. 17, no. 1, pp. 48-52, 2020.

[6] D.J. Smith, "Preprocessing Gait Data Using Machine Learning Techniques", *Proceedings of the 2021 ACM Symposium on AI Applications,* pp. 67-75, 2011.

[7] A.J. Huang, and L.Q. Zhao, "Using AI in Early Detection of Parkinson's Disease via Gait Analysis", *Neurosci. Lett.,* vol. 130, no. 7, pp. 19-23, 2019.

[8] S.K. Bhardwaj, "Gait Anomaly Detection Using AI: A Comprehensive Review", *J. Biomech.,* vol. 68, no. 3, pp. 105-115, 2020.

[9] M. Hollander, and R.P. Langevin, "Risk Prediction in Sports Injuries Through Gait Analysis", *Int. J. Sports Med.,* vol. 19, no. 5, pp. 55-65, 2020.

[10] P. Wang, and C.B. Li, "Wearable Devices for Continuous Gait Monitoring in Health Applications", *IEEE Transactions on Medical Engineering,* vol. 15, no. 2, pp. 92-98, 2021.

[11] A.V. Patel, and L.R. Williams, "Long-term Monitoring of Gait Using Machine Learning", *Healthc. Technol. Lett.,* vol. 9, no. 4, pp. 144-149, 2019.

[12] K. Nakamura, "AI and Performance Enhancement: A Gait Analysis Approach", *Sports Engineering Journal,* vol. 25, no. 1, pp. 11-18, 2021.

[13] S.H. Lee, "Applications of Gait Analysis in Athletic Training Using AI", *J. Sports Sci. Med.,* vol. 19, no. 1, pp. 37-42, 2020.

[14] T.Q. Wang, and M.X. Liu, "AI in Biometric Authentication via Gait Analysis", *IEEE Trans. Inf. Forensics Security,* vol. 16, no. 7, pp. 99-106, 2021.

[15] M. Bala, R. Sharma, and S. Gupta, ""Integration of hybrid nanomaterials and artificial intelligence for sustainable agriculture. "In Technological Applications of Nano-Hybrid Composites", *IGI Global Scientific Publishing,* pp. 97-118, 2024.

[16] N.G. Carlson, "Predictive Gait Analysis for Long-term Health Outcomes", *Computational Methods in Biomechanics,* vol. 25, no. 3, pp. 78-85, 2019.

[17] K. Tran, "Real-Time Gait Monitoring via AI and Wearables", *Proceedings of the 2020 International Symposium on AI and Health,* pp. 132-140, 2020.

[18] L. Yuan, "Advancements in Wearable Technology for Gait Analysis", *J. Med. Eng. Technol.,* vol. 45, no. 2, pp. 201-211, 2021.

[19] S. Ma, "Future Trends in AI-Based Gait Analysis", *Computational Biomechanics Journal,* vol. 24, no. 1, pp. 23-31, 2020.

[20] D.Q. Fernandez, "Gait Analysis and AI: Challenges and Future Prospects", *IEEE Trans. Biomed. Eng.,* vol. 28, no. 3, pp. 65-70, 2021.

CHAPTER 7

Predictive Modeling for Groundwater Contamination using ARIMA as Predictive Model: A Case Study of the Indian Subcontinent

Love Singla[1,*] and **Sheetal**[2]

[1] *Department of Microbiology, Maharaja Agrasen University, Baddi, Himachal Pradesh, India*

[2] *Department of Zoology, Maharaja Agrasen University, Baddi, Himachal Pradesh, India*

Abstract: The availability of clean groundwater is critical for public health and economic development, especially in regions like the Indian subcontinent, where a significant portion of the population relies on this resource for daily use. However, increasing industrialization, agricultural practices, and urbanization have led to groundwater contamination, posing a severe threat to communities. Addressing this challenge requires innovative solutions for monitoring and predicting contamination levels to ensure safe water access. This study explores the use of machine learning models to predict groundwater contamination levels across the Indian subcontinent. Machine learning has emerged as a powerful tool in water resource management due to its ability to analyze large datasets, identify complex patterns, and make accurate predictions. By utilizing models like ARIMA (Auto-Regressive Integrated Moving Average), we aim to forecast the concentrations of key contaminants, such as fluoride and arsenic, prevalent in the region's groundwater. Our approach integrates historical data on groundwater quality and applies advanced predictive algorithms to estimate future contamination trends. These models provide reliable, data-driven insights that can inform policymakers and water management authorities, enabling them to take proactive measures to mitigate health risks and ensure sustainable water usage. By predicting future contamination levels, this research contributes to developing more efficient and informed strategies for groundwater management, ultimately improving water safety and public health outcomes in the Indian subcontinent. It has been shown that in the coming years, there might be a decrease in concentrations of contaminants (such as fluoride and arsenic).

Keywords: Artificial Intelligence (AI), Machine Learning (ML), Prediction Analysis, Predictive analytic models, Water scarcity, Water resource management.

* **Corresponding author Love Singla:** Department of Microbiology, Maharaja Agrasen University, Baddi, Himachal Pradesh, India; E-mail: Lsingla04@gmail.com

Shilpa Gupta, Ritika Sharma & Gokana Mohana Rani (Eds.)

INTRODUCTION

Water from underground is critical to both human and ecological systems. It is one of the primary sources of water used for drinking by many people worldwide, especially those living in rural areas. Groundwater is also crucial for agriculture, industry, and sanitation. But groundwater across the world, especially in the Indian subcontinent, has been pushed into an on-the-edge regime where threats are more, and contamination is higher than before. The pollution of most aquifers because of industrialization, the increase in pace and scale of land cultivation transformation into certain types (intensive farming), and fast urbanization give rise to a significant public health problem. Nowadays, there is an urgent need to treat and clean any instances of groundwater being polluted or contaminated with modern novel ways that focus on safeguarding the sustainability and safety of this fragile resource [1 - 3].

The Growing Threat of Groundwater Contamination

Indeed, contamination of groundwater is one environmental issue that has been observed to have global and social relevance over the past decades. Water bodies are becoming increasingly contaminated with deadly pollutants due to this process, not only in India but on a global scale. Some common contaminants present in the environment include heavy metals from various sources (arsenic, excessive fluoride, nitrate from fertilizers/industrial pollutants). These poisonous effects on human health lead to thousands of diseases and many incurable illnesses, such as cancer, deficiencies, and tooth fluorosis, among the long-term fatal infections [4, 5].

In the Indian subcontinent, this is especially problematic, given that a significant proportion of its inhabitants, particularly in rural regions, mainly rely on groundwater for both drinking and everyday use. The pollution of these water bodies has posed a serious obstacle to providing millions with clean, safe drinking water. These heavy metal exemplars in several areas have shown that these pollutants seriously threaten public health [6]. If left unaddressed and if immediate action is not taken to mitigate the problem, contaminated groundwater could potentially spark extensive health emergencies, especially in vulnerable communities with limited capacity to tap into alternate sources of clean water.

Urgency of Removing Contaminants from Groundwater

Due to the gravity of groundwater contamination, procedures for the elimination and prevention of water pollution are urgently required. Conventional water treatment methods, including chemical and filtration, are generally expensive and difficult to scale up in low-income or rural areas. Furthermore, these methods are reactive in nature and are used to clean up after the contamination has already occurred. Proactive thresholds are required for tunable water managers and policymakers to anticipate possible contamination risks, thus taking measures before these reach alarming values [7].

This is where the need for predictive modeling and data-driven decision-making arises. With advanced knowledge of where contamination is most probable, governments and water management outfits do what they can to protect the quality of their water resources. In doing so, they not only ensure safe drinking water is readily available but also offset potential long-term health risks due to contaminated water supplies [8]. The approach is based on big data analysis of historical groundwater quality information and predictive modeling for forecasting how contamination in the future will develop.

The Role of Machine Learning in Groundwater Management

Machine Learning (ML) has been developed as a ground-breaking feature in environmental science and water resource management over the past years. Since machine learning provides sophisticated techniques for working with large and complex datasets that human cognition cannot, it offers an excellent opportunity to tackle issues of groundwater contamination prediction. Machine learning models can use historical data to predict contamination risks in the future through patterns and trends [9, 10].

Machine learning is highly successful in managing groundwater owing to its capability to process the complexity of data present within the environmental domain. Groundwater contamination arises due to a variety of factors and includes, but is not limited to, soil composition, weather patterns, but also farming practices, and industrial activities [11, 12]. Fig. (**1**) describes the flow of contaminated water from industrial effluents to the ponds. These variables interact non-linearly with each other, making it a challenge to conduct predictions on contamination trends by conventional statistical approaches. There is no limit to the number of relationships that can be taken into account, and machine learning has been in a better position, providing accurate predictions based on understanding such complex networks [13]. In addition, machine learning models can evolve and improve as new data comes in. In the context of groundwater pollution, we need to adapt quickly as land-use changes take place, a result partly driven by climate change and industrial development [14]. Through constant re-fitting of the predictive models with recent data, machine learning provides support to dynamic and real-time forecasting by helping in making decisions at the right time for proper intervention [15].

Fig. (1). The flow of contaminants as industrial effluents to the water bodies.

ARIMA as a Predictive Model for Groundwater Contamination

ARIMA (Auto-Regressive Integrated Moving Average), a machine learning model, has shown promising results in the prediction of contaminant levels. ARIMA is an Auto-Regressive Integrated Moving Averages model that has been very popular in various fields because it can efficiently capture the temporal structure and seasonal decomposition within the data. Especially in the field of groundwater management, it can be used to reexamine historical water quality data and forecast possible contamination levels based on past patterns.

ARIMA can model linear and non-linear relationships in time series data. Particularly, it can be used to accommodate the gradual increase of contaminant levels, seasonal variations resulting from agricultural seasons, or sudden influence due to industrial spills and other environmental occurrences. Table **1** compares ARIMA models to other statistical/machine learning forecasting methods. ARIMA shows its flexibility here and can predict these critical contaminants - fluoride, which ails large parts of the Indian subcontinent, followed by arsenic [16, 17]. The beauty of ARIMA is its simplicity and interpretability. Unlike some other machine learning models that are sometimes referred to as "black boxes" due to their complexity, ARIMA provides a transparent and interpretable framework for forecasting. This is fundamental information to hydrological water management, especially when taking policy actions, because a user must trust statistical procedure results [18].

Table 1. Comparison of ARIMA with other machine learning models.

Feature	ARIMA	Random Forest	Support Vector Machine (SVM)	Neural Networks (RNN/LSTM)
Type of Model	Statistical Time Series Model	Ensemble Learning Model	Classification/Regression Model	Deep Learning Model
Data Requirement	Requires time series data with trends and seasonality	Requires large datasets with labeled outcomes	Requires well-labeled data	Requires large datasets, especially for time series

(Table 1) cont.....

Feature	ARIMA	Random Forest	Support Vector Machine (SVM)	Neural Networks (RNN/LSTM)
Interpretability	High (easy to interpret coefficients)	Moderate (difficult to interpret due to multiple trees)	Moderate to low (depends on kernel functions used)	Low (hard to interpret due to many layers)
Complexity	Low (simple model)	High (complex model with many decision trees)	High (especially with non-linear kernels)	Very High (complex neural network architecture)
Ability to Handle Non-Linear Data	Limited (better for linear data)	Excellent (handles non-linear data well)	Excellent (works well with non-linear data)	Excellent (built for non-linear relationships)
Use of Historical Data	Extensively relies on past values	Not designed for time series data	Not designed for time series data	Excellent at using sequential data
Handling Seasonality	Good at handling seasonal trends	Can model seasonality, but requires feature engineering	It does not inherently handle seasonality	Handles seasonality well, especially LSTM models
Adaptability to New Data	Moderate (can be updated but requires retraining)	High (adapts well as more data is added)	Moderate (requires retraining)	High (can adjust to new data easily)
Computation Time	Low (relatively fast for time series data)	High (computationally expensive with large datasets)	High (especially for large datasets)	Very High (computationally intensive)
Common Use Cases	Forecasting time series data, particularly in economics and environmental modeling	Classification, regression, and decision-making tasks	Classification, regression, and outlier detection	Time series forecasting, speech recognition, and natural language processing
Interpretability	High (easy to interpret coefficients)	Moderate (difficult to interpret due to multiple trees)	Moderate to low (depends on kernel functions used)	Low (hard to interpret due to many layers)
Complexity	Low (simple model)	High (complex model with many decision trees)	High (especially with non-linear kernels)	Very High (complex neural network architecture)
Handling Seasonal Data	Good at handling seasonal trends	Requires feature engineering to handle seasonality	It does not inherently handle seasonality	Handles seasonality well

(Table 1) cont.....

Feature	ARIMA	Random Forest	Support Vector Machine (SVM)	Neural Networks (RNN/LSTM)
Computation Time	Low (relatively fast for time series data)	High (computationally expensive with large datasets)	High (computationally intensive)	Very High (computationally intensive)
Use of Historical Data	Extensively relies on past values	Not designed for time series data	Not designed for time series data	Excellent at using sequential data, but complex

The Importance of Data-Driven Decision-Making

The use of machine learning models, such as the ARIMA, in groundwater management marks a transition to data-driven decision-making. Historically, groundwater contamination management was often reactive, where well closures and emergency water distribution were undertaken after a contaminant had been detected [19]. However, these interventions are not the root of the problem and bring a temporary fix. Predictive modeling is more of a proactive approach. These monitoring systems could help water authorities predict contamination levels in the future and thus implement preventive, more stringent control regarding industrial activities, public health intervention in site-specific areas, or even infrastructural improvement for the purification of contaminated waters [20]. This perspective can thereby protect human welfare and also safeguard the 'near natural state' of groundwater resources, which serves as a study to mark sustainable water use [21].

Predicting and avoiding groundwater contamination is especially important in areas like the Indian sub-continent, considering this region already struggles with clean water availability and preventing the population from severe diseases like skin diseases [22, 23]. However, with the added pressure of climate change and population growth exacerbating already constrained water resources, it has never been so vital that we innovate. The development of these solutions should rely on machine learning due to its efficiency in working with large amounts of data for accurate predictions.

DATA COLLECTION

All the state authorities corroborated the Central Pollution Control Board (CPCB) groundwater data information and ensured an increase in nitrates concerning drilling depth [24]. This chapter takes the values for samples to be evaluated as groundwater contamination levels [25]. This data is collected from the platform (https://cpcb.nic.in/); they possess historical groundwater quality analysis that describes the concentration of different existing pollutants in the Indian subcontinent. The data is a point-wise dataset from January 01, 2012, to September 22, 2023.

Code Run

The machine learning code for future prediction of the contaminant levels of groundwater (using fluoride and arsenic as main pollutants) is based on the ARIMA model. This model is a versatile and powerful tool for time series forecasting tasks, offering flexibility, accuracy, and user-friendliness that caters to diverse forecasting needs, including groundwater contamination concentration level prediction. The link to the code is https://gist.github.com/lovesingla001/c17eb0609625d174d45e953768b0409d .

RESULTS

Results from ARIMA modeling presented in this paper on the prediction of groundwater contamination based on fluoride and arsenic concentrations could improve decision-making towards sustainable water management. Based on the model's predictions, fluoride and arsenic levels are expected to remain in good condition for the next few years (2023–2032), as shown in Fig. (**2**). Such predictions indicate that fluoride will continue to decline slowly, a trend observed in recent years, while arsenic levels are expected not to increase again rapidly after its peak in 2020 and without significant fluctuations.

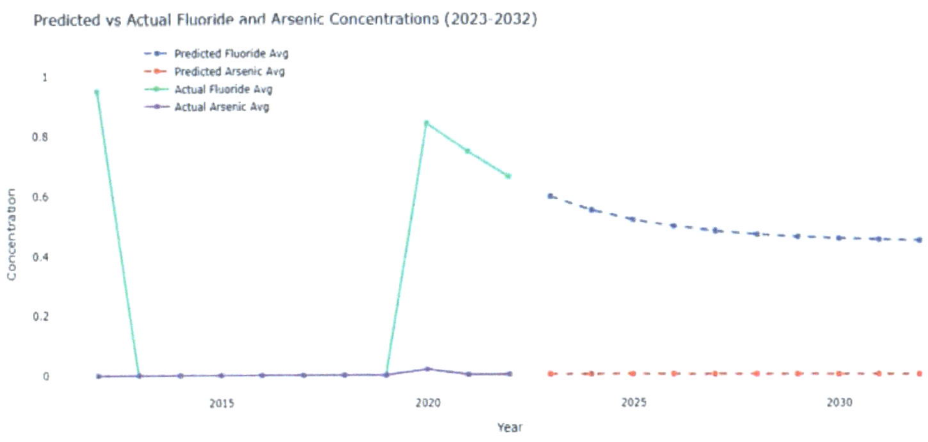

Fig. (2). Predicted vs actual fluoride and arsenic concentrations (2023-2032).

DISCUSSION

This research applies the ARIMA model to predict groundwater fluoride and arsenic pollution levels, which provides a data-intensive means of water-quality management for the Indian subcontinent. According to the model, no evidence exists of either contaminant increasing over time, and fluoride concentrations are projected to decrease slightly as arsenic remains low after a spike in the recent past. This is a beneficial thing as far as the governance of groundwater resources is concerned in the future.

These results show that ARIMA can be employed in predicting using historical data formatted as a time series. However, such an advantage is minimized when non-linear patterns and other unknown mechanisms are highly present concerning clean water, which temporarily occurs mainly due to human activities in some areas or in rare cases. Based on the model prediction, the risk of fluoride and arsenic contamination is not going to go up at an alarming rate in the near future. It is a key insight for policymakers so they can concentrate on staying the course in protecting groundwater rather than reacting to an emergency.

Additionally, as the predictions only indicate what could potentially happen, not what will happen, there should be an ongoing concern for contamination in locales having subpar/poorly regulated water treatment systems or those proximal to industrial/agricultural sources. To ensure our access to safe groundwater, we need proactive policy interventions (stricter regulation of potential pollution sources, public health campaigns, and investments in water purification technologies) and predictive modeling. Utilizing the ARIMA model will improve groundwater management in future strategies and reduce contamination levels reliably over short to medium-term scales. Even when the situation remains challenging, early warnings provide an opportunity for those who decide to be proactive in protecting and preserving water resources, but they should also come under a wider regime of adaptive water management. In high-population areas such as the Indian subcontinent, where millions look to depleted groundwater resources for their daily living, using predictive models integrated with real-time data and taking adaptive policy actions will be key in maintaining the safety and sustainability of this critical resource over the long term.

CONCLUSION

Our stable forecast of contamination levels bodes well for minimal health risk from present contaminants, even in the face of relatively unchanged environmental exposure and industrial practice. ARIMA models are used as alerts to estimate and predict water quality variations. One limitation of ARIMA predictions is that they are based on historical data, and real pollution levels can differ due to environmental changes. Although forecasts suggest adequate groundwater availability in certain parts, regular surveillance and adaptive management would be required to apply water resource strategies successfully.

This has only worsened over time, and innovative solutions are urgently required to solve the groundwater pollution problem. Using this approach, they show that machine learning models such as ARIMA can predict the risk of contamination for large numbers of wells across an entire country. This would allow policymakers to take action promptly before mass contamination becomes critical. Using historical data, ARIMA forecasts the risk of contamination and helps the decision-makers act well in advance to control any damage. Given the escalating demand for drinking water, Machine learning to aid the management of groundwater resources can improve sustainability and longer-term water security. Predictive tools reduce the physical security lapses in defending water resources.

REFERENCES

[1] J.C.O. da Silva, A.M.S. Solano, I.D. Barbosa Segundo, E.V. dos Santos, C.A. Martínez-Huitle, and D.R. da Silva, "Achieving Sustainable Development Goal 6 Electrochemical-Based Solution for Treating Groundwater Polluted by Fuel Station", *Water,* vol. 14, no. 18, p. 2911, 2022. [http://dx.doi.org/10.3390/w14182911]

[2] N. Tanwer, M. Deswal, P. Khyalia, J.S. Laura, and B. Khosla, "Fluoride and nitrate in groundwater: a comprehensive analysis of health risk and potability of groundwater of Jhunjhunu district of Rajasthan, India", *Environ. Monit. Assess.,* vol. 195, no. 2, p. 267, 2023. [http://dx.doi.org/10.1007/s10661-022-10886-z] [PMID: 36602646]

[3] T.A. Kurniawan, W. Lo, X. Liang, H.H. Goh, M.H.D. Othman, K-K. Chong, and K.W. Chew, "Remediation technologies for contaminated groundwater due to arsenic (As), mercury (Hg), and/or fluoride (F): A critical review and way forward to contribute to carbon neutrality", *Separ. Purif. Tech.,* vol. 314, p. 123474, 2023. [http://dx.doi.org/10.1016/j.seppur.2023.123474]

[4] S. Gugulothu, N. Subba Rao, R. Das, L.K. Duvva, and R. Dhakate, "Judging the sources of inferior groundwater quality and health risk problems through intake of groundwater nitrate and fluoride from a rural part of Telangana, India", *Environ. Sci. Pollut. Res. Int.,* vol. 29, no. 32, pp. 49070-49091, 2022. [http://dx.doi.org/10.1007/s11356-022-18967-9] [PMID: 35212895]

[5] A. Ismanto, T. Hadibarata, S. Widada, E. Indrayanti, D.H. Ismunarti, N. Safinatunnajah, W. Kusumastuti, Y. Dwiningsih, and J. Alkahtani, "Groundwater contamination status in Malaysia: level of heavy metal, source, health impact, and remediation technologies", *Bioprocess Biosyst. Eng.,* vol. 46, no. 3, pp. 467-482, 2023. [http://dx.doi.org/10.1007/s00449-022-02826-5] [PMID: 36520279]

[6] M.N. Hoang, P.L. Vo, T.V. Bui, P. Hung, and Q.K. Ha, "Health risk assessment of arsenic in drinking groundwater: A case study in a central high land area of Vietnam", *IOP Conf. Ser. Earth Environ. Sci.,* vol. 964, no. 1, p. 012010, 2022. [http://dx.doi.org/10.1088/1755-1315/964/1/012010]

[7] K Rashi, Fatima Talath, Loni Meenakshi, F. Talath, and L. Meenakshi, "A Comparative Study on the Removal of Fluorides from Groundwater: Strategies and Technologies", *International Research Journal on Advanced Engineering and Management (IRJAEM),* vol. 2, no. 3, pp. 74-78, 2024. [http://dx.doi.org/10.47392/IRJAEM.2024.0012]

[8] J. Olentsova, V. Kukartsev, V. Orlov, E. Semenova, and I. Pinchuk, "Predictive modelling of post-monsoon groundwater quality in Telangana using machine learning techniques", *BIO Web Conf,* vol. 116, p. 03021, 2024. [http://dx.doi.org/10.1051/bioconf/202411603021]

[9] O.C. Akakuru, C.C.Z. Akaolisa, G.O. Aigbadon, M.O. Eyankware, A.I. Opara, P.N. Obasi, I.J. Ofoh, A.O. Njoku, and B.E.B. Akudinobi, "Integrating machine learning and multi-linear regression modeling approaches in groundwater quality assessment around Obosi, SE Nigeria", *Environ. Dev. Sustain.,* vol. 25, no. 12, pp. 14567-14606, 2023. [http://dx.doi.org/10.1007/s10668-022-02679-8]

[10] Y. Huang, L. Ding, W. Liu, H. Niu, M. Yang, G. Lyu, S. Lin, and Q. Hu, "Groundwater Contamination Site Identification Based on Machine Learning: A Case Study of Gas Stations in China", *Water,* vol. 15, no. 7, p. 1326, 2023. [http://dx.doi.org/10.3390/w15071326]

[11] P. Rasaili, S. Rai, K.M. Sachin, B. Saha, and A. Bhattarai, "Arsenic contamination of groundwater sources and a comparative study of its remediation by various conventional and recent approaches in Nepal", *Vietnam J. Chem.,* vol. 62, no. 3, pp. 281-295, 2024. [http://dx.doi.org/10.1002/vjch.202200116]

[12] A. Chatterjee, M.K. Singh, and V.P. Singh, "Groundwater contamination in mega cities with finite sources", *J. Earth Syst. Sci.,* vol. 129, no. 1, pp. 1-10, 2020. [http://dx.doi.org/10.1007/s12040-019-1281-8]

[13] A. Zohud, and L. Alam, "A Review of Groundwater Contamination in West Bank, Palestine: Quality, Sources, Risks, and Management", *Water,* vol. 14, no. 21, p. 3417, 2022. [http://dx.doi.org/10.3390/w14213417]

[14] B.A. Aderemi, T.O. Olwal, J.M. Ndambuki, and S.S. Rwanga, "Groundwater levels forecasting using machine learning models: A case study of the groundwater region 10 at Karst Belt, South Africa", *Systems and Soft Computing,* vol. 5, p. 200049, 2023. [http://dx.doi.org/10.1016/j.sasc.2023.200049]

[15] F. Ghobadi, and D. Kang, "Application of Machine Learning in Water Resources Management: A Systematic Literature Review", *Water,* vol. 15, no. 4, p. 620, 2023. [http://dx.doi.org/10.3390/w15040620]

[16] S.Y. Ganyaglo, A. Gibrilla, E.M. Teye, E.D.G.J. Owusu-Ansah, S. Tettey, P.Y. Diabene, and S. Asimah, "Groundwater fluoride contamination and probabilistic health risk assessment in fluoride endemic areas of the Upper East Region, Ghana", *Chemosphere,* vol. 233, pp. 862-872, 2019. [http://dx.doi.org/10.1016/j.chemosphere.2019.05.276] [PMID: 31340412]

[17] S. Mahammad, A. Islam, P.K. Shit, A.R.M. Towfiqul Islam, and E. Alam, "Groundwater level dynamics in a subtropical fan delta region and its future prediction using machine learning tools: Sustainable groundwater restoration", *J. Hydrol. Reg. Stud.,* vol. 47, p. 101385, 2023. [http://dx.doi.org/10.1016/j.ejrh.2023.101385]

[18] J. Adamowski, H. Fung Chan, S.O. Prasher, B. Ozga-Zielinski, and A. Sliusarieva, "Comparison of multiple linear and nonlinear regression, autoregressive integrated moving average, artificial neural network, and wavelet artificial neural network methods for urban water demand forecasting in Montreal, Canada", *Water Resour. Res.,* vol. 48, no. 1, p. 2010WR009945, 2012. [http://dx.doi.org/10.1029/2010WR009945]

[19] F. Ghobadi, and D. Kang, "Application of Machine Learning in Water Resources Management: A Systematic Literature Review", *Water,* vol. 15, no. 4, p. 620, 2023. [http://dx.doi.org/10.3390/w15040620]

[20] M. Hmoud Al-Adhaileh, and F. Waselallah Alsaade, "Modelling and Prediction of Water Quality by Using Artificial Intelligence", *Sustainability (Basel),* vol. 13, no. 8, p. 4259, 2021. [http://dx.doi.org/10.3390/su13084259]

[21] H. Mosaffa, M. Sadeghi, I. Mallakpour, M. Naghdyzadegan Jahromi, and H.R. Pourghasemi, "Application of machine learning algorithms in hydrology", *Computers in Earth and Environmental Sciences: Artificial Intelligence and Advanced Technologies in Hazards and Risk Management,* no. Jan, pp. 585-591, 2022.

[http://dx.doi.org/10.1016/B978-0-323-89861-4.00027-0]

[22] R. Sharma, and V. Mehan, "Skin Disease Detection Using Image Processing and Soft Computing", *ECS Trans.,* vol. 107, no. 1, pp. 17051-17061, 2022. [http://dx.doi.org/10.1149/10701.17051ecst]

[23] R. Sharma, S.K. Bansal, A. Verma, G. Goyal, and M. Singla, "Multi-Class Deep Learning-Based Enhanced Image Segmentation and Feature Extraction Technique for Early Classification of Skin Diseases", *Communications on Applied Nonlinear Analysis,* 2024.

[24] "CPCB | Central Pollution Control Board." Accessed: December 26, 2023. [Online]. Available from: https://cpcb.nic.in/

[25] "CCR." Accessed: December 26, 2023. [Online]. Available from: https://airquality.cpcb.gov.in/ccr/#/caaqm-dashboard-all/caaqm-landing

CHAPTER 8

Artificial Intelligence in Nanomanufacturing for Optimizing Design, Fabrication, and Quality Control

Sunil Kumar[1,*] and **Harbinder Singh**[2]

[1] *Department of Electrical, Electronics and Communication Engineering, Galgotias University, Greater Noida, UP, India*

[2] *Department of Electronics and Communication Engineering, UCRD, Chandigarh University, Chandigarh, Punjab, India*

Abstract: Together with nanomanufacturing, Digital Manufacturing (DM) is going to set the cutting edge for Industry 4.0, the fourth industrial revolution, as it enables the processing of materials over many dimensions of length. This overview outlines the development of nanomaterials and nanomanufacturing in the digital era, including use cases in consumer electronics, robotics, medical, sensory technologies, and semiconductors. It has also discussed the prospects of possible applications of complex AI algorithms, including expandable artificial intelligence (XAI), reinforced learning, and big data analytics in materials synthesis, innovation in industrial processes, and nanosystem integration. This work provides a thorough assessment of an amalgamation of AI in nanomanufacturing processes, thereby addressing a substantial gap in the field. The challenges of applying machine learning and deep learning to produce reliable and accurate predictions are explained in detail. This chapter examines how AI continues to evolve nanomanufacturing in Industry 4.0 through a thorough assessment, case studies, and data analysis. A detailed literature review is conducted to accumulate existing knowledge on nanomanufacturing, DM, and AI technologies. It also focuses on how AI may improve quality control and process control, including material synthesis in the nanomanufacturing industry. Additionally, it shows how AI may boost market relevance and competitiveness by lowering costs, speeding up time to market, alongside improving product quality. As a result, it provides key knowledge for businesses looking to improve and grow their production capacity.

Keywords: Cyber physical system, Digital manufacturing, Expandable artificial intelligence, Machine learning, Nanomanufacturing, Vapour phase deposition.

* **Corresponding author Sunil Kumar:** Department of Electrical, Electronics and Communication Engineering, Galgotias University, Greater Noida, UP, India; E-mail: sunilrawal22@gmail.com

Shilpa Gupta, Ritika Sharma & Gokana Mohana Rani (Eds.)

INTRODUCTION

Advances in technology that are used at the nanoscale level and have practical uses are referred to as nanotechnology. These technologies operate in dimensions ranging from 1 to 100 nm and include the control and manipulation of matter [1]. It can be further simplified as follows: a substance having a minute operational arrangement within the dimension of a meter can be designed, characterized, manufactured, and applied in a shape and size-controlled manner to create systems, devices, and matter with essentially new properties and functions. In numerous industries and real-life problems, including electronics [2], water treatment [3], nanomanufacturing, and target drug delivery [4], nanotechnology has produced ground-breaking breakthroughs. Nanomaterials, nanomanufacturing, and the use of several systems, including physical, chemical, and biological ones, to develop new materials and devices at the nanoscale exhibiting enhanced properties are the keystones of nanotechnology. The interconnection of various components, such as Digital Manufacturing (DM), Artificial Intelligence (AI), and nanomaterials, along with nanomanufacturing, is depicted in Fig. (**1**).

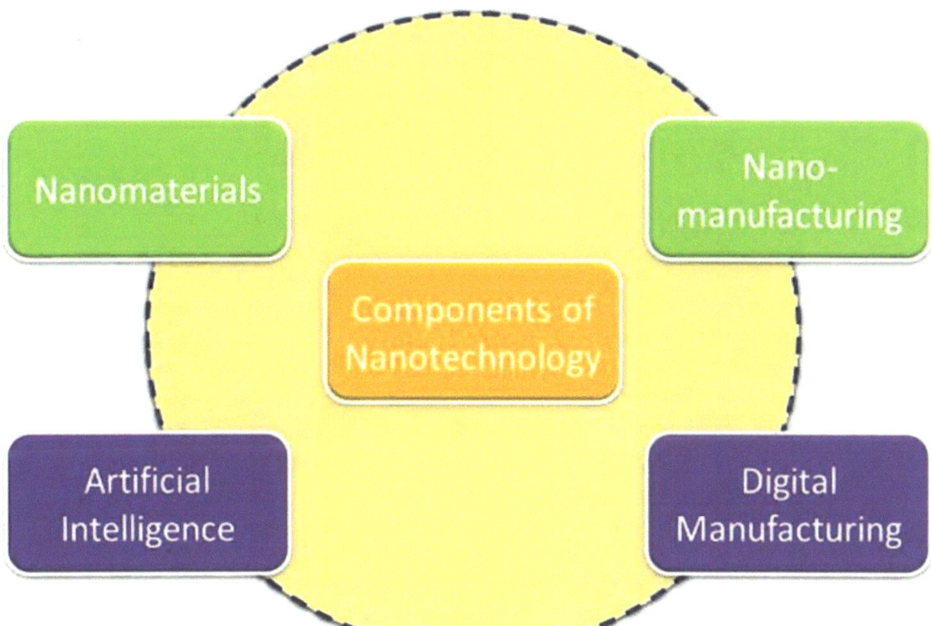

Fig. (1). Interleaved elements of nanotechnology.

Nanomanufacturing

As seen in Fig. (**2**), nanomanufacturing refers to the production techniques used to create nanomaterials, compositions, devices, along systems at a dimension of a billionth of a meter using two ways such as: top-down or bottom-up. The top-down approach begins with a minute substance and works its path down to a more minute point [5]. Top-down techniques such as lithography [6], micromachining, machining, as well as milling are some of the more popular ones [7]. During milling, a soaring energy mill is charged with a particular powder, constituting a suitable milling environment. It is done to mix the particles into new phases and decrease their size. Nanometric material removal, traditional cutting, grinding, and polishing are all included in machining. Top-down lithography works well for creating intricate, mass-producible designs. Using a technique called nanoimprint lithography, a mold's shape can be transferred to target materials by coming into contact with the mold. By employing scanning probe microscope information to supply materials *via* capillary transport, high-quality nanopatterns can be produced in dip-pen lithography [8].

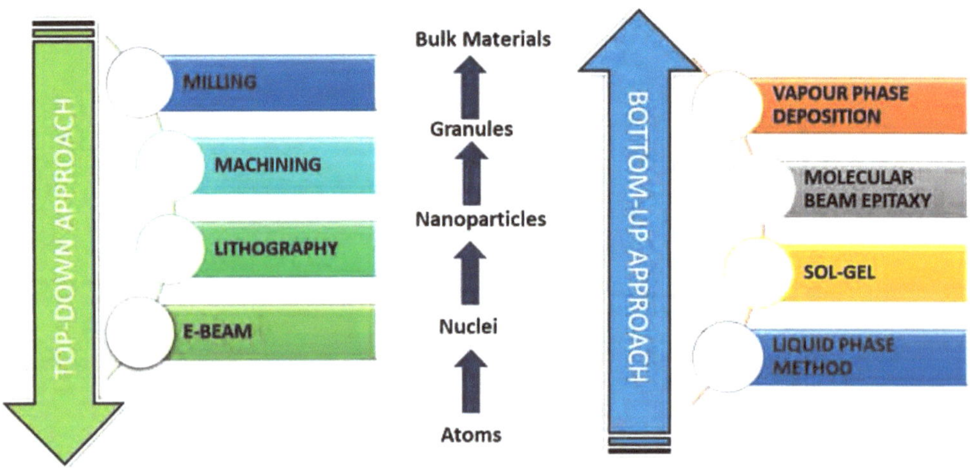

Fig. (2). Fabrication process of nanomaterials.

At the same time, bottom-up approaches start by generating and synthesizing the target molecules by a variety of nanomanufacturing techniques, including molecular beam epitaxy, Vapour Phase Deposition (VPD), liquid-phase techniques, and pulse-laser deposition, including self-assembly [9]. Following bottom-up processes, there are two fundamental techniques: gas-phase synthesis and liquid-phase creation. VPD, molecular beam epitaxy, sol-gel, pulse-laser deposition, as well as magnetron sputtering are a few of these often-used techniques. When a substrate is treated with a couple of volatile precursors during VPD, the substrate breaks down and reacts with the precursors to create the desired deposit [10]. The Molecule beam epitaxy operates on vacuum evaporation, a process in which heated molecule and atomic beams are directly impinged upon in an extremely high vacuum. Metal oxides are created *via* the sol-gel method from tiny solid molecules [11].

During pulse-laser technology, the source material is focused by a pulsed laser beam to be deposited on a substrate within a huge vacuum chamber. An Alternative technique for thin-film installation that is now in practice is called magnetron sputtering, in which intense ions push atoms away from a target. The manufacturing sector uses a variety of nanomanufacturing techniques. The following five nanoscale manufacturing techniques are the most popular such as photolithography, nanomanufacturing of polymer 2D materials, printing of 3D solid materials, and 3D shape memory polymers [12]. The method of printing integrated 3D solid materials is based on the notion of layering melted metals or polymers. To make it easier for the geometric design to transfer from the ideal mask to a substrate, photolithography involves exposing the mask to ultraviolet (UV) light [13]. The microscale production of nanostructured metamaterials involves the assembly of constituents at different scales. Flexible tools adhere to one another by using modulated surface energy to facilitate assembly. Unlike the physical interconnection of mechanical components, trivial actuator mechanisms have been 3D printed, constituting the material's responsiveness towards its surroundings for particular modified shape memory polymers.

Nanomaterials

The fundamental components of nanomanufacturing are nanomaterials, which have a meter-scale size. Because of their shape and size, nanomaterials have unique physicochemical properties, unlike their parent material. Additionally, they display an array of geometric arrangements categorized as one-dimensional (*e.g.*, nanorods), two-dimensional (*e.g.*, films, layers, and sheets), three-dimensional (*e.g.*, nanocomposites, nanowires, and tubes), and even zero-dimensional (*e.g.*, nanoparticles) [14]. Nanomaterials are classified by composition, with form, size, properties, and ingredients being the main points of differentiation. Carbon-based, metal oxide, and semiconductors, along with lipid-based nanomaterials, represent some of the several types of nanomaterials. Silver (Ag), a compound of carbon, as well as tungsten oxide (WO_3), are often utilized in nanomaterials. Because of its biological and physicochemical characteristics, nanosilver is employed in antibacterial applications [15]. Because of their exceptional mechanical and electrical qualities, carbon-based nanomaterials are frequently employed in battery technologies. On the other hand, properties like increased toughness, hardness, and wear-resistance qualities, nanoceramics are utilized in wear-resistant coatings.

Digital Manufacturing

The goal of traditional nanomanufacturing techniques is to improve both the purity along the high quality of the tiny particles, which offers a great deal of potential for improvement. Manufacturing companies in all industries face enormous challenges when it comes to efficiently designing and overseeing contemporary goods. Digital manufacturing is used, with the integration of innovations to create Cyber-Physical Systems (CPSs), including smart industrial units, to handle the complexities involved in the production of modern products [16]. Business organizations are compelled to become more versatile in their goods into different tiny scales as the phase of Industry 4.0 continues to expand, which leads to the adoption of more effective and scalable manufacturing processes. Because of security issues, CPSs are essential in many sectors, including defense systems, automation, electric infrastructure, and robotics. Industry 4.0 states that industries are moving away from traditional, long-standing forms of manufacturing and toward digital manufacturing [17]. Computer systems are used by nanomaterials and DM for product design, simulation, analysis, and production, along with high levels of research and development, as well as extremely sophisticated tools and technology, are needed for the synthesis of nanomaterials and DM [18]. A highly qualified team is also needed to manage and operate the technology. Opportunities for improved production efficiency, cost reductions in expenditure, and customization are provided by both nanomanufacturing and DM. The development of fresh materials and processes could result from the combination of nanomanufacturing and DM for improving production capacity.

Specific use cases are the starting point for a strategic approach to incorporating AI in industrial nanomanufacturing. Machine Learning (ML) algorithms can optimize critical process characteristics, such as temperature or deposition rates, and AI-powered vision systems can improve defect identification and quality control. Manufacturers can increase production efficiency and reduce downtime by using predictive analytics for yield predictions and maintenance. Developing a robust data infrastructure is crucial to the successful utilization of AI. This involves creating centralized storage systems, ensuring data standards, and collecting data in real-time through Internet of Things (IoT) sensors. Moreover, there is a need for investment in workforce development to enable workers to become literate in AI and to foster interdisciplinary collaboration. Organizations could also consider partnerships with educational organizations or AI-centric technology companies to access knowledge and drive innovation.

Artificial Intelligence

AI is a broad field within computer science that focuses primarily on creating intelligent computers capable of doing activities that typically require human intelligence. It is a system that is intrinsically based on data and emphasizes both predictive and autonomous learning. AI excels at performing activities under supervision and stays away from human decision-making [19]. The relationship between AI, ML, and Deep Learning (DL) is depicted in Fig. (**3**). The AI framework, which encompasses sensing, thinking, acting, and adjusting the data applications, is the overall theme and key area of focus. ML is a subfield of artificial intelligence that examines certain methods used to process historical data and extract knowledge from it. ML structures are capable of identifying things in photos, matching products or items with the interests of customers, translating speech into text, and selecting relevant search results [20]. These applications are increasingly utilizing a set of techniques together referred to as DL. As a subset of ML, DL uses multi-layered, organized neural networks to learn from a large amount of data. DL provides breakthroughs in problem-solving that have long posed a significant challenge to the efforts of AI researchers. It has proven to be adept at delving into intricate patterns in large amounts of data and works well with a range of scientific, business, health, along government research domains. Given that it requires less artisanal engineering, it is believed that DL will be much more successful soon. DL can easily adjust and benefit from improvements in the amount of computable data. Since deep neural networks are constantly developing new learning techniques and network architectures, this advancement will happen very quickly [21].

There are several explanations for why investigation into AI structures occurs in the field of nanotechnology. Physical barriers separate nanotechnology from the world of macroscopic scales due to its working scale. This suggests that one of the challenges facing nanotechnology will be how to appropriately evaluate the data produced by tiny systems or devices. In these situations, it may be difficult to produce mathematically computed approximations, and simulation analyses have been widely planned to perform an accurate analysis of investigations. In light of this, AI applications can be crucial to the advancement of science and the development of nanotechnology in the future. Furthermore, AI, which falls within the purview of computer science, can benefit from the growing power that nanotechnology, nanomaterials, and nanodevices will guarantee shortly as effective structures to carry out ML techniques [22]. Additionally, it is more functional and has a quick processing speed. Autonomous driving, healthcare diagnosis, computer vision, automated manufacturing, swarm drones, Unmanned Aerial Vehicles (UAVs) [23], and drug delivery are just a few of the domains where AI has demonstrated its superiority. AI is playing an increasingly important role in the development of nanotechnology as it continues to be incorporated into more and more nanomanufacturing processes, including nano assembly, the synthesis of nanorods, nanomedicine, nanorobotics, and nanobiosensors [24].

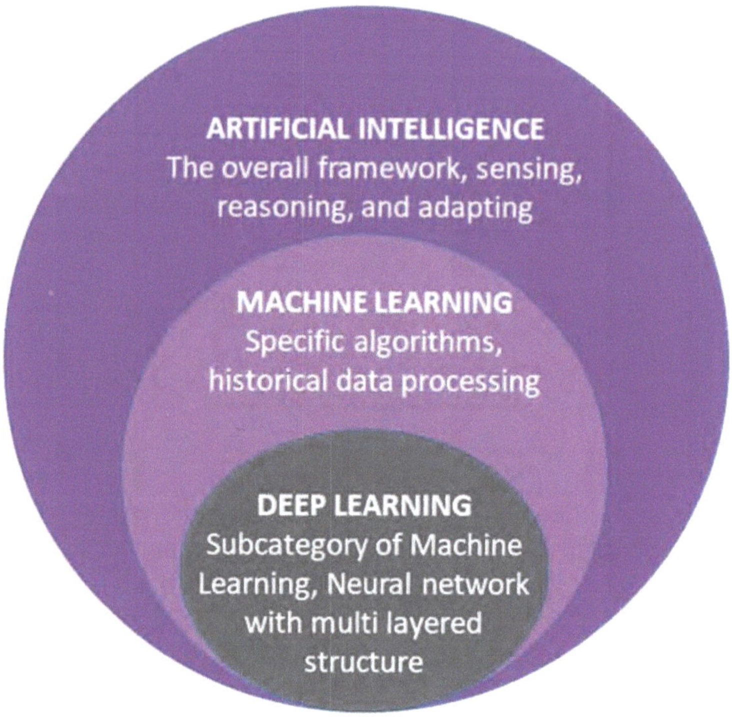

Fig. (3). Convergence relationship of AI, ML, and DL.

Through the use of nanoengineered capsules for prolonged medicine delivery, nanomanufacturing techniques are saving lives. Because these nanoengineered capsules include AI, and they can treat cancer. Cancer patients' clinical profile is facilitated by the mechanical and electrochemical, alongside spectral characteristics of nanosensors, which enable early identification, treatment planning, and disease monitoring [25]. Nanosensors can identify incredibly tiny amounts of cancer biomarkers throughout the diagnostic phase. Combinatory therapies may be recognized through the data analysis process when AI algorithms are integrated. Nanomedicine, also known as nano-capsules, is used to make prescriptions [26]. Notwithstanding the patient's diagnosis and prescribed course of treatment, the drug release rate of the nanomedicine is adjusted to regulate drug dosage. Convolutional neural networks have been routinely employed for nanoparticle-based image processing during the monitoring stage, with follow-up being carried out depending on the AI model's results [27].

INTERRELATIONSHIP OF AI, DM, NANOMATERIALS, AND NANOMANUFACTURING

Industry 4.0 relies heavily on DM, AI, nanomaterials, and nanomanufacturing. ML techniques have opened up new avenues for material optimization and investigation [28]. DM is a potential way to handle issues in complicated configurations, process optimization, and material design [29]. It concerns digital strategy and management of manufacturing processes. This method has brought together the fields of information, computing, sensors, computer programs, networking, and automation to complete certain tasks. AI and DM assisted nanomanufacturing processes jointly, making the course of input data smooth. AI optimizes supply chains, identifies new nanostructured materials, boosts productivity, and guarantees product quality by predictive maintenance. It means manufacturing enterprises can achieve a competitive edge, flexibility, and responsiveness to global time-varying market demands through optimum integration of AI in nanomanufacturing, consistent with Industry 4.0 and DM benchmarks [30]. This also allows opportunities for vast manufacturing process optimization, real-time tracking tools, and the liberty to pursue exploration and progress. The next section in this chapter covers the application of AI in nanomanufacturing.

SYNERGIES BETWEEN NANOMANUFACTURING AND AI

AI is useful in the field of investigating nanomanufacturing since it can rightly predict the characteristics and actions of nanoparticles. In this context, several characteristics of the nanomanufacturing process have been optimized by using AI algorithms, such as reducing defects and improving efficiency. During the conversion process of nanomaterials into finished products, AI is applied rather strategically to ensure maximal efficiency with reduced waste and increased precision. Key important tools applied include Artificial Neural Networks (ANN) combined with Support Vector Machines (SVM) in estimating the correlation between raw materials and nano products created [31]. AI finds application in more aspects beyond just realizing human emotions in the synthesis and characterization of nanoscale structures and metals. The other area where AI, along with nanotechnology, goes well is the domains of nanofabrication and manufacturing. Nanotechnology offers a good deal of production techniques to provide precise material manipulation within the nanoscale. These include top-down techniques like lithography and bottom-up techniques like self-assembly. These processes, however, often require careful control and supervision to guarantee the quality and reproducibility of the created nanostructures [32].

Such claims about the efficiency of AI in nanomanufacturing can be further supported using quantitative analysis along with real-world case studies. For instance, performance metrics such as reduced manufacturing times, less material waste, or more accurate feature sizes illustrate the actual benefits of AI. Simulation experiments may also support these claims, as they inform how AI models enhance throughput and predict results while reducing errors. Moreover, by pointing out some optimizations, such as increased yield rates, reduced operating costs, or energy conservation, comparative analysis can point out how AI performs better than conventional methods.

Real-world case studies provide authentic examples of how AI may transform society. Companies, such as Intel, use AI in semiconductor production to recognize defects and prevent breakdowns and, through predictive maintenance, improve yield and lower downtime. AI-powered nanoscale manufacturing of medication delivery systems and biosensors has vastly accelerated medical research through enhancements in sensitivity and response times [33]. In a similar manner, the application of AI in consumer electronics and robotics has made micro-assembly of nanostructures less complicated, reducing costs and increasing efficiency. Measurable increases in energy conversion efficiency and lifespan costs have been shown in the energy sector as a result of AI's participation in optimizing solar cell manufacturing or enhancing battery technology.

AI-driven techniques address these challenges by enabling process monitoring, control, and optimization in real-time [34]. ML algorithms can analyze the sensor data from nanofabrication processes for anomaly detection, problem prediction, and process parameter adjustment to maximize output and efficiency [35]. Furthermore, AI-assisted robotic techniques can automate nanoassembly and manipulation methods to achieve high-throughput manufacturing.

Material Synthesis

Due to their specialty features, nanoparticles have huge applications in many diverse areas, such as optoelectronic sensing, chemistry, material science, and medicine. In the synthesis of nanoparticles, a wide range of synthetic pathways has to be navigated, whereby it becomes quite difficult to precisely control the particle sizes with the required attributes of the generated nanoparticles [36]. AI and nanotechnology represent two of the most impressive technological leaps available, both having large potential to accelerate innovation and help solve the more pressing issues facing a wide field of applications [37]. The accuracy of nanotechnology, combined with the computational power of AI, can analyze huge datasets and create new substances, devices, and structures with capabilities formerly unimagined.

Materials design and discovery form one area where AI and nanotechnology have the greatest intersection. As such, nanotechnology may be used to create materials at atomic and molecular levels that bear certain specified properties; for instance, improved conductivity, reactivity, and strength. But designing with nanomaterials remains a large and complex domain, requiring sophistication in computational tools to chart a way through it [38]. In addition, using AI-driven computer modeling and simulation allows researchers to study nanomaterial responses under various environments or situations, which enables the optimization of material functionality with performance. By this collaborative approach, the speed at which new materials can be discovered is increased, but it also gives way to an advanced understanding of the nanoscale events leading to innovative materials with earlier, unprecedented properties and applications. In the field of nanomedicine, AI and nanotechnology can do a great deal to change how healthcare is practiced and treated. Nanotechnology has made it possible to come up with very smart drug delivery vehicles [39], improved diagnostic tools, and treatments that improve imaging and targeting, together with therapeutic properties. However, all these technologies need to be specifically tuned with the individual characteristics and illness profiles of each patient to guarantee safety and efficacy. AI-driven techniques that look through huge patient datasets, such as genomes and medical imaging, and classify patient populations concerning prognosis, therapeutic responses, and diseases are precisely what will make personalized healthcare possible. ML algorithms can identify the most effective treatment plans for certain individuals by identifying biomarkers connected to drug response. Innovative methods for sustainability, rehabilitation, and environmental application monitoring are made possible by the integration of AI and nanotechnology [40]. Nanotechnology provides nanomaterials along with nanosensors that can detect and remove pollutants, monitor environmental factors, and help produce renewable energy. The application of these nanotechnologies under real-world conditions, however, requires intelligent systems in terms of data analysis, resource optimization, and decision-making. AI-driven solutions thus offer to solve these problems by providing data-driven insight together with models for prediction in tracking and management of environmental issues. These algorithms of ML can realize the prediction of pollutant levels, identification of hazardous substances, and updating clean-up methods in real-time by analyzing the sensors' data arriving from distributed networks of nanosensors [41]. More importantly, AI-powered optimization algorithms can be used to ensure both high performance and sustainability in nanomaterial-based power systems, including solar cells and batteries, in terms of design and operation [42]. The complementary competencies between AI and nanotechnology represent the intersection of computational intelligence with nanoscale engineering, the opportunities that might pretty much change a great deal of fields [43, 44].

Through this merge of absolute nanoscale accuracy with the computational power of AI, scientists are now capable of solving serious environmental challenges, pushing the limits in materials science, and accelerating new nanofabrication processes.

Design Optimization of Nanomaterials

AI-driven computational modeling combined with simulation is an invaluable tool utilized during the study of complex systems to predict future behavior and its improvement, from the field of materials science and engineering to the health field and environmental sustainability. This technique leverages AI capacities through data computation, trend determination, and model formulations that represent mechanisms' dynamics fully in the system under investigation [45]. One of the most important advantages of computational AI-based modeling, including simulation, is its ability to deal with huge and diversified data sets, and one can take it either way: theoretical predictions, simulated outputs, or experimental measurements. Such databases form the cornerstone through which ML techniques have been applied to find unidentified correlations, patterns, or sequences. AI systems can, through data-driven learning, capture complex relationships and nonlinear dynamics, hence be used to result in more accurate predictions and understanding of the functioning of the system under study [46]. Again, computer modeling and simulation, led by AI, afford research into how systems change across contexts, applications, and parameters, thus easily serving as a platform for running virtual experiments and testing ideas. It thus brings down the high-cost and time-consuming experiments that make possible an accelerated exploration and optimization of materials, equipment, and methods. For instance, AI models in the area of materials science can guide the synthesis of new materials with a set of required properties, predict the attributes of imaginary materials, and increase the parameters of boosting the material synthesis and analyzing parameters for improved performance. Apart from the impression of anticipated results, a computerized model with XAI allows for a real-time investigation and fine-tuning of complicated systems [47].

The ML algorithms can also be used to evaluate real-time sensor data from the system to detect performance anomalies and make adjustments to control settings to realize optimum system performance. This closed-loop feedback control methodology comes in very handy in uses such as cutting-edge manufacturing, power structures, and autonomous vehicles, where all those applications require changes in real time to affect desired outcomes while preserving system integrity [48]. It is in this way that AI-driven computational modeling and simulation drive cross-disciplinary collaboration and knowledge integration by providing a shared framework for the integration of data, models, and information from other fields.

Indeed, only such models can fully capture the multifaceted and multiscale properties of complex systems and lead to landmark innovations and breakthroughs if one can be allowed to merge information emanating from engineering, the life sciences, chemistry, or even physics with AI-empowered data analytics. Coupled with nanotechnology, neural networks are strategic drivers for advancements in the field of neuromorphic electronics [49]. AI algorithms allow the duplication of neural networks to improve the functionality and efficiency of the devices realized from neuromorphic electronics. It is through nanotechnology that materials and structures can be created at the nanoscale, which forms an integral component in having biomimetic properties. Integrated, they shall permit smart construction in intelligent systems that work like the human brain and give life to new opportunities within automation and medical treatment.

Accelerating Novel Material Discovery Using AI

AI is a game-changer in material finding and optimization for the development of drugs because it offers novel approaches for quickly identifying new drug candidates with enhanced safety and efficacy characteristics. Researchers can use AI techniques like ML and DL to analyze large databases of chemical compounds, data from clinical trials, and biological assays to identify novel candidates for medications, predict their properties, and improve their performance [50]. Predictive modelling, along with virtual screening, are the two main ways AI speeds up material discovery for drug development. ML algorithms can search through massive databases of molecular composition and biological activity data to identify substances with potential medical applications. By learning through patterns present in the dataset, the models of AI can predict the action of imaginary drugs for certain pharmacological targets or disorders. This capacity aids in narrowing the exploration area and focusing investigational efforts on the most optimistic scenarios. Moreover, AI-assisted techniques, along with simulation, support the optimization of potential drugs by predicting the properties and behavior of drug candidates. ML algorithms can look at the structure-property relationships of known compounds to predict the properties of new compounds with structures similar to current ones [51]. This process enables scientists to synthesize materials with intended properties, like increased potency, effectiveness, and pharmacokinetic features, which removes the necessity for costly and arduous clinical studies. Along with virtual screening and model-based prediction, AI allows the discovery of new pharmaceutical targets and techniques that operate through data-driven methodologies. ML algorithms can analyze omics data, such as proteomics, metabolomics, and genomics, to identify biomarkers associated with disease pathways and therapy responses.

The optimal pharmacological targets and therapy strategies are chosen with the aid of this knowledge. AI techniques can also be used to find pharmacological compositions and mutual interactions that enhance therapeutic usefulness and lower medicine resistance. Furthermore, AI-driven modification of drug formulations along with delivery techniques considerably aids in improving pharmaceutical efficacy and patient outcomes. Through the analysis of formulation data as well as patient-specific variables, ML algorithms may improve drug dosing procedures and delivery passages, enabling personalized healthcare techniques [52]. Additionally, AI-powered nanomedicine frameworks enable the creation of targeted drug delivery strategies that enhance drug distribution to specific tissues or cells while lowering off-target effects as well as systemic toxicity.

Nanofabrication and Prototyping

By providing cutting-edge techniques to improve scalability, precision, and effectiveness in the fabrication of nanoscale devices, substances, and structures, AI plays a crucial part in nanofabrication and synthesis. AI tools provide smart control, optimization, and computerization of nanofabrication processes, leading to game-changing discoveries across several sectors. One of the primary applications of AI in nanofabrication is for process control and surveillance. Lithography, etching, along deposition are examples of nanofabrication processes that require exact control over variables like temperature, pressure, as well as chemical composition to produce desired results [53]. Real-time process attribute monitoring is made possible by AI-driven techniques, which use sensor data and feedback control systems to optimize performance and adjust process parameters. ML algorithms can analyze sensor data to find anomalies, predict process failures, and improve process conditions for higher yield and better quality of manufactured nanostructures. Furthermore, AI facilitates the design and optimization of nanofabrication processes through the use of predictive modeling and simulation. By examining data from previous fabrication runs, ML algorithms can produce prediction models of the relationships among process, structure, and attribute [54].

These models allow scientists to predict how modifications to a process would impact the properties of the nanostructures that are produced, which aids in the development of manufacturing techniques that are best suited for specific applications. AI-driven simulations also make virtual experimentation easier, allowing researchers to explore the functioning of nanostructures under varied situations and settings, therefore expediting the discovery and advancement of nanomaterials and technologies. AI makes process optimization and control easier, as well as automation and robots in nanofabrication and even production.

With previously unprecedented accuracy and efficiency, AI-driven robots can operate and manufacture complex items at the nanoscale [55]. These robotic systems adapt to changing conditions, learn from their observations, and progressively increase performance through the application of ML algorithms. By automating repetitive and labor-intensive tasks, AI-driven robotics increases throughput, reduces production costs, and optimizes nanofabrication processes. This makes it possible to produce materials and gadgets at the nanoscale on a large scale for use in industry.

Biomaterial Applications

The design, development, and classification of biomaterials having unique properties and capabilities for an enormous variety of biomedical uses are being revolutionized by AI. Owing to AI techniques like ML, DL, and neural networks, scientists may discover and create novel biomaterials for tissue restoration, regenerative healthcare, drug delivery, and healthcare equipment more quickly. In the development and optimization of materials for biomaterial uses, AI is extremely important [56]. Large datasets of material properties, synthesis methods, and performance metrics can be examined by means of ML algorithms to recognize correlations, developments, and patterns that guide the creation of innovative biomaterials. By learning from data, AI models may quickly identify materials with intended properties like mechanical strength, biological compatibility, and degradation kinetics [57]. They can also optimize material compositions along with processing settings. Investigators may use AI-assisted modeling along with simulation to learn more about the functioning of biomaterials at the atomic and subatomic scales. The biological structures and protein-ligand interactions, including cellular reactions, can all be analyzed by ML algorithms to predict the biocompatibility, immunogenicity, as well as biological activity of biomaterials [58]. By simulating the relationships involving biomaterials and biological systems, AI models direct the fabrication of biomaterials for specific biomedical uses.

The basic processes governing host response, regeneration of tissue, and cell-material interactions are made explicit by these models. AI optimizes biomaterials, enabling tissue engineering and drug delivery uses in addition to assisting with material design. Tissue absorption pathways, medicine release kinetics, along diffusion mechanisms can all be examined by ML algorithms to optimize the formulation of drug delivery systems, including hydrogels and nanoparticles [59]. Through the prediction of release patterns and targeting capabilities of drug-loaded biomaterials, AI models enable the development of more effective and personalized drug delivery solutions for a variety of therapeutic usage. Additionally, biomaterials may be characterized and their quality tracked throughout the entire production process thanks to AI techniques. AI is also revolutionizing the medical field in several ways. AI also speeds up the pursuit of biomarkers for disorders like cancer and enhances early disease detection by using nanodevices and image analysis through medical imaging. AI also accelerates drug discovery by predicting protein structures and creating new nanomolecules, which further revolutionizes precision medicine [60].

Environmental Sustainability

AI-assisted nanomanufacturing for cleaner energy is one novel approach to addressing two critical issues: climate change and the sustainability of energy [61]. Researchers may accelerate the creation of nanomaterials having enhanced properties for the production, storing, and utilization of renewable energy through the use of AI approaches such as ML and DL, along with neural networks. Two of AI's primary roles in the optimization of nanomaterials towards sustainable energy are materials design and exploration. ML algorithms can analyze massive datasets of material properties, synthesis methods, and operational assessments and identify patterns, trends, and correlations that can be used in the creation of novel nanomaterials for energy-related purposes. In addition to materials design, AI aids in the optimization of nanomaterial-based devices and systems to obtain sustainable energy solutions. ML techniques that assess sensor data, functional conditions, and operational metrics can be used to optimize the designs and functions of energy devices, such as solar cells, electrochemical cells, along catalytic reactors [62]. By predicting device performance under varied operational settings and environmental conditions, AI models contribute to the development of more dependable, affordable, and efficient energy solutions. Because of AI techniques, nanomaterials can also be incorporated into the energy as well as infrastructure systems of grid-scale applications.

CHALLENGES AND FUTURE PROSPECTS

Considering AI utilization in nanomanufacturing is still in its beginning stages, there are several implementation-related obstacles to overcome, including those related to data availability, accessibility, security, and regulatory compliance. Researchers have developed AI methods, such as convolutional as well as deep neural networks, resulting in are more effective than conventional algorithms like classifiers and regression frameworks, to address all of the issues.

Issues and Prospective Solutions

Even while nanotechnology has enormous potential in a variety of fields, it is necessary to overcome the issues with data organization and assembly that now exist to support the development of AI models. An AI model requires a lot of high-quality data to work well, but this can be difficult to acquire in abundance. The intentional or unintentional inclusion of incorrect data in training sets has a significant impact on the model's and predictions' accuracy. The researchers also observed that maintaining several dataset versions is a challenging effort and that mistakes made in this process are frequently difficult to determine and rectify. The outcomes of AI and ML can occasionally be ambiguous and frequently uncertain. This could result in conducting sensitive investigations during nano-characterization being very challenging. AI implementation will be difficult for a complicated process with multiple influencing variables, multi-scale impacts, and stochastic and unpredictable outcomes. Multiscale modeling is extremely sophisticated and involves integrating models at many scales to create a comprehensive understanding of manufacturing processes because of its predictive potential. Similar to any other kind of computer model, all AI models are susceptible to adversarial prediction-generating attacks.

Encryption, data anonymization, and rigorous cybersecurity measures, when used effectively, can greatly reduce possible security concerns. Enacting suitable legislative laws and promoting awareness are crucial steps toward guaranteeing security and privacy in AI models. Many investigations have demonstrated the effectiveness of DL models as a technique for detecting and mitigating adversarial data poisoning. For AI systems to perform effectively, they need a lot of training. In the highly complex field of nanomanufacturing, intensive training would be necessary. Additionally, higher system training would be necessary for modifications, advancements, or adjustments to production processes. AI can only attain tasks for which it is properly trained, and its application in environments such as nanomanufacturing, wherein several tasks may require rapid decisions and unforeseen problem-solving, may be difficult. One of the main challenges in real-time computing is managing and transferring computer resources to analyze options on time.

Future Prospects and Discussion

The integration of AI technologies into the design, fabrication, and characterization of nanoscale materials and systems is the process of merging nanomanufacturing with AI. The integration of AI technology through nanoscale manufacturing systems has the potential to revolutionize the industry, as this chapter highlights. Through the provision of improved capabilities in material exploration, process optimization, and quality control, including predictive modeling, this combination holds the potential to transform the area of nanomanufacturing. Some important points that were taken into consideration for this study are: to produce materials including devices at the nanoscale, nanomanufacturing is discussed in this study as a crucial element of Industry 4.0.

It talks about how the development of novel items with special features and capabilities is made possible by nanomanufacturing, which paves the way for the incorporation of cutting-edge technology like AI. AI integration in nanomanufacturing carries with it numerous types of opportunities and challenges that are still being worked out. Concerns about data availability and effectiveness, the understanding of AI and ML results, the additional complexity of multiscale modeling, confidentiality and privacy concerns, training difficulties, technical difficulties in real-time decision-making, strict regulations, equipment compatibility, prices, and material property variability are a few of the major challenges. However, new advances in AI indicate that the manufacturing sector could change thanks to the application of sophisticated analytical instruments. The creation of traditional modeling and control processes, computer vision-dependent AI models, and reinforcement learning are some potential remedies that academics have suggested. Algorithms and frameworks like explainable AI are guided by physics. Investigating these novel Potential solutions could lessen the difficulties and make room for future advancement.

CONCLUSION

This chapter provides a thorough assessment of the incorporation of AI in nanomanufacturing processes, thereby addressing a significant gap in the field. It focuses on how AI may improve quality control and process control, including material synthesis, when applied to the nanomanufacturing industry. Additionally, it shows how AI may boost market relevance and competitiveness by lowering costs, speeding up time to market, and boosting product quality. As a result, it provides strategic insights for businesses looking to improve and grow their manufacturing capabilities. This review's discussion of AI's compatibility with Industry 4.0 principles, which place a strong emphasis on digitalization, automation, and data-driven assistance in nanomanufacturing, is another important factor in its justification. These initiatives have the potential to advance nanomanufacturing technology by encouraging collaboration and knowledge sharing among professionals in materials science, engineering, and AI. This chapter additionally functions as a roadmap for additional research and creativity in this dynamically developing field by highlighting important challenges, prospects, and developing trends.

REFERENCES

[1] S. Malik, K. Muhammad, and Y. Waheed, "Nanotechnology: A Revolution in Modern Industry," Molecules, vol. 28, no. 2, p. 661, 2023. [Online]. Available: https://doi.org/10.3390/molecules 28020661
[http://dx.doi.org/10.3390/molecules28020661]

[2] Payal, and P. Pandey, "Role of Nanotechnology in Electronics: A Review of Recent Developments and Patents", *Recent Pat. Nanotechnol.*, vol. 16, no. 1, pp. 45-66, 2022.

[http://dx.doi.org/10.2174/1872210515666210120114504] [PMID: 33494686]

[3] Nishu, and S. Kumar, "Smart and innovative nanotechnology applications for water purification", *Hybrid Advances,* vol. 3, p. 100044, 2023. [http://dx.doi.org/10.1016/j.hybadv.2023.100044]

[4] X. Cheng, Q. Xie, and Y. Sun, "Advances in nanomaterial-based targeted drug delivery systems," Frontiers in Bioengineering and Biotechnology, vol. 11. Frontiers Media S.A., p. 1177151, Apr. 13, 2023. [http://dx.doi.org/10.3389/fbioe.2023.1177151]

[5] A. Biswas, I. S. Bayer, A. S. Biris, T. Wang, E. Dervishi, and F. Faupel, "Advances in top-down and bottom-up surface nanofabrication: Techniques, applications & future prospects," Advances in Colloid and Interface Science, vol. 170, no. 1–2. Elsevier, pp. 2–27, Jan. 15, 2012. [http://dx.doi.org/10.1016/j.cis.2011.11.001]

[6] J.A. Liddle, and G.M. Gallatin, "Lithography, metrology and nanomanufacturing", *Nanoscale,* vol. 3, no. 7, pp. 2679-2688, 2011. [http://dx.doi.org/10.1039/c1nr10046g] [PMID: 21487581]

[7] V. K. Jain et al., "Micro-machining: An overview (Part II)," Journal of Micromanufacturing, vol. 5, no. 1. SAGE PublicationsSage India: New Delhi, India, pp. 46–73, Oct. 06, 2022. [http://dx.doi.org/10.1177/25165984211045244]

[8] G. Liu, S. H. Petrosko, Z. Zheng, and C. A. Mirkin, "Evolution of Dip-Pen Nanolithography (DPN): From Molecular Patterning to Materials Discovery," Chemical Reviews, vol. 120, no. 13. American Chemical Society, pp. 6009–6047, Jul. 08, 2020. [http://dx.doi.org/10.1021/acs.chemrev.9b00725]

[9] S. Kumar, P. Bhushan, and S. Bhattacharya, "Fabrication of Nanostructures with Bottom-up Approach and Their Utility in Diagnostics, Therapeutics, and Others," in Energy, Environment, and Sustainability, Nature Publishing Group, 2018, pp. 167–198. [http://dx.doi.org/10.1007/978-981-10-7751-7_8]

[10] L. Duta and I. N. Mihailescu, "Advances and Challenges in Pulsed Laser Deposition for Complex Material Applications," Coatings, vol. 13, no. 2. MDPI, Feb. 01, 2023. [http://dx.doi.org/10.3390/coatings13020393]

[11] V. G. Kessler and G. A. Seisenbaeva, "Molecular mechanisms of the metal oxide sol-gel process and their application in approaches to thermodynamically challenging complex oxide materials," Journal of Sol-Gel Science and Technology, vol. 107, no. 1. Springer, pp. 190–200, Jul. 01, 2023. [http://dx.doi.org/10.1007/s10971-023-06120-y]

[12] J.Y. Choi, S. Das, N.D. Theodore, I. Kim, C. Honsberg, H.W. Choi, and T.L. Alford, "Advances in 2D/3D Printing of Functional Nanomaterials and Their Applications", *ECS J. Solid State Sci. Technol.,* vol. 4, no. 4, pp. P3001-P3009, 2015. [http://dx.doi.org/10.1149/2.0011504jss]

[13] S. Srikanth, J.M. Mohan, S. Dudala, S.K. Dubey, A. Javed, and S. Goel, "Direct UV laser writing system to photolithographically fabricate optimal microfluidic geometries: Experimental investigations", *Mater. Today Proc.,* vol. 28, pp. 799-803, 2020. [http://dx.doi.org/10.1016/j.matpr.2019.12.301]

[14] A. Saravanan, P.S. Kumar, R.V. Hemavathy, S. Jeevanantham, M.J. Jawahar, J.P. Neshaanthini, and R. Saravanan, "A review on synthesis methods and recent applications of nanomaterial in wastewater treatment: Challenges and future perspectives", *Chemosphere,* vol. 307, no. Pt 1, p. 135713, 2022. [http://dx.doi.org/10.1016/j.chemosphere.2022.135713] [PMID: 35843436]

[15] A. Dhaka, S. Chand Mali, S. Sharma, and R. Trivedi, "A review on biological synthesis of silver nanoparticles and their potential applications", In: *Results in Chemistry.* vol. Vol. 6. Elsevier, 2023, p. 101108. [http://dx.doi.org/10.1016/j.rechem.2023.101108]

[16] S.J. Oks, "Cyber-Physical Systems in the Context of Industry 4.0: A Review, Categorization and Outlook", *Inf. Syst. Front.*, vol. 1, pp. 1-42, 2022.
[http://dx.doi.org/10.1007/s10796-022-10252-x]

[17] N. Agrawal, and R. Kumar, "Security Perspective Analysis of Industrial Cyber Physical Systems (I-CPS): A Decade-wide Survey", *ISA Trans.*, vol. 130, pp. 10-24, 2022.
[http://dx.doi.org/10.1016/j.isatra.2022.03.018] [PMID: 35396141]

[18] L. Lin, P. S. Kollipara, and Y. Zheng, "Digital manufacturing of advanced materials: Challenges and perspective," Materials Today, vol. 28. Elsevier, pp. 49–62, Sep. 01, 2019.
[http://dx.doi.org/10.1016/j.mattod.2019.05.022]

[19] A. Haleem, M. Javaid, M. Asim Qadri, R. Pratap Singh, and R. Suman, "Artificial intelligence (AI) applications for marketing: A literature-based study," International Journal of Intelligent Networks, vol. 3. Elsevier, pp. 119–132, Jan. 01, 2022.
[http://dx.doi.org/10.1016/j.ijin.2022.08.005]

[20] S. K. Baduge *et al.*, "Artificial intelligence and smart vision for building and construction 4.0: Machine and deep learning methods and applications," Automation in Construction, vol. 141. Elsevier, p. 104440, Sep. 01, 2022.
[http://dx.doi.org/10.1016/j.autcon.2022.104440]

[21] J. Vamathevan *et al.*, "Applications of machine learning in drug discovery and development," Nature Reviews Drug Discovery, vol. 18, no. 6. NIH Public Access, pp. 463–477, Jun. 01, 2019.
[http://dx.doi.org/10.1038/s41573-019-0024-5]

[22] O. Adir *et al.*, "Integrating Artificial Intelligence and Nanotechnology for Precision Cancer Medicine," Advanced Materials, vol. 32, no. 13. Europe PMC Funders, p. e1901989, Jul. 07, 2020.
[http://dx.doi.org/10.1002/adma.201901989]

[23] M.H. Rahman, M.A.S. Sejan, M.A. Aziz, R. Tabassum, J.I. Baik, and H.K. Song, "A Comprehensive Survey of Unmanned Aerial Vehicles Detection and Classification Using Machine Learning Approach: Challenges, Solutions, and Future Directions", *Remote Sens. (Basel),* vol. 16, no. 5, p. 879, 2024.
[http://dx.doi.org/10.3390/rs16050879]

[24] S. Kumar, H. Singh, J. Feder-Kubis, and D.D. Nguyen, "Recent advances in nanobiosensors for sustainable healthcare applications: A systematic literature review", *Environ. Res.,* vol. 238, no. Pt 2, p. 117177, 2023.
[http://dx.doi.org/10.1016/j.envres.2023.117177] [PMID: 37751831]

[25] M. Nandipati, O. Fatoki, and S. Desai, "Bridging Nanomanufacturing and Artificial Intelligence—A Comprehensive Review," Materials, vol. 17, no. 7. Multidisciplinary Digital Publishing Institute, p. 1621, Apr. 02, 2024
[http://dx.doi.org/10.3390/ma17071621]

[26] L.A. Kolahalam, I.V. Kasi Viswanath, B.S. Diwakar, B. Govindh, V. Reddy, and Y.L.N. Murthy, "Review on nanomaterials: Synthesis and applications", *Mater. Today Proc.,* vol. 18, pp. 2182-2190, 2019.
[http://dx.doi.org/10.1016/j.matpr.2019.07.371]

[27] H. Wang *et al.*, "Scientific discovery in the age of artificial intelligence," Nature, vol. 620, no. 7972. Nature Research, pp. 47–60, Aug. 03, 2023.
[http://dx.doi.org/10.1038/s41586-023-06221-2]

[28] S. Kumar, H. Singh, and S. Singh, *Introduction to optimization techniques commonly used in materials science.* Metaheuristics-Based Mater. Optim, 2025, pp. 131-168.
[http://dx.doi.org/10.1016/B978-0-443-29162-3.00005-8]

[29] A.V. Singh, M. Varma, P. Laux, S. Choudhary, A.K. Datusalia, N. Gupta, A. Luch, A. Gandhi, P. Kulkarni, and B. Nath, "Artificial intelligence and machine learning disciplines with the potential to

improve the nanotoxicology and nanomedicine fields: a comprehensive review," Arch. Toxicol., vol. 97, pp. 963–979, Mar. 2023. [Online].
[http://dx.doi.org/10.1007/s00204-023-03471-x]

[30] Y. Xu, X. Liu, X. Cao, C. Huang, E. Liu, S. Qian, X. Liu, Y. Wu, F. Dong, C.-W. Qiu, J. Qiu, K. Hua, W. Su, J. Wu, H. Xu, Y. Han, C. Fu, Z. Yin, M. Liu, R. Roepman, S. Dietmann, M. Virta, F. Kengara, Z. Zhang, L. Zhang, T. Zhao, J. Dai, J. Yang, L. Lan, M. Luo, Z. Liu, T. An, B. Zhang, X. He, S. Cong, X. Liu, W. Zhang, J. P. Lewis, J. M. Tiedje, Q. Wang, Z. An, F. Wang, L. Zhang, T. Huang, C. Lu, Z. Cai, F. Wang, and J. Zhang, "Artificial intelligence: A powerful paradigm for scientific research," The Innovation, vol. 2, no. 4, p. 100179, Nov. 2021. [Online]. Available: https://doi.org/10.1016/j.xinn.2021.100179.
[http://dx.doi.org/10.1016/j.xinn.2021.100179]

[31] O. I. Abiodun, A. Jantan, A. E. Omolara, K. V. Dada, N. A. E. Mohamed, and H. Arshad, "State-o--the-art in artificial neural network applications: A survey," Heliyon, vol. 4, no. 11. Elsevier, p. e00938, Nov. 01, 2018.
[http://dx.doi.org/10.1016/j.heliyon.2018.e00938]

[32] C. Cao *et al.*, "Deep Learning and Its Applications in Biomedicine," Genomics, Proteomics and Bioinformatics, vol. 16, no. 1. Beijing Genomics Institute, pp. 17–32, Feb. 01, 2018.
[http://dx.doi.org/10.1016/j.gpb.2017.07.003]

[33] S. Kumar, H. Singh, and D. K. Singh, "Metasurfaces in Optical Biosensing: Revolutionizing Detection Techniques and Shaping the Future," Photonics, vol. 12, no. 4. Multidisciplinary Digital Publishing Institute (MDPI), pp. 12–31, Apr. 01, 2025.
[http://dx.doi.org/10.3390/photonics12040360]

[34] S. Kumar and H. Singh, "Antenna Array Pattern Synthesis Using Nature-Inspired Computational Techniques: A Review," Archives of Computational Methods in Engineering, vol. 30, no. 5. Springer, pp. 3235–3269, Mar. 10, 2023.
[http://dx.doi.org/10.1007/s11831-023-09900-5]

[35] M. Javaid, A. Haleem, R. Pratap Singh, R. Suman, and S. Rab, "Significance of machine learning in healthcare: Features, pillars and applications", *International Journal of Intelligent Networks,* vol. 3, pp. 58-73, 2022.
[http://dx.doi.org/10.1016/j.ijin.2022.05.002]

[36] S. Kumar, H. Singh, H. Singh, H. Soni, M. Bechelany, and J. Singh, "Extraction of Metallic Nanoparticles from Electronic Waste for Biomedical Applications: Pioneering Sustainable Technological Progress," Sustainability (Switzerland), vol. 17, no. 5. Multidisciplinary Digital Publishing Institute (MDPI), pp. 9–23, Mar. 01, 2025.
[http://dx.doi.org/10.3390/su17052100]

[37] M.M. Mariani, I. Machado, V. Magrelli, and Y.K. Dwivedi, "Artificial intelligence in innovation research: A systematic review, conceptual framework, and future research directions", *Technovation,* vol. 122, p. 102623, 2023.
[http://dx.doi.org/10.1016/j.technovation.2022.102623]

[38] N. Korin, M. J. Gounis, A. K. Wakhloo, and D. E. Ingber, "Targeted drug delivery to flow-obstructed blood vessels using mechanically activated nanotherapeutics," JAMA Neurology, vol. 72, no. 1. American Medical Association, pp. 119–122, Jan. 01, 2015.
[http://dx.doi.org/10.1001/jamaneurol.2014.2886]

[39] S. Sim, and N. Wong, "Nanotechnology and its use in imaging and drug delivery (Review)", *Biomed. Rep.,* vol. 14, no. 5, p. 42, 2021.
[http://dx.doi.org/10.3892/br.2021.1418] [PMID: 33728048]

[40] D.S. Char, M.D. Abràmoff, and C. Feudtner, "Identifying Ethical Considerations for Machine Learning Healthcare Applications", *Am. J. Bioeth.,* vol. 20, no. 11, pp. 7-17, 2020.
[http://dx.doi.org/10.1080/15265161.2020.1819469] [PMID: 33103967]

[41] G. Manogaran, and D. Lopez, "A survey of big data architectures and machine learning algorithms in healthcare", *Int. J. Biomed. Eng. Technol.*, vol. 25, no. 2/3/4, pp. 182-211, 2017. [http://dx.doi.org/10.1504/IJBET.2017.087722]

[42] S. Kumar, and H. Singh, "Evaluation of Multiple Element Failure Correction in Antenna Array with Metaheuristic Approach", *2024 IEEE International Conference on Interdisciplinary Approaches in Technology and Management for Social Innovation, IATMSI 2024,* 2024. [http://dx.doi.org/10.1109/IATMSI60426.2024.10503033]

[43] R. Bhardwaj, A. R. Nambiar, and D. Dutta, "A Study of Machine Learning in Healthcare," in Proceedings - International Computer Software and Applications Conference, Sep. 2017, vol. 2, pp. 236–241 [http://dx.doi.org/10.1109/COMPSAC.2017.164]

[44] T.J. Saleem, and M.A. Chishti, "Exploring the Applications of Machine Learning in Healthcare", *Int. J. Sensors Wirel. Commun. Control,* vol. 10, no. 4, pp. 458-472, 2020. [http://dx.doi.org/10.2174/2210327910666191220103417]

[45] S. T. Mueller, R. R. Hoffman, W. Clancey, A. Emrey, and G. Klein, "Explanation in Human-AI Systems: A Literature Meta-Review, Synopsis of Key Ideas and Publications, and Bibliography for Explainable AI," Feb. 2019, Accessed: Aug. 26, 2024. [Online]. Available from: http://arxiv.org/abs/1902.01876

[46] S. Siddique, and J.C.L. Chow, "Machine Learning in Healthcare Communication", *Encyclopedia,* vol. 1, no. 1, pp. 220-239, 2021. [http://dx.doi.org/10.3390/encyclopedia1010021]

[47] R. R. Hoffman, S. T. Mueller, G. Klein, and J. Litman, "Measures for explainable AI: Explanation goodness, user satisfaction, mental models, curiosity, trust, and human-AI performance," Frontiers in Computer Science, vol. 5. Frontiers Media S.A., p. 1096257, Feb. 06, 2023. [http://dx.doi.org/10.3389/fcomp.2023.1096257]

[48] D. R. Gunasegaram *et al.*, "Machine learning-assisted in-situ adaptive strategies for the control of defects and anomalies in metal additive manufacturing," Additive Manufacturing, vol. 81. Elsevier, p. 104013, Feb. 05, 2024. [http://dx.doi.org/10.1016/j.addma.2024.104013]

[49] M. K. Kim, Y. Park, I. J. Kim, and J. S. Lee, "Emerging Materials for Neuromorphic Devices and Systems," iScience, vol. 23, no. 12. Elsevier, p. 101846, Dec. 18, 2020. [http://dx.doi.org/10.1016/j.isci.2020.101846]

[50] G.M. Sacha, and P. Varona, "Artificial intelligence in nanotechnology", *Nanotechnology,* vol. 24, no. 45, p. 452002, 2013. [http://dx.doi.org/10.1088/0957-4484/24/45/452002] [PMID: 24121558]

[51] K. K. Mak and M. R. Pichika, "Artificial intelligence in drug development: present status and future prospects," Drug Discovery Today, vol. 24, no. 3. Elsevier Ltd, pp. 773–780, Mar. 01, 2019. [http://dx.doi.org/10.1016/j.drudis.2018.11.014]

[52] P. Hassanzadeh, F. Atyabi, and R. Dinarvand, "The significance of artificial intelligence in drug delivery system design," Advanced Drug Delivery Reviews, vol. 151–152. Elsevier B.V., pp. 169–190, Nov. 01, 2019. [http://dx.doi.org/10.1016/j.addr.2019.05.001]

[53] K. Stokes, K. Clark, D. Odetade, M. Hardy, and P. Goldberg Oppenheimer, "Advances in lithographic techniques for precision nanostructure fabrication in biomedical applications," *Discover Nano*, vol. 18, no. 1. Springer, p. 153, Dec. 01, 2023. [http://dx.doi.org/10.1186/s11671-023-03938-x]

[54] L. K. Vora, A. D. Gholap, K. Jetha, R. R. S. Thakur, H. K. Solanki, and V. P. Chavda, "Artificial Intelligence in Pharmaceutical Technology and Drug Delivery Design," *Pharmaceutics*, vol. 15, no. 7.

Multidisciplinary Digital Publishing Institute (MDPI), Jul. 01, 2023.
[http://dx.doi.org/10.3390/pharmaceutics15071916]

[55] R.G.L. da Silva, "The advancement of artificial intelligence in biomedical research and health innovation: challenges and opportunities in emerging economies", *Global. Health,* vol. 20, no. 1, p. 44, 2024.
[http://dx.doi.org/10.1186/s12992-024-01049-5] [PMID: 38773458]

[56] L. M. Petrick and N. Shomron, "AI/ML-driven advances in untargeted metabolomics and exposomics for biomedical applications," Cell Reports Physical Science, vol. 3, no. 7. Cell Press, Jul. 20, 2022.
[http://dx.doi.org/10.1016/j.xcrp.2022.100978]

[57] L. David, A. Thakkar, R. Mercado, and O. Engkvist, "Molecular representations in AI-driven drug discovery: a review and practical guide," Journal of Cheminformatics, vol. 12, no. 1. BioMed Central Ltd, Sep. 17, 2020.
[http://dx.doi.org/10.1186/s13321-020-00460-5]

[58] A. Holzinger, K. Keiblinger, P. Holub, K. Zatloukal, and H. Müller, "AI for life: Trends in artificial intelligence for biotechnology", *N. Biotechnol.,* vol. 74, pp. 16-24, 2023.
[http://dx.doi.org/10.1016/j.nbt.2023.02.001] [PMID: 36754147]

[59] H. Kim, "AI, big data, and robots for the evolution of biotechnology", *Genomics Inform.,* vol. 17, no. 4, p. e44, 2019.
[http://dx.doi.org/10.5808/GI.2019.17.4.e44] [PMID: 31896244]

[60] A.L. Oliveira, "Biotechnology, Big Data and Artificial Intelligence", *Biotechnol. J.,* vol. 14, no. 8, p. 1800613, 2019.
[http://dx.doi.org/10.1002/biot.201800613] [PMID: 30927505]

[61] S. Kumar, V. Vaid, and G. Thakur, "A Comprehensive Review of 5G Networks for Sustainable and Smart Cities", *Recent Adv. Electr. Electron. Eng.,* vol. 17, no. 6, pp. 535-543, 2024.
[http://dx.doi.org/10.2174/2352096516666230720164542]

[62] A. Bennagi, O. AlHousrya, D. T. Cotfas, and P. A. Cotfas, "Comprehensive study of the artificial intelligence applied in renewable energy," Energy Strategy Reviews, vol. 54. Elsevier, p. 101446, Jul. 01, 2024.
[http://dx.doi.org/10.1016/j.esr.2024.101446]

CHAPTER 9

Smart Mobility through a Human Lens: Addressing Urban Transportation Challenges with a People-First Approach

Ranjit Kumar Bindal[1,*], **Vaibhav**[1] and **Vaibhav JaDon**[1]

[1] *Department of Electrical Engineering, Chandigarh University, Chandigarh, Punjab, India*

Abstract: Rapid urbanization comes with an increasing demand on transportation systems, which are increasingly being subjected to great environmental concerns and changing mobility needs. This paper advances a human-centric approach for smart mobility by concentrating the solution on user experience, accessibility, and community well-being. This study takes an outlook on how people-first design can transform the available technology into a different paradigm for reshaping urban mobility in light of current urban transportation challenges, such as congestion, pollution, and inefficiencies. By using case studies and data analysis, it is brought out how the integration of intelligent transportation systems, shared mobility solutions, and multimodal networks can create sustainable and inclusive urban environments. Our findings suggest that human-centered design-based smart mobility solutions provide not only user satisfaction but also support resiliency and addictiveness in the transportation ecosystem.

Keywords: Human-centric approach, Intelligent transportation systems, Multimodal networks, People-first design, Smart mobility, Sustainable mobility, Shared mobility, Transportation challenges, Urban transportation, Urbanization.

INTRODUCTION

Although the rate of growth is unprecedented, it is bound to put enormous strains on urban transportation systems in terms of accommodating increased population densities and mobility demands. It is estimated that nearly 70% of the world's population will live within an urban region-immersing the demand for efficient, reliable, and sustainable transportation solutions by 2050. The traditional models of urban transportation often fail, leading to a negative impact such as traffic congestion and much longer commute times, pollution, and so forth. To address

* **Corresponding author Ranjit Kumar Bindal:** Department of Electrical Engineering, Chandigarh University, Chandigarh, Punjab, India; E-mail: ranjitbindal.eee@cumail.in

Shilpa Gupta, Ritika Sharma & Gokana Mohana Rani (Eds.)

these complex challenges, cities are reaching out to what has been known as "smart mobility": advanced technologies and data-driven approaches to renovate the urban mobility framework.

Smart Mobility involves the use of digital technologies, data analytics, and IoT to streamline transportation systems and enhance urban transit. It brings about a gamut of solutions: Intelligent Transportation Systems (ITS), shared mobility platforms, and electric or even autonomous vehicles, to name a few. While an important enabler of smart mobility, technology alone cannot fulfill the variety of needs that urban residents have. A human-centered approach, therefore, is to fold in principles into smart mobility systems, so they can be equally effective and inclusive. A human-centric approach to transportation is based on the main idea of designing systems around the needs, preferences, and behavior of people.

In a human-centric model, the real-world challenges of real people, such as accessibility, safety, and comfort, are tackled when designing transportation solutions. This is contrary to the traditional model, which focuses more on infrastructure and technology than end-user experience. This brings cities to create solutions to mobility issues that are not only technologically advanced but also adaptable for different user groups, including the elderly and people with disabilities, and those who are economically disadvantaged.

Fig. (**1**). Shows some important Aspects of smart mobility, i.e., artificial intelligence, vehicle-to-grid, intelligent system, among others. Cities often experience problems in urban transportation systems like traffic congestion, pollution, lack of safety, and a lack of decently reliable options for transit. Issues such as these reduce not only the quality of life for residents living in urban areas but also contribute to degrading the environment and creating inefficiencies in the economy. Moreover, many of the currently implemented transportation systems lack the ability to dynamically respond to the needs of modern urban populations. Human-centric smart mobility efforts address all these issues by basing transportation solutions on a holistic view of social, economic, and environmental factors, which are in tune with the needs of the communities in cities. While technology serves as the backbone of intelligent mobility, success depends on how well it is incorporated into human-centered design.

The emerging technologies of IoT, AI, and machine learning enable real-time collection and analysis; specifically, the deployment and design of these technologies should lead to maximized user experience and accessibility.

Smart mobility applications can be employed to provide real-time information and updates regarding public transit presence, routes, and traffic conditions, thereby making it easier for users to navigate their commute time and reduce the stress they experience while in transit. Human-centric smart mobility is also a pathway toward a more eco-friendly approach to urban transportation. Electric as well as shared vehicles, along with the promotion of multimodal transit networks, reduce carbon footprints in the city and also improve air quality. Another aspect of human-centred initiatives of mobility includes equity through distribution and equal access to transport services, with special attention given to the less privileged groups.

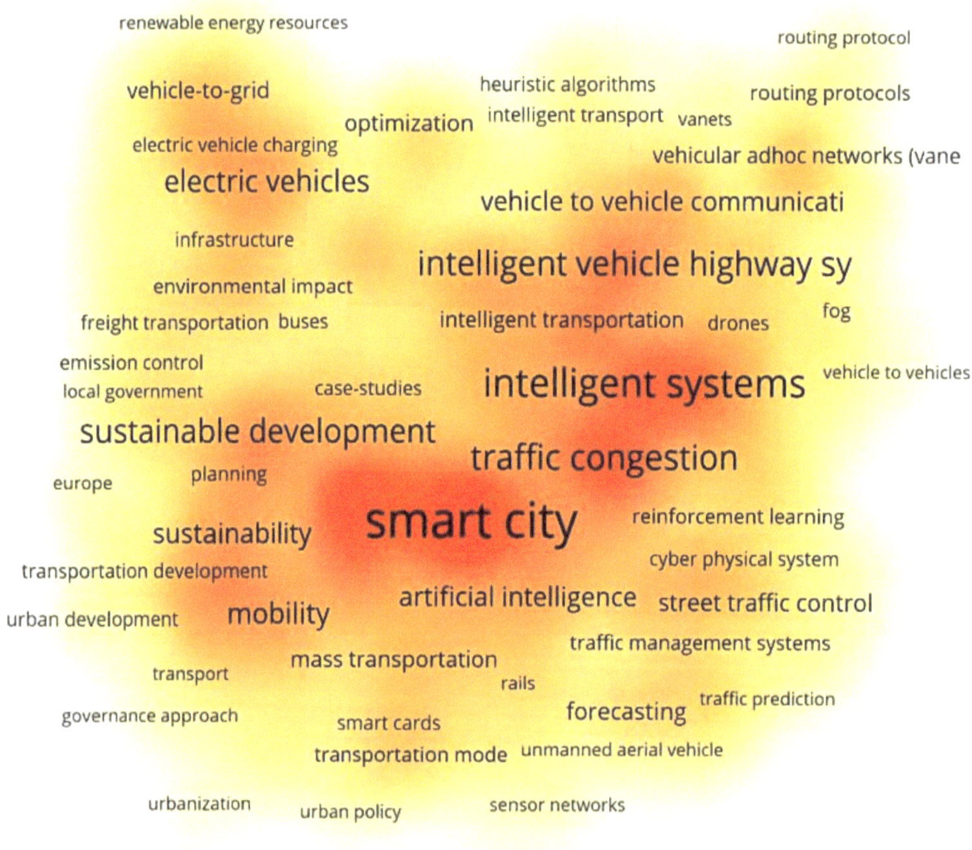

Fig. (1). Some important aspects.

Sustainable, inclusive urban mobility can be regarded as a structure that conceives moving people not only in its literal meaning but as a social equity and economic opportunity enabler. Shared mobility like car-sharing, ride-hailing, and bike-sharing is one of the transformative elements of smart mobility. These services provide alternative, flexible ways of transport. They reduce the dependency on private vehicles and decrease traffic congestion in general. Multimodal solutions consist of several transport modes put together, such as buses, trains, bikes, and walking paths. This presents users with hassle-free alternatives for transition. Shared and multimodal mobility is approached with a human-centric attitude, with great emphasis on user accessibility, comfort, and convenience, making urban transportation more attractive and practicable to diverse populations. In the human-centred framework of mobility, safety and accessibility remain basic elements. The safety of all road users-pedestrians, cyclists, and motorists is rooted in a trusted system of transportation that is broadly adopted. Human-centric design mitigates and minimizes potential hazards, thereby making safe interaction among different modes of transport possible.

LITERATURE REVIEW

In this review, it is written that navigating the role of IoT technologies in the development of smart cities defines fundamental applications such as traffic management, environmental monitoring, and smart infrastructure, but highlights the importance of IoT for better quality of urban living [1]. The paper intends to examine how blockchain technology plays an indispensable role in the development of smart cities, while sharpening transparency and security and increasing the efficiency of urban services such as transportation, supply chain management, and governance [2]. This article reviews the integration of AI and IoT in smart traffic systems to analyze the impact on optimizing flow, reducing congestion, and ensuring the safety of the roads of the smart city [3]. This article reviews the integration of AI into applications of smart cities, namely traffic control, healthcare, and urban planning. It gives much emphasis on how AI would be built into a smarter, more efficient, and responsive urban environment [4]. The review focuses on sustainable transportation systems in smart cities, detailing innovations in electric vehicles, shared mobility, and green infrastructure. It also addresses how these technologies contribute to reducing urban carbon footprints [5]. This chapter discusses how IoT devices assist in energy management within the smart city. It reviews the systems that optimize energy consumption, reduce waste, and integrate renewable energy sources into the urban grid [6].

Review on smart homes and buildings, keenly observe to find them as an integral part of the infrastructure for smart cities. The technologies that power these innovations are outlined, including IoT, automation, and AI. It also proceeds with these and their improvement of energy efficiency and quality of life [7]. This review addresses the role of big data in the development of smart cities, proving how data-driven insights increase improvements in urban planning, resource management, and citizen engagement in smart cities. It raises challenges about managing large urban data [8]. The paper reviews AI-based solutions for urban mobility, such as self-driving vehicles, traffic prediction systems, and mobility-a-

-a-service (MaaS) models. AI is changing the face of transportation in smart cities, making it much more efficient and decongested [9].

Fig. (**2**) shows the publication trend graph from 2009 to 2024. It shows that the documents are increasing on a yearly basis. In the year 2019, the maximum peak point is observed, and after that, it starts decreasing. This review talks about the application of IoT in health services within smart cities, especially leveraging connected devices to track health conditions of patients, management of medical resources, and improvement in the delivery of urban health services [10]. This paper is an overview of how the current energy distribution within the city is transformed into a smarter approach through smart grids, thus integrating advanced metering, real-time monitoring, and predictive analytics in pursuit of energy efficiency and reliability [11]. Table **1** shows the literature review of relevant studies.

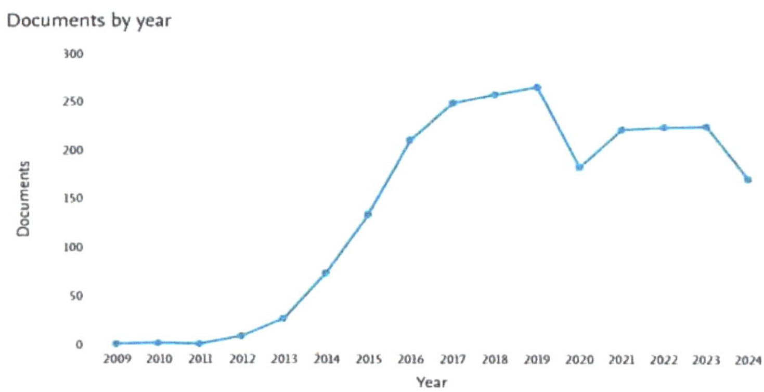

Fig. (2). Publication trend graph.

Table 1. Literature review of relevant studies.

S. No.	**Author(s) & Year**	**Title**	**Key Findings**	**Summary**
1	S. Chowduri, S. Midlam-Mohler, K. P. Singh (2024) [1]	"Design, prototyping, and implementation of a vehicle-to-infrastructure (V2I) system for eco-approach and departure through connected and smart corridors"	This study focuses on V2I systems designed to reduce environmental impacts and enhance traffic flow.	The research demonstrates the benefits of real-time communication between vehicles and infrastructure to promote eco-friendly driving patterns and improve traffic flow in urban areas.

(Table 1) cont.....

S. No.	Author(s) & Year	Title	Key Findings	Summary
2	S. Tahir, B. Abdulrazak, D. Baillargeon, S. B. Givi, C. Girard, H. Pigot, V. Provencher (2024) [2]	"Towards smart and inclusive cities: MOBILAÎNÉS project - Innovating age-friendly mobility solutions for older adults"	Focuses on creating mobility solutions for older adults in smart cities.	The study emphasizes the need for age-friendly mobility solutions and highlights the development of inclusive transportation systems to meet the needs of senior citizens.
3	Y. K. K. Rajnath (2024) [3]	"E-mobility in electrical energy systems for sustainability"	Explores the role of e-mobility in supporting sustainable energy systems.	The study discusses how Electric Vehicles (EVs) can contribute to reducing carbon footprints and improving energy grid efficiency by integrating renewable energy sources.
4	E. Faliagka, E. Christopoulou, D. Ringas, T. Politi, N. Kostis, D. Leonardos, C. Tranoris, C. P. Antonopoulos, S. Denazis, N. Voros (2024) [4]	"Trends in digital twin framework architectures for smart cities: A case study in smart mobility"	Reviews the role of digital twin technologies in optimizing urban mobility.	The paper highlights the application of digital twins in simulating and improving transportation systems in smart cities, providing valuable insights into real-time monitoring and forecasting.
5	T. Poongodi, N. S. Pasupuleti, B. Balusamy (2024) [5]	"Smart Mobility and Intelligent Transportation Systems for Commercial and Hazardous Vehicles"	Focuses on applying smart mobility to improve safety and efficiency in the transportation of goods, especially hazardous materials.	The study emphasizes how intelligent transportation systems can optimize commercial vehicle operations, ensuring safety and reducing environmental impact in sensitive transportation contexts.

This paper discusses innovative urban waste management solutions based on IoT sensors and AI technologies related to waste generation monitoring, optimized collection routes, and improved recycling processes within a smart city [12]. The review discusses the critical issue of cybersecurity in smart cities. It identifies vulnerabilities associated with IoT devices and other smart infrastructure. It also explores strategies to protect the urban systems from cyber threats [13]. This article reviews the application of data analytics to transportation systems in smart cities. Several methods are employed to analyze traffic data, predict congestion, and optimize routes further improve mobility as well as reduce environmental impacts [14]. Considering the rising trends toward the future of urban agriculture, the paper would also study the future application where technology, IoT, AI, and automation could be deployed as an optimum way for agriculture optimization, waste reduction, and food security in cities [15]. The applications of AI in healthcare in a smart city, which include diagnostic tools, predictive health trends analytics, and patient management systems, are reviewed. Challenges in the adoption of AI in healthcare are discussed [16]. The integration of AVs in urban mobility networks is reviewed, including impacts on traffic flow, infrastructure, and, consequently, planning for urban areas. The benefits and challenges of integrating AVs into a smart city are discussed in the text [17]. This review explains how AI technologies are used to optimize the traffic flow and deal with congestion in smart cities. This incorporates, among others, machine learning models, live analysis of traffic, and adaptive traffic signal systems [18]. The aim of this paper is to review the techniques used in machine learning for smart city applications related to the prediction of traffic accidents. This deals with types of weather and traffic conditions concerning models that would be used to avoid accidents [19, 20]. The paper undertakes an analysis of blockchain technology as an enabler for increasing Mobility as a Service in smart cities. It is focused on how blockchain technology can serve to improve security, enhance transparency, and increase the efficiency of urban transportation systems [21].

Methodology

It will have a mixed-methods approach to research human-centered smart mobility solutions and their role in transportation schemes in towns. The approach will combine the study of quantitative statistical analysis of data in transportation data with insights through the use of selected case studies, consumer surveys, and user interviews. With regard to current urban mobility behavior and to identify the challenges for such mobility patterns in terms of congestion, accessibility, and environmental impact, data were gathered based on sources like city transportation departments, traffic monitoring systems, and public datasets. Surveys with urban residents were also carried out with regard to the preferences, pain points, and perceptions concerning the existing transportation options. These findings serve as a benchmark for the evaluation of human-centered design in smart mobility endeavors.

The quantitative analysis will apply data from intelligent transportation systems, ride-sharing services, and multimodal networks for evaluation purposes. Average travel time, frequency of usage, and carbon emission represent some of the performance indicators applied in measuring effectiveness when smart mobility solutions were employed. Spatial and Geographic Information System (GIS) tools are used to map transit accessibility and bring attention to underserved populations who would benefit greatly from mobility choices. Such spatial analysis will be understood in order to understand how well the current systems serve different demographic groups and the gaps where human-centric solutions can be made more effective. As such, it links these data points with some feedback from the survey study to provide a holistic view of transportation challenges and potential improvements.

Fig. (**3**) shows the methodology being used in flow chart form. This flow chart shows that cases were analyzed to create qualitative insights into cities that have been successful in human-centric smart mobility initiatives. Cases of cities such

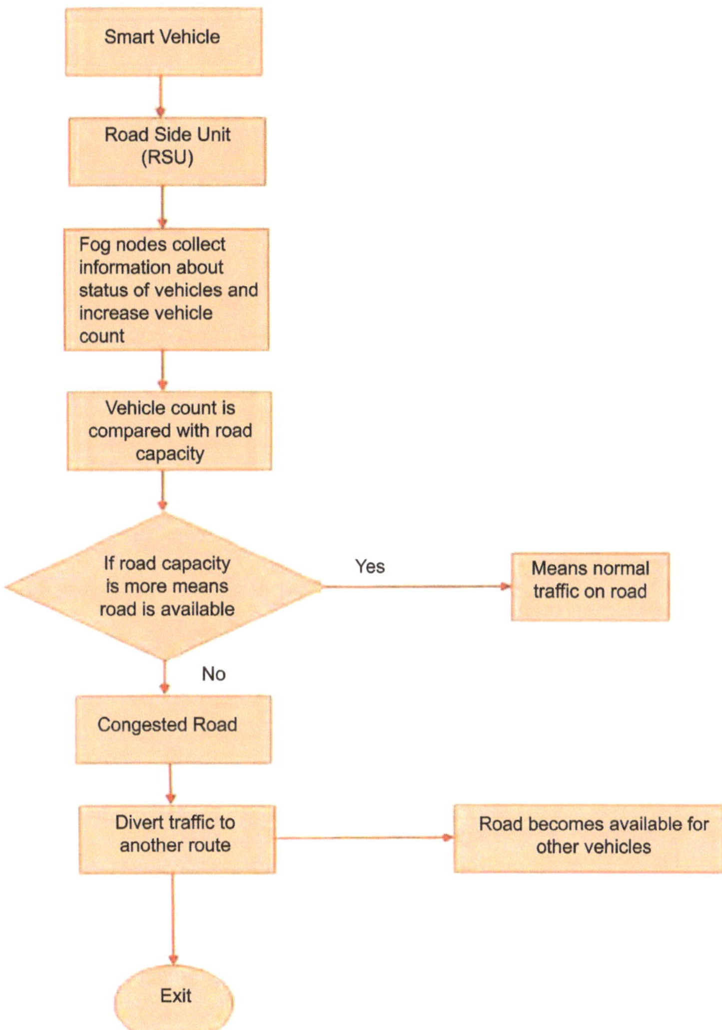

Fig. (3). Methodology.

as Amsterdam, Singapore, and Stockholm were considered because they had been the first among their peers in deploying technology-driven, people-focused transport systems. Interviews with policymakers, urban planners, and technology providers in these cities provided a level of depth in the strategies aimed at enhancing inclusiveness, safety, and environmental sustainability in urban transport. These case studies illustrate best practices and challenges associated with human-centered mobility solutions, and are of immense value to cities seeking similar approaches.

Thirdly, user feedback and preferences were included to evaluate the social and behavioral impacts of smart mobility solutions. This research compares data from surveys, case studies, and transportation metrics in assessing how far human-centered ways can ease the problems afflicting the challenges of urban transportation. These findings will yield evidence-based recommendations to design smart mobility systems that are adaptive, sustainable, and responsive to human needs. Methodology identifies ways by which the distinction between advancement in technology and delivery of user experience can be filled, and contributes as such to a framework guiding future urban mobility planning and policy-making in rapidly growing cities.

RESULT AND EVALUATION

The analysis of transportation data reveals a significant improvement in travel efficiency and user satisfaction in human-centered smart mobility solutions. The mean commuting time dropped to 20% of traditional systems in cities that implemented Fig. (**4**) and Table **2** present the results for human-centric smart mobility solutions within Singapore's multimodal networks. The results are shown in a bar graph (Fig. (**4**)) and in a table of values (Table **2**). Much of this was due to easy interchanges between modes of transport and real-time transit information, helping users choose the optimal route more efficiently. A response survey from people in these cities revealed that 78% preferred multi-stream systems, as opposed to single-stream systems; this suggests the worth of heterogeneity in city travel. Environmental effects are also presented in the car-sharing and bike-sharing shared mobility solutions and accounted for a reduction of carbon emissions by 15% in cities under study. For instance, shared electric scooters and bike-sharing programs in Stockholm reduced the percentage of private vehicles on the roads, bringing cleaner air and lower emissiona. GIS data analysis indicated that, in regions with high shares of shared mobility adoption, there was a 30% reduction in traffic congestion as well, which reflects the general benefits of sharing mobility in air quality and road traffic.

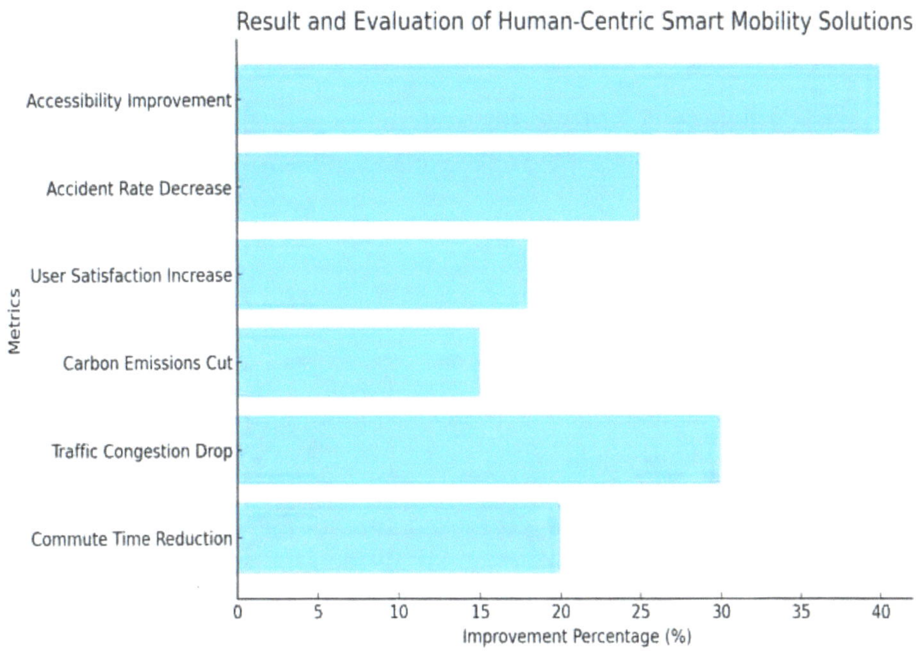

Fig. (4). Result and evaluation of human-centric smart mobility solutions.

Table 2. Result and evaluation of human-centric smart mobility solutions.

Metric	City Example	Improvement (%)	Observation
Commute Time Reduction	Singapore	20%	Reduced wait and smoother transitions with multimodal.
Traffic Congestion Drop	Stockholm	30%	Fewer private vehicles on roads due to shared mobility.
Carbon Emissions Cut	Stockholm	15%	Electric/shared vehicles contributed to lower emissions.
User Satisfaction Increase	Multiple Cities	18%	Real-time data and multimodal improved convenience.
Accident Rate Decrease	Amsterdam	25%	Protected lanes reduced cyclist and pedestrian accidents.
Accessibility Improvement	Amsterdam	40%	Step-free transit improved access for all.

As a result of human-centric mobility initiatives, metrics of safety and accessibility also improved. It was considered that the number of cyclist-pedestrian accidents declined by 25% in Amsterdam with the implementation of bike lanes and pedestrian-friendly zones. As discussed above, accessibility measures, such as step-free access for passenger stations increased accessibility up to 40% for individuals with disabilities, thus opening up the city further to facilitate transport for a larger mobility contingent.

Based on survey data, 85\% of the respondents said that they appreciated these safety improvements; thus, people-first design elements prove to be pretty relevant in building trust and satisfaction amongst urban commuters. The findings clearly highlight the fact that people-first strategies of smart mobility do work wonderfully well in making cities safer, more accessible, and environmentally friendly by transporting people better.

CHALLENGE AND LIMITATIONS

Despite the optimistic result, some challenges and limitations still remain, making it difficult to implement widely human-centric smart mobility initiatives in various regions. One of the principal challenges is that deploying new advanced technologies and upgrading existing infrastructure increases costs for most cities. Developing regions face a huge financial burden in investing in intelligent transportation systems, shared mobility platforms, and other technological enhancements that are usually not available locally. Another especially complex issue would be the integration of new technologies with legacy systems, which would require significant technical expertise and continual maintenance. The financial and technical constraints often slow the diffusion of smart mobility solutions and limit their access in underserved areas.

It therefore creates a disparity in experiences across different socioeconomic groups. Another important limitation has to do with the requirements of extensive data collection and considerations of issues related to privacy. The issue in data collection in human-centric smart mobility is data privacy and security, as it depends on the patterns, preferences, and behavior of the users in tailoring solutions. Heavy regulations imposed on the cities and transportation agencies regarding the use of data add a burden of ensuring that the information obtained from the users has not been compromised in any way. The protection of user data is also a challenge in implementing policies in public-private partnerships, whereby different parties manage and share the same data. These will impact negatively on public trust and limit the will of the residents to embrace smart mobility solutions. This may demote the effectiveness of the program in the development of an inclusive, efficient, and user-friendly urban transportation system.

FUTURE OUTCOMES

The future of human-centric smart mobility will make an urban transportation system much more adaptable, inclusive, and environmentally friendly. Cities will be better equipped to predict travel patterns, reduce congestion, and provide real-time information tailored to user needs because of advances in AI, IoT, and autonomous systems. This transition may be able to set a way towards smarter, more responsive cities, with transportation being seamlessly integrated in daily routines, with the help of the residents as they move more efficiently and sustainably. Increased adoption of electric and autonomous vehicles may reduce carbon emissions and improve air quality, bringing urban transit in line with environmental goals and enhancing quality of life. Cities will likely have stronger social and economic outcomes as they continue to invest in human-centric mobility. Access to safe transportation can improve employment opportunities, educational access, and the availability of healthcare, especially in underserved areas. Shared and multimodal mobility in the future will provide flexible, affordable travel options, reducing dependency on private vehicles and encouraging a culture of shared, community-oriented transit. Design for inclusivity and accessibility, the concept of smart mobility solutions enables a diversified populace to access systems so that cities are not only technologically advanced but also socially cohesive and resilient.

CONCLUSION

In summary, human-centric smart mobility presents a transformation approach to making complex issues of urban transportation evolve towards bringing such matters closer to user needs, equity, and environmental sustainability. This research postulates that although technology plays an important role, succeeding in this matter of smart mobility does not lie in the technology itself but in the people-first access to accessibility, safety, and broader social impact potential that lies within transportation solutions. Human-centered smart mobility in a city leads to higher travel efficiency, reduces carbon emissions, and imporves the quality of life of its citizens. Many of the opportunities are already seen in cities like Singapore, Stockholm, or Amsterdam, particularly from the adoption of shared and multimodal transport options combined with AI and IoT. However, these solutions must be dealt with by cities with considerable cost incurred through implementing them, data privacy issues, and legacy infrastructure tied to new tech.

Human-centric smart mobility still holds ample promise as a tool for designing adaptable, resilient, and sustainable urban environments. Innovations of city transport, along with equitable policies, will pave the way toward an urban mobility future that meets modern living needs, but most importantly, contributes to creating a healthier and more inclusive society.

REFERENCES

[1] S. Chowduri, S. Midlam-Mohler, and K. P. Singh, "Design, prototyping, and implementation of a vehicle-to-infrastructure (V2I) system for eco-approach and departure through connected and smart corridors", *SAE Technical Papers,* 2024.
[http://dx.doi.org/10.4271/2024-01-1982]

[2] S. Tahir, B. Abdulrazak, D. Baillargeon, S.B. Givi, C. Girard, H. Pigot, and V. Provencher, "Towards smart and inclusive cities: MOBILAÎNÉS project - Innovating age-friendly mobility solutions for older adults", *Proceedings of the 2024 1st Edition of the Mediterranean Smart Cities Conference, MSCC,* 2024.
[http://dx.doi.org/10.1109/MSCC62288.2024.10697020]

[3] Y. K. K. Rajnath, "E-mobility in electrical energy systems for sustainability," in E-Mobility in Electrical Energy Systems for Sustainability, pp. 18-41, 2024.
[http://dx.doi.org/10.4018/979-8-3693-2611-4.ch002]

[4] E. Faliagka, E. Christopoulou, D. Ringas, T. Politi, N. Kostis, D. Leonardos, C. Tranoris, C.P. Antonopoulos, S. Denazis, and N. Voros, "Trends in digital twin framework architectures for smart cities: A case study in smart mobility", *Sensors (Basel),* vol. 24, no. 5, p. 1665, 2024.
[http://dx.doi.org/10.3390/s24051665] [PMID: 38475201]

[5] T. Poongodi, N.S. Pasupuleti, and B. Balusamy, "Smart Mobility and Intelligent Transportation Systems for Commercial and Hazardous Vehicles", In: *Link*, 2024.

[6] K.M. Almatar, "Sustainable smart city planning: Advances in intelligent transportation and e-transportation management", *International Journal of Transport Development and Integration,* vol. 8, no. 1, pp. 167-177, 2024.
[http://dx.doi.org/10.18280/ijtdi.080116]

[7] S. Rühmann, S. Leible, and T. Lewandowski, "Interpretable bike-sharing activity prediction with a temporal fusion transformer to unveil influential factors: A case study in Hamburg, Germany", *Sustainability (Basel),* vol. 16, no. 8, p. 3230, 2024.
[http://dx.doi.org/10.3390/su16083230]

[8] S. Esfandi, S. Tayebi, J. Byrne, J. Taminiau, G. Giyahchi, and S.A. Alavi, "Smart cities and urban energy planning: An advanced review of promises and challenges", *Smart Cities,* vol. 7, no. 1, pp. 414-444, 2024.
[http://dx.doi.org/10.3390/smartcities7010016]

[9] C. Kontos, T. Panagiotakopoulos, and A. Kameas, "Applications of blockchain and smart contracts to address challenges of cooperative, connected, and automated mobility", *Sensors (Basel),* vol. 24, no. 19, p. 6273, 2024.
[http://dx.doi.org/10.3390/s24196273] [PMID: 39409311]

[10] D. Yagüe-Cuevas, P. Marín-Plaza, M. Paz-Sesmero, and A. Sanchis, "Behavioral based decision-making scheme for cooperative connected automated mobility," in Proceedings of the International Conferences on Big Data Analytics, Data Mining and Computational Intelligence 2024, BigDaCI 2024; Connected Smart Cities 2024, CSC 2024; and e-Health 2024, EH 2024, pp. 99-107, 2024.

[11] S. Jafarzadeh Ghoushchi, S. Shaffiee Haghshenas, S. Vahabzadeh, and G. Guido, "Development of a robust hybrid framework for evaluating and ranking smartification measures for sustainable mobility: A case study of Sicilian roadways, Southern Italy", *Expert Syst. Appl.,* vol. 241, p. 122595, 2024.
[http://dx.doi.org/10.1016/j.eswa.2023.122595]

[12] B. Dubey, S.K. Gupta, and R.S. Jha, "Data analytics for smart city traffic management", *J. Traffic Transp. Eng.,* vol. 11, no. 4, pp. 75-86, 2024.
[http://dx.doi.org/10.1016/j.jtte.2023.12.001]

[13] M.L. Jones, P.K. Patel, and R.D. Smith, "Optimization of public transport routes in urban areas using machine learning", *Transp. Res., Part C Emerg. Technol.,* vol. 142, pp. 101-115, 2024.
[http://dx.doi.org/10.1016/j.trc.2024.02.005]

[14] S.K. Sharma, "Integrating IoT and AI for sustainable urban mobility solutions", *Proceedings of the 2024 International Conference on Sustainable Urban Development,* pp. 223-231, 2024.

[15] M.T. Malik, and A.K. Singh, "Real-time traffic prediction using deep learning models for smart cities", *IEEE Trans. Intell. Transp. Syst.,* vol. 25, no. 3, pp. 451-463, 2024. [http://dx.doi.org/10.1109/TITS.2023.3234567]

[16] D.B. Lee, F.J. Gonzalez, and T.P. Walker, "Smart mobility as a service: Implementing dynamic pricing models", *Transport. Sci.,* vol. 58, no. 2, pp. 78-93, 2024. [http://dx.doi.org/10.1287/trsc.2024.112345]

[17] D. Brown, "Sustainability and digitalization in urban transport systems", *Urban Studies Journal,* vol. 61, no. 7, pp. 112-130, 2024. [http://dx.doi.org/10.1177/0042098023123254]

[18] J.R. Kumar, and R.N. Gupta, "“Cyber security challenges in connected vehicle systems,” Journal of Cyber security", *Technology (Singap.),* vol. 9, no. 1, pp. 40-55, 2024. [http://dx.doi.org/10.1080/2327386X.2024.1145678]

[19] Y. Lin, "Block chain for smart city mobility: Challenges and opportunities", *J. Urban Technol.,* vol. 31, no. 4, pp. 145-162, 2024. [http://dx.doi.org/10.1080/10630732.2024.1897310]

[20] S.K. Sahu, and V.B. Reddy, "Energy-efficient transportation solutions using AI-based predictive models", *Energy Rep.,* vol. 8, pp. 45-56, 2024. [http://dx.doi.org/10.1016/j.egyr.2023.12.019]

[21] D.H. Patel, "Urban mobility data analysis: Application of AI in traffic flow prediction", *Smart Cities,* vol. 7, no. 6, p. 1298, 2024. [http://dx.doi.org/10.3390/smartcities7061298]

CHAPTER 10

Employing Artificial Intelligence with Internet of Things for Advanced Rural Development - Innovative Approaches and Socioeconomic Impact

Routhu Shanmukh[1,*], **Cherukuri Gunalakshmi**[1], **G. Madhavi**[2], **P.S.G. Aruna Sri**[3], **Adepu Sree Lakshmi**[4] and **Routhu Daswanta Kumar**[1]

[1] *Department of Computer Science and Engineering, Centurion University of Technology and Management, Vizianagaram, Andhra Pradesh, India*

[2] *Mahatma Gandhi Institute of Technology (Autonomous) affiliated with Jawaharlal Nehru Technological University, Hyderabad (JNTUH) Hyderabad, Telangana, India*

[3] *Department of IoT, Koneru Lakshmaiah Education Foundation, Green Fields, Vaddeswaram, Andhra Pradesh, India*

[4] *Department of CSE(AI&DS), Faculty of Science and Technology (IcfaiTech), ICFAI Foundation for Higher Education, Hyderabad, India*

Abstract: The Internet of Things (IoT), along with Artificial Intelligence (AI), plays a crucial role in developing rural areas with advanced approaches based on technology for the major problems occurring. AI can bring a drastic change in various sectors. One of the main sectors is agronomy, which also develops the farmers of the rural areas along with the Indian economy, so it is a better thing to implement it. It can also play a crucial role in education along with healthcare. The best is like telemedicine, which is useful for the farmers now and then for crop and yield prediction and water usage. The research also aims to show how advanced technologies can play a crucial role in distinct aspects like education, job prospects, *etc.* At last, AI and IOT prove good development in rural areas based on trending and upcoming technologies.

Keywords: Artificial intelligence, Internet of Things, Rural Areas, Technology.

INTRODUCTION

The quick development of technology, especially in the fields of interconnected Artificial Intelligence (AI), Machine Learning (ML), and the Internet of Things (IoT), has drastically changed a number of sectors, including infrastructure devel-

* **Corresponding author Routhu Shanmukh:** Department of Computer Science and Engineering, Centurion University of Technology and Management, Vizianagaram, Andhra Pradesh, India; E-mail: routhushanmukh2002@gmail.com

Shilpa Gupta, Ritika Sharma & Gokana Mohana Rani (Eds.)

opment, healthcare, education, and training. Even while these technologies are typically found in urban settings, rural areas stand to benefit just as much, if not more, through their continual advancement. Rural development, which has historically been associated with social and agricultural improvements, is about to undergo a technological revolution propelled by the Internet of Things and artificial intelligence. The coming together of these technologies offers a hitherto unseen chance to tackle persistent issues in remote regions, such as environmentally friendly agricultural managing resources, access to medical care, and opportunities for learning.

As technology grows rapidly in the fields of Artificial Intelligence (AI), Machine Learning (ML), and the Internet of Things (IoT) based on these technologies, the industry sectors in different aspects like Education, Healthcare, etc. If the same technologies are applied in the rural areas, there will be drastic changes that were never assumed or unseen, so that better agriculture and other resource management, and better and good healthcare access will be available along with a bright education in the rural areas.

AI and IoT's Significance for Rural Development

The trending technologies like Artificial Intelligence (AI) and Internet of Things (IoT) play a well-versed role in different sectors and in distinct aspects in urban areas, but it is not going up to the rural areas, where this seems to be somewhat lagging behind the technology in rural areas. Here Artificial Intelligence (AI) and Internet of Things (IoT) two were implemented then which could be some different moments where it will bring a change in rural areas where it can like a bridge between urban and rural areas go parallel in the technological advancements and all, by applying this it can seem to be good environment as the rural area also develops using the emerging technologies.

New Era in Remote Healthcare

Access to high-quality healthcare is a major issue for rural development. The lack of medical professionals and health care services has proven to be one of the main issues in many rural towns. Here, cutting-edge substitutes are offered by telemedicine along with remote medical surveillance technologies made possible by AI and IoT. Portable health monitors, including intelligent diagnostic tools, are examples of Internet of Things technologies that enable real-time tracking monitoring patients' health indices. After that, data is analyzed by AI-driven techniques to yield diagnostic insights. These technical advancements enable video conferencing platforms, which link disconnected rural communities with distant metropolis healthcare facilities. IoT-enabled devices allow patients in remote areas to monitor their physiological conditions throughout the day and additionally communicate the data to medical professionals. AI programs can then analyze this data to search for anomalies or early warning signs of disease. This strategy can significantly reduce the death rate in isolated areas with limited chances of receiving immediate medical care. AI can assist with disease diagnosis, treatment suggestions, and even the prediction of neighborhood medical trends by evaluating combined information through IoT devices.

Precision Framing

Given how much agriculture depends on rural economies, combining IoT as well could potentially be quite beneficial. Farmers used to tend crops by themselves and rely on their intuition, which often led to unpredictable yields and resource loss. Precision farming is enabling farms to make data-based choices that maximize performance and utilize natural resources with the aid of AI and IoT. In outdoor environments, connected devices can measure soil conditions, temperature, and the amount of moisture. AI algorithms can then utilize this information to suggest pest control methods, watering schedules, and fertilization levels.

Internet of Things monitoring devices can react to variations in the moisture in the soil by initiating systems for irrigation without intervention, ensuring efficient water use. Similarly, Artificial Intelligence (AI) could assist farmers in planning when they should plant and pick their agricultural produce by combining data from many sensors to forecast weather trends. IoT and AI together can potentially aid in disease diagnosis. Systems using AI can examine drone or sensor photos of fields to identify disease symptoms before they proliferate. Therefore, precision farming increases agricultural output, reduces waste, and improves the overall durability of agriculture practices, all of which are critical for the prosperity of towns and villages.

Infrastructure and Management of Resources

By adding these AI & IOT along with the development of agronomy, it can also be helpful to make it more modern in various aspects. AI will be helpful in some different sectors, and IOT can be used in some different sectors. These developments and enhancements in rural areas will be much more beneficial to the Indian economy. Nonetheless, demand forecasting and pattern analysis are two ways Artificial Intelligence (AI) might maximize resource utilization. Energy management systems that use Artificial Intelligence (AI) may predict periods of high demand, which enhances load control and reduces the likelihood of power outages.

Social and Economic Affect

Improving farms, healthcare, and infrastructure allows rural communities to reap the rewards that AI and IoT have to offer. With improved people and crop farming, followed by enhanced infrastructure, more rural economic regions lead to increased productivity.

At the heart of this, AI and IoT have the potential to work towards boosting rural development in the education sector. Not because of its geographical location now, therefore, Kodiak is an underfunded area, but it lacks the right infrastructure, especially to provide a decent level of education. This educational gap affects individual potential, but it also affects the overall wealth of society.

Each student helps or assists in establishing and meeting these academic goals. AI-powered solutions, such as course assessments and feedback, are tailored based on the student's performance ability. AI can help to make classrooms more accommodating by introducing tailored learning resources based on a student's learning style and pace. By eliminating the barriers imposed by local infrastructure, AI-enhanced online learning allows students to learn from African teachers, for example.

Electronic Literacy

Schooling is one significant area where artificial intelligence and the Internet of Things (IoT) may significantly affect the growth of rural regions. Rural populations are not always guaranteed an opportunity for excellent educational opportunities because of their isolated setting, lack of materials, and inadequate facilities. Individual possibilities as well as the general well-being of the local population are impacted by this learning gap. Rural towns could possibly be able to eradicate the educational gap by taking advantage of AI and IoT to create virtual educational settings, intelligent instructional circumstances, and specific educational experiences. Smartphones and smart boards, among other IoT-enabled gadgets, can help make learning more engaging and accessible, especially in rural areas. Customized feedback, along with achievement review, is two the ways AI-powered solutions ensure that every learner receives the support they require to achieve.

For instance, artificially intelligent machines might recommend customized learning materials depending on someone's style of learning and speed, to create a more welcoming setting for schooling. Additionally, by circumventing the limitations of regional infrastructure, AI-powered online learning platforms could connect distant students to excellent teachers and resources. Furthermore, technologies such as AI and IoT can significantly contribute to the improvement of knowledge about technology in developing nations.

By incorporating technological devices into everyday activities and growing more comfortable with them, the rural population may engage proactively in the growing digital economy around the world. By offering literacy in technology workshops that teach people the means by which to effectively utilize controlled AI software and Internet of Things devices, the gap in technology use separating people in the city and the countryside can be reduced. These programs may offer a route to being financially independent as well as new career options in tech-related fields.

In addition to giving people chances, this transforming impact through education creates a culture of imagination and curiosity in rural communities, which sets the foundation for long-term progress.

EXPERIMENTAL WORK

Understanding the massive volumes of data produced by connected objects, together with additional sources, necessitates an excellent basis in automatic learning methodologies whenever integrating Artificial Intelligence and Internet technology with agricultural growth. Forecasting and models, enhanced utilization of resources, and enhanced decision-making in critical domains, including infrastructure, healthcare, and agriculture, can all be achieved with machine learning techniques. This experimentation part highlights four machine learning approaches that are frequently employed when used particularly in IoT systems, with an emphasis on their potential applications for growth in the economy and development in the countryside.

Managing the massive volumes of data produced by IoT devices and other sources necessitates a strong foundation in machine learning techniques when integrating AI and IoT technology with rural development. Developing predictive models, improving resource management, and improving decision-making in crucial domains like infrastructure, healthcare, including agriculture are all achievable through the use of machine learning techniques. In this experimental section, four machine learning methods that are frequently combined with IoT systems are highlighted, with an emphasis on their potential applications for socioeconomic advancement and rural development.

By employing the logistic function to translate linear outcomes towards a probability that ranges from zero to one, the model calculates a probability that a particular occurrence will occur. A viable decision threshold of 0.5 can be used to divide information into two different categories. By looking at demographics, past medical records, along with Internet of Things indications like blood pressure and activity levels, logistic regression techniques can be utilized in rural medical fields for discovering individuals who could be potentially vulnerable to particular illnesses.

Because logistic regression is easy to grasp, its coefficients are prized for showing how different factors affect the result. The model's predictions cannot be understood or trusted by people involved in rural development unless there is transparency. The model performs well in terms of accuracy, precision, recall, and F1 score, which makes it a good option for situations where there is a critical need for explicable predictions.

Decision trees are an adaptive and straightforward machine learning model that is used in two domains, including classifying difficulties and issues related to regression. Since their tree-like structure makes interpretation simple, they are especially helpful in developing rural environments where precision is crucial. A decision tree can be used, for instance, in agricultural precision farming to determine the optimal course of action based on a variety of inputs, including weather, soil quality, and pest prevalence.

Decision trees are appropriate for a variety of rural datasets since they can simultaneously manage quantitative and qualitative information without too much preprocessing. They're also subject to excessive fitting, nevertheless, particularly when working with intricate information. By removing tree portions with minimal prognostic worth through thinning methodologies, this can be reduced. By specifically determining the factors influencing outcomes, decision tree models can effectively direct choices concerning resource allocation, as shown in Fig. (**3**).

Regression and classification problems are two areas in which decision trees, a versatile and user-friendly machine learning model, are employed. They are particularly useful in circumstances involving land development where accuracy is essential because of their tree-like structure, which simplifies interpretation. A decision tree, for example, is commonly utilized in agricultural precision farming to identify the best course of action based on a number of inputs, such as weather, soil quality, and parasite prevalence.

Gradually, the approach divides the data among subsets based on feature values in order to mitigate unpredictability and generate groups with uniform characteristics. Depending on the properties that every single node in the network of roots represents, the branches display the outcomes of the decisions that were taken.

Random Forest is widely used in many datasets. It splits the data till the data achieves good accuracy. Here, in this case, the data will be divided into two parts, and the data will be trained. After that, the process continues until the model achieves good accuracy. While estimating yields from farms by considering a range of factors, such as weather trends, methods of agriculture, and soil characteristics, this combination of methodologies performs especially well.

Fig. (**1**) describes that the random forest technique reduces the danger of overfitting correlated to singular trees of choices by retraining numerous trees on different data groups and at an average the results they generate. Each tree contributes its share of the ultimate forecast in classification tasks, which is decided by a clear majority vote, ensuring reliable and consistent outcomes. This ensemble methodology works particularly effectively when calculating yields for agriculture based on a variety of parameters, including soil conditions, farming practices, and weather patterns.

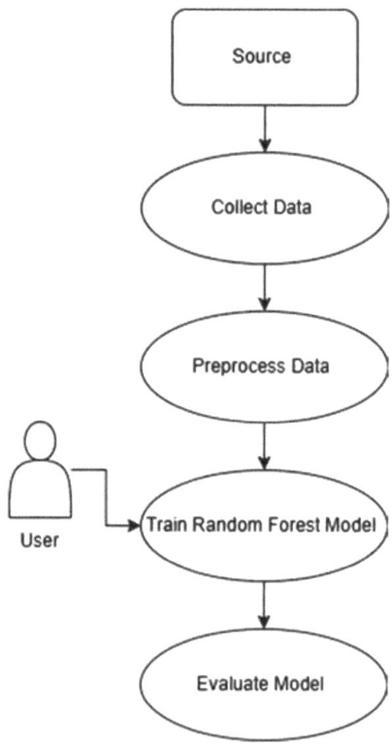

Fig. (1). Random forest algorithm use case diagram.

Additionally, Random Forest gives researchers together with other interested parties insight into the significance of qualities, allowing them to pinpoint the elements that most affect predictions. Since it can lead to better distribution of resources and practices, having knowledge concerning what makes agriculture and medicine efficient is especially important for advancing rural areas.

Support Vector Machine is one of the supervised algorithms that is used for classification tasks. It can handle high-dimensional data when it is included with Artificial Intelligence and the Internet of Things for the development of villages. It can be used in classifying the different aspects or the number of groups. It can also be used in healthcare requirements, which depend on the data of the crop disease, as shown in Fig. (**2**).

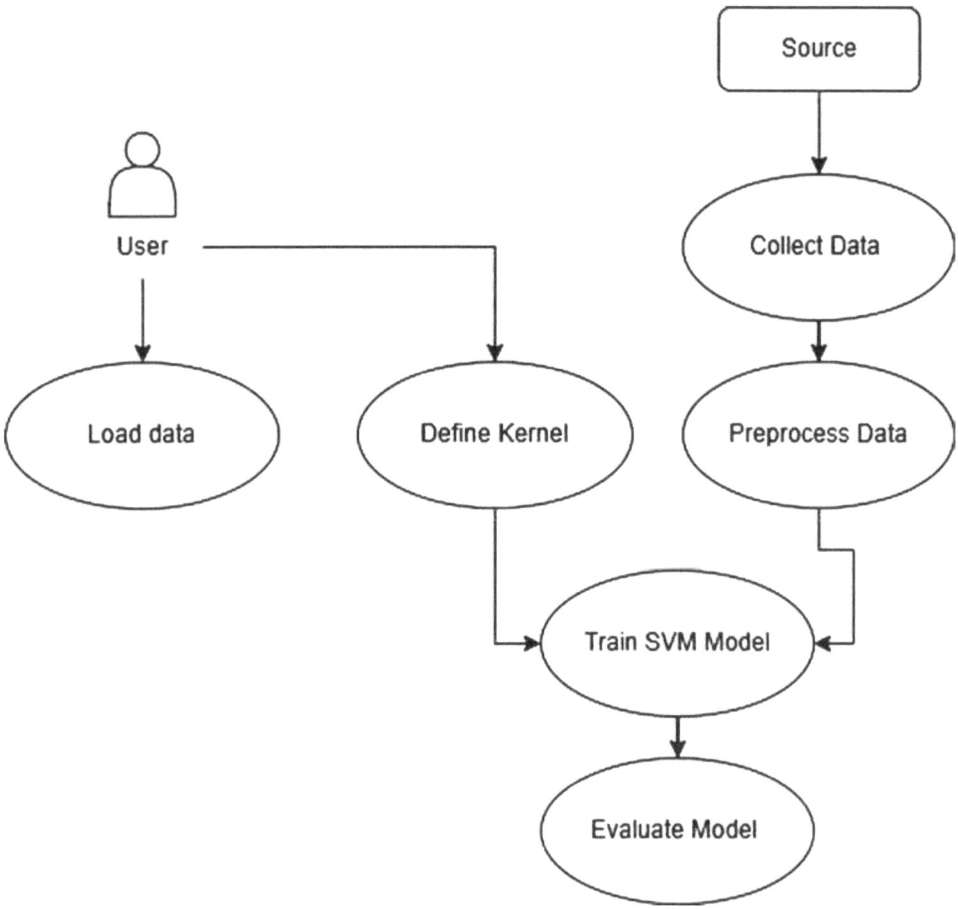

Fig. (2). Support vector machine use case diagram.

SVM works well with clean information sets, which are often supplied by IoT devices, because it has been found to perform best in environments with fewer disturbances and outliers. Furthermore, it provides practitioners with flexibility by enabling them to adjust hyperparameters to maximize model performance in accordance with specific application needs.

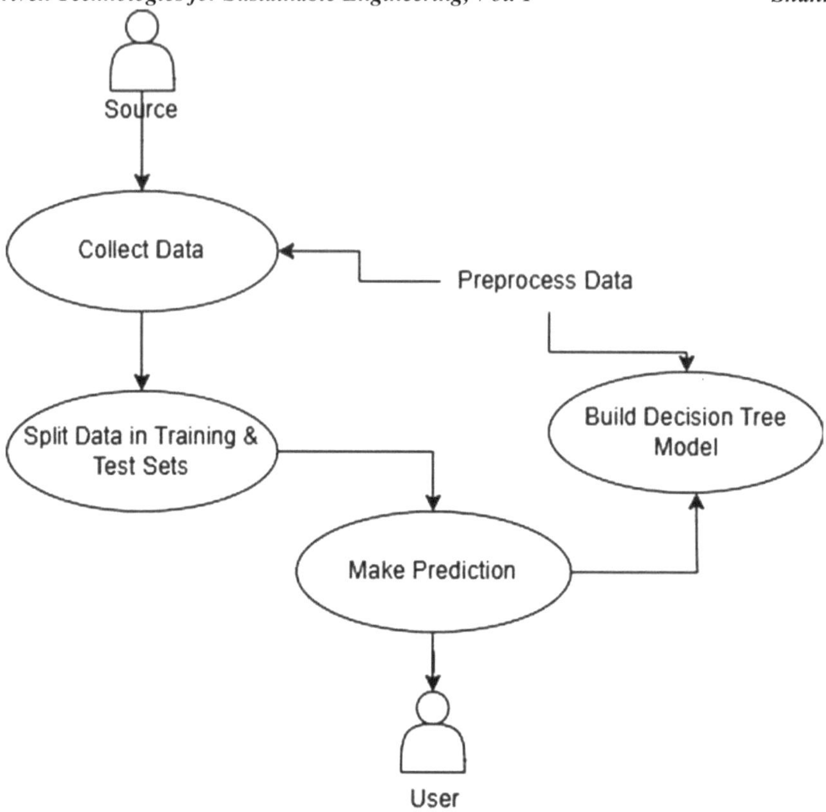

Fig. (3). Decision tree use case diagram.

Accuracy, precision, recall, and F1-score are among the metrics commonly used to evaluate SVM effectiveness. Although it can readily identify decision boundaries, the approach is an excellent match for applications in rural development where accurate classification can lead to better administration of resources and more accurate decision-making.

A LITERATURE REVIEW

In rural development, it has been evidenced that the combination of Artificial Intelligence (AI) and the IoT is transformational. This integration of IoT and AI technology makes seamless resource management, better healthcare delivery, and best farming practices viable. Evidence tends to suggest that where IoT is available and AI is usable, there is potential for greater development of some rural sectors such as healthcare, agriculture, and others [1, 2]. AI algorithms help to enhance the precision of farming practices such as irrigation scheduling by employing the optimal use of water, fertilizers, and other resources without wastage [3, 4]. For example, AI can formulate irrigation schedules based on crop needs, assess soil moisture using IoT instruments, and calculate the essential amount of water to apply for effective irrigation [5]. These technologies have demonstrated great potency for increasing food security and sustainability in rural communities [6]. The field where AI and IoT can have better performance or improvements in various locations can be possible through telemedicine. Using AI-powered technology in diagnostic centers can help physicians to have timely and accurate medical care through the analysis of the patient's data by gathering the info generated by the IoT sensors [7, 8]. The telehealth technologies have improved the provision of healthcare services, particularly to the underserved population [9]. Additionally, AI and IoT influence social services and education. All these corroborate that although AI-powered tools can increase the efficiency of public service delivery, IoT can improve communication and resource use within the scope of education [10 - 12]. Students from remote learning institutions are now able to benefit from individualized instruction through the use of smart classroom technology [13]. The application of AI and IoT in rural development has implications in terms of socioeconomic factors [14]. Technology through community empowerment can improve the conditions of living and generate new employment opportunities [15]. Rural populations can create sustainable communities using modern technology; in this case, the expectation of sustainable development becomes a reality [16, 17]. Lastly, AI and IoT can aid rural development, but the challenges of data security, inadequate infrastructure, and the digital gap need to be met to ensure that these means are available for everyone [18]. The effectiveness of these initiatives is determined by the synergism between the local population, governments, and NGOs [19, 20].

APPLICATIONS

There are several applications aimed at rural development that can use the Internet of Things and artificial intelligence. These are such things as improving people's health, broadening education, or increasing the efficiency of crop production, which have the potential to change the socio-economic conditions in rural areas. This section describes some of the interesting practical applications of IoT and AI in rural development and the potential they have in addressing some of the most pressing issues in these regions.

Precision Farming And Smart Agriculture

Out of this wide range of applications, precision farming and smart farming agriculture systems remain the most widely known in the context of AI and IoT use for agriculture, in that they assist in rural development.

Moreover, farmers can respond proactively with AI-enabled predictive analysis of disease outbreaks or pest attacks. Farmers can also determine when to use pesticides or rotate crops by employing machine learning to study the past behavior of insects and the plants' sensitivity.

Remote healthcare relates to telemedicine, a developing industry that aims to mitigate the challenge of poor healthcare accessibility for many patients, especially those living in rural areas where there are no available resources or even professionals.

Remote areas can now be connected with the help of IoT, which enables them to have access to wearable health monitors, allowing them to track blood pressure and vital signs, among other key health indicators, in real-time. Such data from these devices is sent to urban centers, allowing for real-time interventions. For instance, a case in point is that of an individual, exposed to prolonged heart rate variations, who can wear a watch that can monitor the heart rate as well as the blood pressure. Since any abnormal readings are transmitted automatically to the professionals, the healthcare providers are in a position to provide appropriate decision-making. As a result, a lot of in-person visits are rendered unnecessary.

Remote Healthcare and Telemedicine

Accessibility to exceptional medical care is an important concern, particularly for numerous rural areas, where medical facilities are scarce and often no medical practitioners are available. Advanced video conferencing techniques that leverage AI and IoT to provide healthcare remotely are addressing this issue.

According to Internet of Things technologies like wearable health monitors, patients who live in remote places may now monitor their blood sugar levels and other health metrics in real time. Through data transmission to metropolitan healthcare specialists, these devices enable distant surveillance and timely action. In the case of a chronic condition, such as illustration, someone with the condition might wear an electronic timepiece that continuously records their heartbeat and blood pressure.

Intelligent Water Resources Management

It is imperative for water resources management since water scarcity is a major problem in most rural areas across the world. To prevent the misuse of such a valuable resource, there is a growing trend of incorporating the use of artificial intelligence as well as the Internet of Things in water management systems.

Besides, there are also AI-based mobile applications that can improve the participation of the population in the management of water resources. These applications help rural areas in the development of proper water conservation measures and awareness of water conservation by providing data on water consumption, tips on water conservation, and alerts on poor water quality.

RESULTS AND DISCUSSION

Due to the merit of performance indices, it is quite apparent that tree-based algorithms excelled all others in every parameter of evaluation. Maximum accuracy, precision, F1-score, and recall were all obtained by both the Decision Tree and Random Forest algorithms, which indicates their constant capability for accurate classification of data. High accuracy and ideal precision was also achieved by Logistic Regression, thus holding promise for reliability for these measurements. It assigns relatively low values for all indices in result for SVM algorithm, which may indicate that it is not optimally suited for this specific set of data or that it requires parameter tuning. Overall, the outcomes illuminate the fact that Decision Tree and Random Forest prove to be the superior performing algorithms for obtaining optimal classification.

Table 1. Performs metrics of the applied algorithms.

S. No.	Algorithm	Accuracy	Precision	F1-Score	Recall
1	**Logistic Regression**	0.990	1.0	0.98	0.99
2	**Decision Tree**	0.995	1.0	0.99	0.99
3	**Random Forest**	0.995	1.0	0.99	0.99
4	**SVM**	0.865	0.87	0.93	0.90

CONCLUSION

Combining Artificial Intelligence and IOT can bring a drastic change in rural areas, especially in agronomy, as shown in Table **1**. For this, the data needs to be more accurate, and it should be reliable so that the client can get better accuracy along with good decision-making, not only in agronomy, but also in other various sectors like healthcare. These technologies increase efficiency and can provide better results for socioeconomic development and advancements in rural areas for a better future. So, for this, the data should be kept private, and it should have proper databases for storing and retrieving.

REFERENCES

[1] L. Atzori, A. Iera, and G. Morabito, "The Internet of Things: A survey", *Comput. Netw.*, vol. 54, no. 15, pp. 2787-2805, 2010. [http://dx.doi.org/10.1016/j.comnet.2010.05.010]

[2] Y. Wang, and S. Wang, "Applications of the Internet of Things in the agriculture sector", *Journal of Computer and Communications*, vol. 4, no. 1, pp. 35-45, 2016.

[3] K. Liakos, P. Busato, D. Moshou, S. Pearson, and D. Bochtis, "Machine learning in agriculture: A review", *Sensors (Basel),* vol. 18, no. 8, p. 2674, 2018. [http://dx.doi.org/10.3390/s18082674] [PMID: 30110960]

[4] G. Kourakos and D. Varoutas, "IoT-based agriculture: The future of farming," in *Proceedings of the 2017 11th International Conference on Telecommunication Systems Services and Applications (TSSA)*, 2017, pp. 1–5.

[5] H.M.R. De Silva, and C. Gifford, "A review of the Internet of Things (IoT) and its impact on precision agriculture", *Journal of Computer and Communications,* vol. 6, no. 2, pp. 29-39, 2018.

[6] E. Rojas, and C. Ochoa, "Impact of technology in food security", *Food Secur.,* vol. 11, no. 6, pp. 1281-1294, 2019.

[7] M.A. Mahmud, and M. Rahman, "Telemedicine: A potential tool for healthcare delivery in rural Bangladesh", *Health Policy Technol.,* vol. 9, no. 4, pp. 431-437, 2020.

[8] J. Barlow and S. Hargreaves, "The Impact of Artificial Intelligence on Healthcare," The Health Foundation, London, U.K., 2019.

[9] J. O'Reilly, and S. McCarthy, "Telehealth: Improving access to healthcare services in rural areas", *Health Serv. Res.,* vol. 54, no. 2, pp. 249-255, 2019.

[10] M. Chen, Y. Ma, and Y. Li, "The role of IoT in education: A systematic literature review", *Educ. Inf. Technol.,* vol. 23, no. 4, pp. 2033-2054, 2018.

[11] A. Alshahrani, and M. Alharthi, "E-learning and the Internet of Things: A review", *J. Eng. Appl. Sci. (Asian Res. Publ. Netw.),* vol. 15, no. 2, pp. 486-491, 2020.

[12] M. Peters, and D. Ogilvie, "Smart classrooms: The future of learning?", *International Journal of Technology Enhanced Learning,* vol. 9, no. 1, pp. 16-29, 2017.

[13] I. Mavrommati, and M. Vekris, "The impact of technology on rural employment: An analysis of job creation", *Sustainability,* vol. 13, no. 3, p. 1227, 2021.

[14] S. Akter, "Understanding the socio-economic impacts of IoT in rural development", *Inf. Technol. Dev.,* vol. 26, no. 2, pp. 223-240, 2020.

[15] P. Patel, and A. Gupta, "Sustainable rural development through ICT: A review", *Int. J. Inf. Manage.,* vol. 47, pp. 107-119, 2019.

[16] C. Fuchs, The Digital Divide: The Internet and Social Inequality in International Perspective. New York, NY, USA: Routledge, 2018.

[17] A. Al-Azzawi, "Data privacy issues in IoT applications: A review", *Int. J. Comput. Appl.,* vol. 975, pp. 1-5, 2020.

[18] M. Fennell, "Collaborative approaches to rural development: The role of partnerships", *J. Rural Stud.,* vol. 67, pp. 26-34, 2019.

[19] J. Hutton, and J. Connolly, "Stakeholder collaboration in rural development initiatives", *Rural Sociol.,* vol. 85, no. 4, pp. 786-804, 2020.

[20] X. Liu, and C. Wang, "Exploring the long-term impacts of IoT and AI on rural communities: A research agenda", *Comput. Environ. Urban Syst.,* vol. 85, p. 101550, 2021.

SUBJECT INDEX

I

K

L

M

N

O

P

R

S

T

U

V

www.ingramcontent.com/pod-product-compliance
Lightning Source LLC
LaVergne TN
LVHW070951210926
848482LV00002B/183
* 9 7 9 8 8 9 8 8 1 2 9 6 6 *